Race Relations in the United States, 1980–2000

Race Relations in the United States
Ronald H. Bayor, General Editor

Race Relations in the United States, 1980–2000

TIMOTHY MESSER-KRUSE

Race Relations in the United States
Ronald H. Bayor, General Editor

GREENWOOD PRESS
Westport, Connecticut • London

Library of Congress Cataloging-in-Publication Data

Messer-Kruse, Timothy.
   Race relations in the United States, 1980–2000 / Timothy Messer-Kruse.
     p. cm. — (Race relations in the United States)
   Includes bibliographical references and index.
   ISBN-13: 978–0–313–34311–7 (alk. paper)
   ISBN-13: 978–0–313–33717–8 (set : alk. paper)
  1. United States—Race relations—History—20th century. 2. Racism—United
States—History—20th century. 3. Minorities—United States—Social conditions—
20th century. 4. African Americans—Social conditions—20th century. 5. United
States—Social conditions—1980– I. Title.
   E184.A1M44   2008
   305.800973—dc22   2008007492

British Library Cataloguing in Publication Data is available.

Library of Congress Catalog Card Number: 2008007492
ISBN: 978–0–313–34311–7 (vol.)
      978–0–313–33717–8 (set)

First published in 2008

Greenwood Press, 88 Post Road West, Westport, CT 06881
An imprint of Greenwood Publishing Group, Inc.
www.greenwood.com

Printed in the United States of America

The paper used in this book complies with the
Permanent Paper Standard issued by the National
Information Standards Organization (Z39.48–1984).

10 9 8 7 6 5 4 3 2 1

Contents

Series Foreword

W.E.B. Du Bois, an influential African American civil rights activist, educator, and scholar, wrote in 1903 that "the problem of the twentieth century is the problem of the color line." Although Du Bois spoke only of the situation affecting African Americans, we now know that the twentieth century brought issues to the fore that affected all of America's racial and ethnic groups. It was a century that started with vicious attacks on blacks and other minority Americans, as evident in the 1906 Atlanta race riot, and included within its years substantial civil rights gains in legislation and public attitudes as revealed by the Civil Rights Act of 1964 and the Voting Rights Act of 1965. Everything that occurred took place during the time of two world wars, the Great Depression, the Cold War, the turbulent 1960s, the Civil Rights and Women's movements, the rise of the Conservative movement, and the Persian Gulf and Iraqi wars.

The first volumes in the *Race Relations in the United States* series include coverage of significant events, influential voices, race relations history, legislation, media influences, culture, and theories of intergroup interactions that have been evident in the twentieth century and related to race. Each volume covers two decades and encapsulates the state of race relations by decade. A standard format is followed per decade, allowing comparison of topics through the century. Historians have written the topical essays in an encyclopedic style, to give students and general readers a concise, yet authoritative overview of race relations for the decade studied.

Coverage per decade includes a Timeline, Overview, Key Events, Voices of the Decade, Race Relations by Group, Law and Government, Media and Mass Communications, Cultural Scene, Influential Theories and Views on Race, and a Resource Guide. Furthermore, each volume contains an introduction for the two decades and a selected bibliography and index. Historical photos complement the set.

The volumes not only deal with African Americans, Native Americans, Latinos, and Asian Americans but also with religious entities such as Jewish Americans. The history is a fascinating story that deals with such personalities as Henry

Ford, Marcus Garvey, Martin Luther King Jr., Cesar Chavez and Dolores Huerta, Russell Means, and George Wallace; defining events such as the imprisonment of Japanese Americans during World War II, the 1943 Zoot suit riots in California against Mexican Americans, the Selma to Montgomery Civil Rights march in 1965, and the American Indian Movement's occupation of Wounded Knee, South Dakota in 1973; and legislation and court cases deciding who could enter the country and who could become a citizen. The 1960s as a decade of new civil rights acts, immigration laws, and cultural changes are covered along with the increase in new immigration that marked the 1980s and 1990s. The volumes familiarize readers with the role of the Ku Klux Klan, the fear of a "Yellow Peril," and the stereotypes that impeded the attainment of equality for many minorities.

The books' focus will enable readers to understand the progress that has been made in the face of relentless persecution and oppression. As the year 2000 approached and passed, the United States was a different country than it had been in 1900. Many problems remained in relation to immigration and civil rights, but the days of lynching, racially discriminatory laws, and culturally negative stereotypes have largely faded. The story is a positive one of growth and change, but one that provides lessons on the present and future role of race relations.

One of the enduring changes that can be seen is on TV where the human landscape has evolved from ugly images of racial and ethnic groups to more multicultural and accepting views. When television first appeared, African Americans, Native Americans, Asian Americans, and Hispanic Americans were portrayed in negative ways. Blacks were often portrayed as ignorant servants and Native Americans as savages. "Stepin Fetchit," Charlie Chan, wild Indians, and the "Frito Bandito" are gone. These negative images evident in the 1950s would not find a place in today's media. By itself, that represents a significant change in attitudes and indicates the progress that has been made in intergroup relations. How this happened is what students and general readers will find in these volumes.

Ronald H. Bayor
Series Editor

Preface

In this volume I have attempted to compile and describe a selection of events that seem to be landmarks in the race relations among different communities as defined by race, ethnicity, and government policy in the last fifth of the twentieth century. I do not pretend that this is a comprehensive survey of events; indeed, there are many instances that reveal important truths about the status and meaning of race at the end of the twentieth century that I have not recounted for lack of space. But I hope that I have chosen enough of the most important events and changes in policy to portray accurately the general trend and character of this time. Admittedly, more attention is given to what ethnic studies scholars refer to as the black-white binary over the experiences of other ethnic minorities in America. This approach seems necessary because at the end of the century, as at its beginning, the continuing impact of the stereotypes and misperceptions of the white community toward the African American community, as well as the uniquely disadvantaged economic status of blacks in America remains one of the most formative, if well disguised, forces in American society, culture, politics, law, and government policy. The trends of the 1980s and 1990s, such as the replacement of African Americans by Hispanics as the nation's largest minority group in the 1990s, suggest that perhaps this situation will change in the next century.

With just seven years of hindsight, the direction and meaning of the trends of the last decades of the twentieth century are challenging to discern. In some respects, being close to the events that one studies seems to allow a clearer and more unobstructed view than can be glimpsed of more distant periods. But although the view may be clearer, the meaning of what one sees is cloudier. To historians, the distance of time is a great comfort: time not only winnows the volume of material that must be considered but also slowly shows us which events are truly important and which are merely singular outbursts and misleading symbols of historical paths and possibilities unrealized.

One of the trends and developments of the decades under consideration, the rise of new electronic communications through the Internet and the proliferation of electronic databases, has both facilitated the sifting of great quantities of sources and allowed for the preservation of a greater volume of material than ever before. Simultaneously, the ease of obtaining any historical scrap—newspaper columns, television clips, government reports—has increased along with the size of the mountain of material that was potentially relevant. In the end, the ability of the researcher to embrace such a wide subject as "race relations" over a 20-year period is not improved. Discreet and individual events or subjects can be plumbed to greater depths, but the confidence one has that any selection of events is representative or comprehensive is equally diminished. Does the rise of the East Coast/West Coast Hip-Hop rivalry, Tupac versus B.I.G., say something more important about the dynamics of America at the end of the century than the politics of Cuban identity in Miami, the mysterious arsons of black churches in the South, the frequent outbursts of racial invective from sports stars, or the establishment of nuclear waste dumps on Indian lands? (I chose to leave out Hip-Hop's civil war, but include the tensions of Miami's Cuban American and African American communities. Only time will tell whether I made the right choice.) How confident can anyone be from the near vantage point of 2007 that any of these occurrences will prove to reveal anything significant about the meaning of race in America at the end of the twentieth century? The power of integrated databases allows access to an overwhelming volume of chatter and reported events and even suggests some relationships among them, but it also makes far more complicated the act of choosing which of these points on the timeline are more representative, more descriptive, or more significant than the others.

Some alert or partisan readers may note that the titanic political struggle that was the 2000 presidential election—an election that in many ways revealed the continuing salience of race and the deep racial divisions within the American electorate, as well as the continuing political oppression of racially defined groups—is omitted from my account of the 1990s. After much struggle with this question, I chose not to include it here because it better represents the starting point of another volume that takes these same issues forward into the first decades of the twenty-first century than it does an end point of the 1990s. Whether this author or some other has the privilege of chronicling the decades that are now the present, the 2000 election will surely be the starting point of that analysis. With a tip of my hat I therefore leave those events in the hands of another.

In culling journalistic reports from a variety of databases, I have taken the liberty of citing only the newspaper sources used in this book rather then the electronic indexes and particular services from which they were retrieved. Those sources accessed through general Internet searches rather than dedicated library databases are cited by their Web addresses.

Acknowledgments

I would like to thank Aisha McGriff and Crishawn Marsh for their help in compiling and collecting some of the sources used in this book. I also appreciate Stephanie Rader's cheerful office assistance. Thanks to Ronald Bayor for showing confidence in me and also to Wendi Schnaufer for her patience and encouragement. Finally, this book is dedicated to all of my colleagues and students in the department of ethnic studies at Bowling Green State University who daily remind me of the relevance and importance of this subject.

Introduction

Nearly 40 years had passed since Thurgood Marshall had presented the case against legalized segregation in the landmark Supreme Court decision of *Brown v. Board of Education of Topeka, Kansas* when he stood in Independence Hall on the Fourth of July, 1992, and reflected on the state of race relations at the end of the century. Marshall, America's first and only African American justice until his retirement from the Supreme Court the year before, had observed the uneven course of America's journey away from overt racial oppression from that most unique vantage point since his appointment in 1967, a time when the country's consciousness of the issue of race and the government's commitment to the eradication of Jim Crow was at its height. Looking out over his audience, summing up his experience and applying it to that moment in time, Marshall had this to say about America in 1992: "I wish I could say that this nation had traveled far along the road to social justice and that liberty and equality were just around the corner....But as I look around, I see not a nation of unity, but a nation of division: Afro and White, indigenous and immigrant, rich and poor, educated and illiterate. Even many educated white people and successful Negroes have given up on integration, and lost hope in equality....America can do better, because America has no choice but to do better."

Marshall did not detail the reasons he had such a dim view of the progress America had made in overcoming its racial divisions at the end of the twentieth century. He did not have to. By every measure African Americans, Latinos, and Native Americas remained poorer, less well educated, less healthy, and physically segregated from the white majority. In terms of law, in Marshall's view, the last half of his Supreme Court tenure represented a retreat from an earlier commitment to rooting out racial oppression and fulfilling the Constitution's mandate of equal protection. He understood that law and society could not be separated—that all law existed within social structures and contexts that fixed their meaning and force. Laws, seemingly neutral in their language, could have profoundly discriminatory and unequal effects when they operated within racist environments. The Supreme Court's increasingly tough scrutiny of government attempts to overturn systems of racial discrimination through court supervision of school districts and elections, or administrative incentives to minority hiring and retention, were, to him, examples of upholding the letter of the law at the expense of its substance.

Marshall's summation of the status of race relations may have been more appropriate in the realm of law than culture. Important symbolic progress was made in the last fifth of the century as American society overcame the last vestiges of resistance to the establishment of a holiday for the Rev. Martin Luther King Jr. and the banishing of the Confederate flag from atop southern capitols. In the realms of music, fashion, movies, and literature, the interests and tastes of people of all racial and ethnic backgrounds crossed over and mingled more than ever before in the twentieth century. Bill Cosby, Connie Chung, and Oprah Winfrey represented a new era in television; Michael Jordan and Tiger Woods changed the equations of their respective sports; and Alice Walker and Toni Morrison extended a strong and long tradition of African American literary achievements. All of these figures united in their diverse audiences. Other indications of a slow but significant shift in racial beliefs among the American populace were evident in the strong challenge of Jesse Jackson for the Democratic nomination for president and later in the election of William Jefferson Clinton, a politician who more than any other in the past seemed to genuinely sympathize with and understand the problems as well as the joys and spirit of the black community.

Still alongside this blending of cultures, there were constant reminders that the outlooks and situations of people of different racial backgrounds remained stubbornly divergent. It was seen that the relationship between minority communities and the police who were charged with keeping those communities safe was far more antagonistic and rife with conflict than was the case in most white neighborhoods. Police harassment and brutality underlay the urban explosions of the 1980s and 1990s in Miami, Los Angeles, New York, and in dozens of smaller eruptions around the nation. Such outbreaks of collective violence forced governments to reexamine the procedures of policing and placed the issue of racial profiling solidly on the national agenda.

Although overt expressions of racism were surely less tolerated in public discourse in these decades than in the past, there were constant indications that racial stereotypes and unspoken racist beliefs continued to underlie the behavior and outlook of many whites. Individual acts of racial hatred and intolerance by some measures even seemed to increase. Such was the continuing problem of racist violence that dozens of states and the federal government passed new laws establishing stronger penalties for crimes committed with racial malice. The deeply embedded differences in white and black perceptions, residual structures of three centuries of racial oppression, were profoundly exposed in the contrasting responses of whites and African Americans to the jury's verdict in the murder trial of O. J. Simpson.

Social beliefs and behaviors do not change swiftly over time. Rather, they move as a consequence of deeper tectonic shifts in social reality. Demographics, economics, and technologies all configure and shape social patterns and collective understanding. In the last two decades of the twentieth century, the United States became an even more diverse country with millions of new immigrants arriving from Asia, Latin America, and the Caribbean. An immigrant influx that in many places, most notably in the nation's two largest cities and greatest immigrant entrepôts, provoked new racial conflicts between minority communities, especially East Asians and African Americans. The socially defined boundaries of racial groups became less clearly demarcated as the number of interracial marriages and the number of people who rejected single racial categories for their own self-definition increased year by year. In 2000, the United States Census institutionalized this trend by allowing individuals to define their own racial status by selecting more than one racial label at a time.

The resistance of some whites to the sharing of powers and privileges manifested itself in several new ways. President Ronald Reagan brought urban white ethnics and southern white voters out of the Democratic Party and into the Republican column by deftly using a racially coded language that opposed "welfare queens" and "ghetto hoodlums" against "decent, hard-working Americans." Attempts to exclude noncitizens and those without documented legal residency status from government benefits and government services proved a powerful political movement in those states with burgeoning Latino populations. Other movements to establish English as an official language (and implicitly the exclusion of all other tongues from public discourse) also grew and were successful in some places. Most successful was the movement to amend state constitutions so as to outlaw all government initiatives aimed at redressing historical racial oppression through what were loosely called as "affirmative action" programs. By the end of the century such movements could claim not only to have succeeded on the grassroots and state levels but to have powerfully influenced the rulings of the Supreme Court, which all but abolished them in practice if not in principle.

On the other side of the ledger many initiatives of racial reconciliation sprang up. President Clinton in his second term announced his intention to lead a national discussion of race to address the continuing corrosive effects of racism in America. Some conservative protestant denominations, Southern Baptists and Pentecostals, united racially divided branches of their faiths as their white members apologized for the actions of their churches in the past and sought atonement and communion with their black co-religionists. A large evangelical Christian movement known as the Promise Keepers made healing racial divisions one of the center pieces of their ministry. On their own initiative, a number of school boards, state departments of education, and universities moved to eliminate Indian mascots and change Indian-themed sports team names out of an increasing sensitivity to their demeaning nature.

The twentieth century began with the prescient observation that W.E.B. Du Bois made to the Pan-African Congress in 1900: "the problem of the twentieth century is the problem of the color-line." While many of the most extreme problems that Du Bois faced in his own time—legal segregation, lynching, wholesale economic exclusion, an openly racist public and popular culture, and political disenfranchisement—were with heroic effort gradually overcome, the lines he referred to in 1900 remained in 2000, although often submerged and hidden from view. As the twenty-first century dawns, Du Bois's problem remains to be solved.

1980s

TIMELINE

1980   Refugee Act of 1980 relaxes immigration restrictions and leads
                to a marked increase in the number of immigrants to the United
                States.

                President Jimmy Carter vetoes a law that would have banned
                the Justice Department from using busing as a remedy for school
                segregation.

                By a 6–3 vote, the Supreme Court in *City of Mobile v. Bolden* af-
                firms an electoral districting arrangement that had been shown to
                have significantly reduced the political representation of African
                Americans. The Court ruled that in order to challenge a system
                of electoral districting, discriminatory intent must be shown.

April 4   A federal district court rules that the state of Mississippi can-
                not ban a prize-winning ninth-grade textbook from the public
                schools just because it highlighted that state's role in slavery
                and racial discrimination.

May 17–19   Liberty City riots shake Miami, Florida and revive images of
                cities in flames not seen in a decade. Roots of the riot lie in
                urban segregation, economic marginalization of the African
                American community (unemployment in Liberty City triples
                from 1968), and the issue of police brutality raised by the police
                beating and killing of Arthur McDuffey.

November 5   Republican Ronald Reagan defeats Democrat Jimmy Carter in
                a presidential election that many saw as pivoting on issues of
                race and affirmative action.

November 18   Six members of the Ku Klux Klan and the American Nazi Party who were tried for the shooting murder of five activists at a "Death to the Klan" rally in Greensboro, North Carolina in 1979, are acquitted.

1981

January 12   In a reversal of a policy begun by President Richard M. Nixon, the Reagan administration orders the Treasury Department to stop denying tax-exempt status to private schools that practice discrimination, saying such tax policy should be the subject of Congressional legislation, not administrative policy.

Maya Lin, a 21-year-old Chinese American design student at Yale University, surpasses 1,425 other entrants and wins the international competition to design the Vietnam Veteran's Memorial in Washington, D.C. Although the announcement was much criticized at the time, the 246-foot wall of black granite bearing the names of more than 58,000 dead and missing Americans has since proven to be one of the most moving and often visited of Washington's many monuments.

June 5   President Reagan nominates William Bradford Reynolds to head the Civil Rights Division of the Justice Department. The 38-year-old Reynolds, heir to part of the DuPont family fortune, had no experience in civil rights law or litigation, unlike all his predecessors. Bradford indicates that he would not pursue remedies to discrimination such as court-ordered busing or hiring quotas.

1982

June   Chinese American Vincent Chin, mistaken for a Japanese, is murdered by two auto workers in suburban Detroit who blamed him for the loss of auto jobs to Japan. Although found guilty of manslaughter, neither assailant went to prison.

June 29   President Reagan signs into law a 25-year extension of the Voting Rights Act of 1965. The Reagan administration originally proposed extending this landmark legislation for 10 years and to increase the burden of proof required to prove discrimination in voting, but the Senate passes the tougher law 85 to 8.

1983   Alice Walker wins the Pulitzer Prize for Literature for her novel, *The Color Purple*.

Michael Stewart, a young black man arrested by New York Transit Police for scrawling graffiti on a train, dies in police custody.

African American community leaders demand justice and six officers are tried for negligent homicide but are acquitted.

The Supreme Court, in *Grove City College v. Bell*, limits the ability of the federal government to withhold grants from colleges that discriminated, a ruling that Congress will overturn five years later with passage of the Civil Rights Restoration Act of 1988.

In another case centered on a college that practiced racial discrimination, in this case by prohibiting interracial dating, the highest court rules in *Bob Jones University v. United States* that the Internal Revenue Service could terminate the tax-exempt status of schools that discriminate on the basis of race. The Reagan administration sides with Bob Jones University on this case and prohibits its Justice Department from representing the United States as a plaintiff. In this unusual situation, the Supreme Court appoints a private attorney to argue the case on behalf of the American people.

Vanessa Williams is crowned "Miss America," the first African American to be so honored. Less than a year later her title is revoked when *Penthouse* magazine publishes nude photographs of her that had been taken long before the Miss America competition.

Lily Lee Chen becomes the first Chinese American woman to become mayor of an American city. Chen was born in Tianjin, China and fled to Taiwan with her family ahead of the Communist revolution in 1949. She came to the United States to attend college and became a prominent Asian American activist in the Los Angeles area. She made her home in Monterey Park, a Los Angeles suburb that had become a magnet for Chinese immigrants in the 1970s and by 1980 had an Asian majority of its 61,000 population.

April 11   Governor Charles S. Robb appoints John Charles Thomas to a vacant seat on the Virginia Supreme Court, making Thomas the first African American to sit on Virginia's highest court.

April 20   Chancellor Porter L. Fortune Jr. announces that the University of Mississippi will no longer display the Confederate flag at university functions. Only about 7 percent of the "Ole Miss" student body is African American.

Against all expectations, President Reagan signs the controversial bill making the Reverend Martin Luther King Day the first new federal holiday since the 1940s and only the second named for an individual person.

April 21   Harold Washington is sworn in as Chicago's first African American mayor.

1984   William K. Coors, chairman of the Coors Brewing Company of Colorado, gives a speech to African American businessmen in which he is quoted as saying that the best thing white slave traders did "was to drag your ancestors here in chains" and that blacks in Africa "lack the intellectual capacity to succeed." Civil rights and community organizations respond by calling for a nationwide boycott of Coors beer.

Nike signs basketball star Michael Jordan to an exclusive endorsement contract and demonstrates the marketing power of sports superstardom. The NBA bans Jordan's "nonstandard" footwear for not matching his team's uniforms, providing even more free publicity to the shoe company. After 1986, Jordan's edgy television commercials are directed by Spike Lee, whose independent films help define a new urban cinema.

Longtime civil rights activist Jesse Jackson makes a strong run for the Democratic nomination for president.

1985   Philadelphia Mayor W. Wilson Goode orders the police to crack down on a black nationalist organization known as MOVE (not an acronym), which had been noisily disrupting the peace in their neighborhood. Police move to close down the MOVE headquarters and commune that had long been a thorn in the side of the city's police and administration. After a pitched gun battle, the police drop a bomb on the structure located in a densely populated neighborhood, killing 11 members of the MOVE organization, including five children, and leading to a conflagration that destroyed six city blocks of townhouses.

August   Federal District Judge W. Arthur Garrity Jr. announces he is ending his oversight of the Boston public schools after 11 years of direct court supervision. Management of Boston's schools was taken out of the elected school board's hands in 1974 after the court determined that the city had segregated black children into inferior facilities. Since 1974, many white parents had placed their children in private schools and Boston's percentage of pupils who were white dropped from 65 to 28 percent in a decade.

November 22   Mayor W. Wilson Goode declares a state of emergency in Philadelphia in response to the gathering of white mobs who threaten several African American couples who had recently moved into predominately white Elmwood neighborhoods. Mayor Goode's order prohibits any street gatherings of more than four people in the area.

1986

November   Congress passes the Immigration Reform and Control Act, which gives amnesty to those who entered the United States before January 1, 1982. Three million people, mostly from Mexico, Central America, and various Asian nations, obtain permanent legal residency in the United States as a result.

President Reagan nominates William Rehnquist to be chief justice of the Supreme Court, replacing the retiring Warren Burger. During Rehnquist's Senate confirmation process, it is revealed that as a Supreme Court clerk in 1952, he had written in support of the "separate but equal" doctrine of racial segregation, that he had owned a home in Arizona with a racially restrictive covenant restricting its sale to "Caucasians," and that he had worked to suppress black and Hispanic voter turnout in his early political career. The Senate votes to confirm him by the smallest margin of any chief justice in the twentieth century.

December   White youths in the Howard Beach neighborhood of Queens, New York attack three African American men who were seen walking through their neighborhood, chasing one onto a freeway where he was struck and killed. Mayor Edward Koch describes the attack as "racial lynching."

December 2   Harry Lee, sheriff of Jefferson Parish, Louisiana, a mostly white community bordering on the city of New Orleans, tells a reporter "if there are some young blacks driving a car late at night in a predominately white area, they will be stopped." A subsequent opinion poll found 70 percent of local residents think favorably of Sheriff Lee.

1987

June   Bernard Goetz, a white man who shot four black youths on a New York subway car in 1984 and later told police he did so because he feared they were about to rob him, is acquitted of attempted murder and assault charges, sparking protest from civil rights organizations around the country.

The Supreme Court, in the case of *McCleskey v. Kemp*, rules that challenges to capital punishment cannot be brought on evidence that racial minorities were disproportionately sentenced to death compared to whites. An extensive study of Georgia's record of death sentences conclusively shows that blacks who killed whites where four times more likely to be sentenced to death than whites who killed blacks. Justice Lewis Powell rules that to overturn the death penalty in such a case, it must be proven that there was racially discriminatory intent in either Georgia's law or in the particular actions of the judge or jury.

A report from the Commission on Racial Justice is released documenting that toxic dumps, chemical plants, and other poison hazards were far more likely to be situated near minority communities than white ones. This report opens a new front in the battle for racial equality, pointing out the need to fight against environmental racism that endangers the health of minority communities.

Ben Nighthorse Campbell (Dem.-Colorado), the great-grandson of a Cheyenne who rode with Crazy Horse and died at the battle of the Little Big Horn, takes his seat in the U.S. House of Representatives, the first Native American to serve in Congress since 1971 and only the second to be elected to Congress since the 1940s.

Rita Dove, a poet from Akron, Ohio, wins the Pulitzer Prize for poetry, becoming the second African American to be so distinguished after Gwendolyn Brooks who took this honor in 1950.

November 25   Mayor Harold Washington suffers a heart attack and dies early in his second term as mayor of Chicago, Illinois.

1988

January 15   Jimmy "The Greek" Snyder, a popular CBS sports analyst, provokes controversy when he says in an interview that black athletes outperform whites because "they were bred to be that way" by slave owners.

March 16   The Vatican announces the appointment of Eugene Antonio Marino as the archbishop of Atlanta. Marino is the first African American to become a Catholic Archbishop in U.S. history. Fewer than 3 percent of American Catholics are African American.

Jaime Escalante, a mathematics teacher in a tough East Los Angeles high school, is awarded the Presidential Medal for Excellence in Teaching by President Reagan. Escalante gained national notoriety in 1982 when 14 of his calculus students passed their advanced placement tests but were accused of cheating by the Educational Testing Service who doubted that so many students could do so in one class. His students were required to take an additional test and again they passed. The next year twice as many of Escalante's students passed the AP calculus exam. Escalante's experiences in the classroom were then popularized by the Hollywood film, *Stand and Deliver* (1988).

George Bush's presidential campaign releases a political advertisement featuring "Willy Horton," a notorious rapist and murderer in Massachusetts who committed some of his worst crimes while on furlough from prison under a program initiated by Bush's Democratic opponent, Michael Dukakis. Such ads, featuring images of fierce-looking black men leaving prison through a revolving door, were widely denounced for exploiting racial stereotypes for political advantage.

October   Congress passes the Indian Gaming Regulatory Act, which paves the way for the expression of native sovereignty by allowing tribes to establish and regulate gambling operations in their own nations.

Congress passes the Civil Rights Restoration Act of 1988, overturning the Supreme Court's ruling in *Grove City College v. Bell* and banning federal financial aid and grants to colleges that practice discrimination.

Headlines are dominated by the case of Tawana Brawley, a 15-year-old African American girl who claimed she was raped and demeaned by three white men including a New York City police officer. The case divides the nation and becomes the springboard for the appearance of new black leaders including the Reverend Al Sharpton.

1989

June   Spike Lee's *Do the Right Thing* debuts, a movie that powerfully explores the complexities of race relations in New York. Although it wins the internationally prestigious Golden Palm award at the Cannes Film Festival, it wins no awards at the 1990 Academy Awards.

August 22   The former leader of the Black Panther Party, Huey Newton, is gunned down in Oakland, California by a notorious drug dealer. Thus ends one chapter in the history of black radicalism and social activism.

A group of up to 30 baseball-bat-wielding white youths attack and kill black teenager Yusef Hawkins, believing that he had come to their Bensonhurst, New York neighborhood to date a white girl.

General Colin Powell is appointed chairman of the Joint Chiefs of Staff of the U.S. Defense Department by President George Bush, becoming the first African American to hold the top position in the U.S. military.

Michigan Representative John Conyers introduces a bill in Congress establishing a commission to examine the legacy of slavery and its lingering economic effects on African American communities. The commission would attempt to determine the potential monetary damages owed African Americans. The bill never makes it to a full floor vote.

September   The Virginia National Guard is called to Virginia Beach to quell rioting by thousands of black college students angered at police harassment and what they describe as the racial insults of local residents. The annual Labor Day "Greekfest" gathering in Virginia Beach had been a tradition among African American college students for a decade before the unrest.

After many attempts over nearly 15 years of campaigns, David Duke, former Grand Wizard of the Ku Klux Klan, is elected state senator in Louisiana. He serves one term.

December   Judge Robert S. Vance, a U.S. appeals court judge in Birmingham, Alabama, who had recently concluded a case that led to the conviction of 10 Ku Klux Klan members, and Robert Robinson, a black civil rights attorney in Savannah, Georgia, are killed within 48 hours of each other by similar letter bombs. Walter LeRoy Moody, Jr., a white supremacist, was convicted of the crime and sentenced to life without the possibility of parole.

OVERVIEW

When the decade of the 1980s began, a quarter century had passed since legalized segregation was struck down in *Brown v. Board of Education,* and the federal Civil Rights Act had been in effect for 16 years. Images of the 1960s—club-wielding southern sheriffs, urban ghettoes aflame, black power salutes, and white-sheeted vigilantes—seemed a sharp but fading memory as many Americans began to believe that racial problems and institutional discrimination were

a thing of the past. As they opened their respective campaigns for president, neither Jimmy Carter, a southern Democrat, nor Ronald Reagan, former California
governor and B-list movie actor, said much about race or racial relations as they
set out on the campaign trail. Carter was quoted at a news conference saying
that "the Presidential campaign is no place for the reviving of the issue of racism
under any circumstances."[1]

But race seemed as politically powerful and relevant as ever, and in the midst of
fevered summer campaigning it flared hot. In July the Ku Klux Klan issued its unwanted endorsement of Reagan, saying that his platform, which opposed school
integration by busing and affirmative action programs to redress historical employment discrimination, "reads as if it were written by a Klansman." Although
Reagan immediately rejected any harmony of interests with the KKK, less than a
week later he made a campaign stop in Philadelphia, Mississippi, site of the murder of three Civil Rights campaigners in 1964, and mentioned that he "believed
in states rights" to the mostly white crowd, a phrase that many felt was code for
resistance to racial integration. Speaking to a more integrated audience on Labor
Day in Detroit, Reagan accused his opponent of insensitivity for announcing the
start of his campaign in the city that was the birthplace of the Klan.[2] For all the
progress that had been made since *Brown,* issues of race seemed as divisive and
powerful as they had ever been.

Claiming to champion "colorblind" principles by opposing racial quotas and
affirmative action programs, Reagan galvanized the Republican popular base and
wooed many former southern Democrats into the GOP. Overwhelmingly, African Americans viewed Reagan's candidacy with alarm, but Carter's weak record
on issues of importance to the black community led to more political apathy at
the polls rather than a greater turnout for the Democrats. A few prominent African American leaders, most notably Ralph Abernathy, leader of the Southern
Christian Leadership Council, endorsed Ronald Reagan. In the end, a smaller
percentage of black voters cast their ballots for Jimmy Carter in 1980 than in
1976. Nearly half of Hispanic voters chose Reagan.

With the election of Ronald Reagan, the 1980s would become a decade of
retreat from governmental initiatives to overcome the effects of historical racial
discrimination. The 1980s was a decade in which America's popular culture and
mass media displayed greater racial tolerance, but American cities, neighborhoods, schools, and businesses continued to be deeply divided by race. Ironically,
as President Reagan would declare that America had become a society where
everyone of whatever racial heritage stood equally before the law and enjoyed
the same legal rights, it also became a nation that was more racially conscious
and divided along new and numerous racial fault-lines. Tensions between minority communities—African Americans and Koreans, Hassidic Jews and Afro-
Caribbean immigrants, Hispanics and blacks in Los Angeles—highlighted the
continuing challenges of race in America as it neared the end of the twentieth
century.

KEY EVENTS

MIAMI RIOT OF 1980

In the wake of an explosion of urban rioting in 1967, President Lyndon B. Johnson appointed a blue-ribbon commission to investigate the causes and potential solutions to these shocking events. The Kerner Commission Report identified the source of these violent outbursts as the inevitable outcome of racist political and social institutions. In its most famous passage, the Kerner Commission noted that "Our nation is moving toward two societies, one black, one white—separate and unequal." This drift was not only the result of the legacy of racial oppression but also the continued apathy of the nation's majority to its effects: "What white Americans have never fully understood—but what the Negro can never forget—is that white society is deeply implicated in the ghetto. White institutions created it, white institutions maintain it, and white society condones it." As violent clashes over the U.S. war in Vietnam took center stage in the following decade of the 1970s, the issues of urban racism and racial violence receded from view. Rather than implementing the recommendations of the Kerner Commission to invest in new public housing, job programs, and business incentives for the inner city, the government retreated from many of the "War on Poverty" initiatives of the 1960s. But as the 1970s produced no riots on the scale of those that prompted the Kerner Commission report, by the dawn of the 1980s, many white Americans had come to believe that such outbreaks of collective violence were a thing of the past.

On December 17, 1980, Arthur McDuffie, a 33-year-old Miami insurance salesman and father of two, borrowed his cousin's motorcycle. When he passed a patrol car late that night that flipped on its lights, McDuffie make the fateful choice to speed away. No one knows why he fled, whether it was his suspended driver's license, the confidence of an ex-Marine, or the many stories about other black motorists being abused by Miami police at routine traffic stops that twisted the throttle. After an eight-minute chase, McDuffie rolled to a stop, raised his hands, and shouted, "I give up." Police officers pulled him to the ground, ripped off his helmet, handcuffed his hands behind his back, and began kicking and beating him with their heavy flashlights. A crowd of a dozen or more policemen participated or watched as McDuffie was struck at least five times in the head with such force that, according to the medical examiner, his head "cracked like an egg." The police then ran over McDuffie's motorcycle with their cruiser in a clumsy attempt to make McDuffie's injuries appear to be a road accident. McDuffie lapsed into a coma and died four days later.

Five white police officers were indicted for crimes related to McDuffie's slaying. A local judge expressed fear at the level of tension the incident was causing in the Miami black community. Saying "The case is a time bomb," he granted a motion to move the trial to Tampa. Defense lawyers successfully used all their preemptory challenges to keep all 10 African Americans off the jury. After a seven-week trial that seemed almost repetitious in the amount of evidence and eye-witness testimony prosecutors introduced, the jury deliberated for a few hours and found all defendants "not guilty" five months to the day that Arthur McDuffie was beaten to death.

News of the verdict spread quickly and seemed to many of Miami's African American residents certain confirmation of the racist nature of the state's legal apparatus. It was just the spark needed to set off the frustrations of a community falling behind Miami's prosperity. In the previous decade, Liberty City's unemployment doubled to nearly 18 percent, the numbers of high school dropouts and single-parent families increased, and the number of people living below the poverty line increased from 28 to 52 percent.

A protest rally held in Liberty City African Square Park (the location a smaller riot in 1968 at the time that Richard Nixon was nominated to be president at the Republican National Convention held just across the Julia Tuttle Causeway in nearby Miami Beach) quickly escalated into violence. The black neighborhood of Liberty City, an 18-square mile enclave nestled between interstate ramps on the northwest corner of Miami and one of the poorest areas in the county, erupted in rioting.

Unlike those involved in the urban explosions of the 1960s, the rioters who expressed their rage in Miami over the next two nights targeted people more than property. Of the more than 100 people killed during the worst 1960s riots in Watts, Detroit, and Newark, only a handful of whites were purposefully killed by black rioters. Most of the anger of oppressed neighborhoods in the 1960s was expressed in arson and attacks on police or other authorities, but in Miami the initial targets of the mobs were whites passing through black neighborhoods. Before any fires were set or widespread looting began, scores of whites were pulled from their cars and beaten or burned to death. Eight people were killed in this way and hundreds were injured. One hospital used 35 gallons of blood in treating the victims brought in the first night of rioting.

Later that night as the burning and looting began (at least 51 major structures would be destroyed and 240 damaged over the next 48 hours), the police and the initial deployment of national guard moved to cordon off the worst affected areas and to disperse crowds. It was then that the identity of the riot's casualties shifted. All nine of those killed on the second and third day of the riot were African Americans, three of whom were shot down by white vigilantes, and the rest by police and security guards. A total of 855 individuals were arrested and charged that weekend with various crimes, but of these only three individuals were sentenced to jail. Later, after subsequent investigations, five rioters were convicted of murder, although the white vigilantes who randomly shot blacks were never found.[3]

Media coverage of the Miami riot was intense and exaggerated. Many newspapers carried headlines falsely proclaiming that it was the costliest in American history. Lurid coverage of the mob beatings of whites did not always mention the actions of other black residents in helping victims to flee or in driving them to the hospital.

Although much of the press coverage connected the rioting to neighborhood frustration over the influx of Cuban refugees to Miami in the preceding months (the so-called Mariel Boatlift), this was apparently not the perception among Miami's black citizens, only 4 percent of whom in a poll conducted soon after the riot thought the increasing Cuban presence was a factor.[4]

As 1980 was an important election year and Florida was a hotly contested state, politicians at all levels made promises of reconstruction that they did not keep. The first local reconstruction funds went to consultants whose comprehensive studies and plans ultimately proved to be not guidelines for action but dusty, unread volumes. The state of Florida provided tax credits for businesses to rebuild in the riot zones, but only two businesses employing fewer than 50 employees took advantage of the offer. Slightly more than $1 million in grants was allocated to 11 community development corporations. On the federal level, $40 million in small business loans were authorized by the Carter administration, but only half that amount was applied for, and nearly all of that went to white and Hispanic entrepreneurs, most of whom used the money to establish or expand business outside the actual riot areas. Another $6 million was allocated for federal job training programs for residents of riot-affected areas, but these programs proved of marginal use, as most of their graduates were unable to secure jobs that took advantage of their new skills.[5]

Even before it was clear that government development efforts would prove inadequate or misdirected, many were suspicious of the sincerity of those promoting them. Three weeks after the riots, President Jimmy Carter's motorcade pulled into the James Scott community center in Liberty City to discuss rebuilding efforts with local leaders. The meeting quickly turned ugly and secret service agents ushered all reporters out of the room. As Carter's limousine pulled away, a crowd booed, gestured, and threw trash. One beer bottle bounced off the limousine's roof. Such anger was not containable by a handful of scattershot programs, and the neighborhood would see rioting again before the decade of the 1980s was over.

MARTIN LUTHER KING JR. HOLIDAY

On November 3, 1983, an unusual crowd filled the White House Rose Garden. Milling about were Kansas Senator Robert Dole, African American leader Jesse Jackson, the widow of slain Civil Rights leader Rev. Martin Luther King Jr., Coretta Scott King, and President Reagan. Reagan signed his name to a bill making every third Monday in January a paid legal holiday for all federal employees in honor of the Rev. Martin Luther King Jr. As Reagan finished, a chorus sang "We Shall Overcome." Reagan had just returned from a weekend of golf at the all-white Augusta National Golf Course and just days before had fired three members of the U.S. Commission on Civil Rights for being too critical of the administration's civil rights record.[6]

It was an unlikely culmination of 15 years of legislative efforts, demonstrating the tremendous political pressure the demand for a holiday to honor King had accrued since it was first proposed just days after he was assassinated in 1968. The pressure proved powerful enough to cause Reagan to change his position on the issue. Just one month earlier, Reagan corresponded with a close political associate, Meldrim Thomson Jr., the former Republican governor of New Hampshire, who denounced a holiday honoring King because he believed King was "immoral" and a tool of communists. Reagan wrote that "I have the reservations you have, but here the perception of too many people is based on an image, not reality. Indeed to them, the perception is reality. We hope some modifications might still take place in Congress."[7]

The idea for a national holiday commemorating King was first mentioned just days after King was assassinated in Memphis on April 4, 1968. Dr. Samuel L. Woodard, a young Temple University education professor, was quoted in the *New York Times* that week suggesting that such a national holiday would help to bind up the wounds of America in the wake of that terrible loss and perhaps even help put an end to the riots that still burned in its wake. When King was buried on April 9, many black schoolchildren stayed away from their schools, effectively shutting down many schools and enforcing the first "holiday" of a sort.

As the first anniversary of King's birthday approached that coming January, the idea of a King holiday resurfaced. The Southern Christian Leadership Conference (SCLC), the civil rights organization King had co-founded, announced that it was making the designation of January 15 as a King holiday one of its priorities and encouraged churches throughout America to observe "MLK Sunday" the second Sunday of January. Some high school students went further and demanded that their schools close in honor of the occasion. At Lawrence high school in Cedarhurst, New York, all 200 black students boycotted their classes until the principal agreed to send a letter requesting such a holiday to their school board. In Greenburgh, New York, students were successful in forcing their school commission to declare January 15 a holiday. In response to student, teacher, and community demands, one of the largest school districts in the nation, that of New York City, announced in April that it would recognize King day.

The next year Representative John Conyers, a Michigan Democrat and leader of the Congressional Black Caucus, introduced legislation to designate a federal holiday in honor of King. Hoping to draw national attention to the bill, the Rev. Ralph Abernathy, King's successor at the SCLC, led a petition drive that garnered 3 million signatures urging Congress to create a King holiday and delivered them to the steps of Congress in a mule-drawn cart, symbolic of the long broken promise of "40 acres and a mule" once made to those freed from slavery. When the bill never even made it out of committee, the 24 members of the Congressional Black Caucus urged the nation's mayors to issue local proclamations declaring

January 15 a holiday. Conyers would introduce similar legislation in every session of Congress until it eventually passed in 1983.

At that time politicians remained exceptionally timid about endorsing what was essentially a symbolic gesture of respect to the black community. The governors of three states, Michigan, Georgia, and Florida, chose to declare January 15 "Human Relations Day" rather than credit King by name. Connecticut Governor Thomas J. Meskill vetoed a bill declaring January 15 a holiday honoring King. Georgia Governor Jimmy Carter, then making his plans to run for president, announced that he would not support a bill establishing a King holiday in his state. South Carolina adopted legislation allowing state employees to elect to take Martin Luther King Jr. day off, although if they did so they could not enjoy one of the state's other three paid holidays: Robert E. Lee's birthday, Jefferson Davis Day, or Confederate Memorial Day. In 1978, Virginia passed a bill declaring January 1 a holiday honoring Martin Luther King, choosing a day that was already a day off for state workers. One Virginia legislator publicly wondered why King got a day for himself when Virginia's heroes Robert E. Lee and General "Stonewall" Jackson had to share one day. Another group of Virginia delegates attempted to amend the bill to honor Thomas Jefferson and Patrick Henry rather than King. Because the District of Columbia had established a King day in 1975 and Virginia's Lee-Jackson day designated for the third Monday of January happened to fall on January 15 in 1978, in an ironic reprise of the fundamental faultlines of the Civil War, that year Martin Luther King day was celebrated north of the Potomac River and Lee-Jackson day was observed south of it.[8]

The most effective pressure for King holiday legislation came not from civil rights organizations or churches but from labor unions whose black members began pushing their leaders to demand a King holiday as part of their labor contracts. As early as 1969, a group of workers led a wildcat strike at a General Motors factory demanding paid time off for King's birthday. Hospital employees in New York City also went on strike that year and won a paid holiday on January 15. Chicago teachers went on strike in the spring of 1971 when the Chicago school board refused their union demands to give paid time off for King's birthday. The International Longshoreman's Union made similar demands and struck the Port of Newark, one of the nation's busiest, shutting it completely on January 15 to emphasize their point. By the mid-1970s, many unions including the United Automobile Workers, a union that had long been at the forefront of civil rights activities in America, and the American Federation of State, County, and Municipal Employees, perhaps the union with the greatest stake in the passage of a federal paid holiday, routinely placed a demand for a King holiday on the table as part of their contract negotiations.[9]

The King holiday movement used the occasion of the slain civil rights leader's 50th birthday in 1979 to make a concerted push for Congressional action. A massive birthday commemoration was held in Atlanta, King's hometown and the home of King's widow, Coretta. Atlanta also housed a civil rights foundation in his name and observed a King holiday, although the state did not. (Georgia gave paid days off to all state employees on Robert E. Lee day and Jefferson Davis day.) During the six-day commemoration, Senator Edward Kennedy told a large crowd that, as chairman of the Senate Judiciary committee, he would "insure that legislation is enacted...declaring that the birthday of Martin Luther King is a national holiday in every city, town and village of these United States." President Jimmy Carter also spoke in Atlanta and pledged his support for a King holiday bill.[10]

Later that year Kennedy shepherded a King holiday bill out of committee and onto the floor where the full Senate delayed action to see what the House of Representatives would do. House leaders attempted to forestall Republican attempts to amend the bill by moving for a suspension of the rules, a critical procedural ploy. Coretta Scott King watched from the House chamber gallery as the motion failed by four votes. Opponents of the holiday then moved quickly to amend the law, moving it permanently to the second Sunday in January, reducing its significance as a national holiday and giving King the same degree of recognition as Lief Erickson and Stephen Foster. This maneuver forced the congressional leadership to kill the bill.

Just when it seemed that the possibility of achieving a federal holiday for King was at its lowest point—the congressional failure in 1979 had shown that the opposition to the proposal was firm and powerful and, with the election of Ronald Reagan, the White House was occupied by an opponent of the idea—new life was breathed into the movement from a direction perhaps more powerful than partisan politics—music. In the fall of 1980, musician Stevie Wonder released his album, *Hotter than July*, the concluding track was an upbeat musical appeal for a King holiday entitled "Happy Birthday." Musicians often say that political campaigns and music don't often mix well, but "Happy Birthday" managed to be both a catchy pop tune and a direct call for action.

Wonder led a mass march through Washington the following January, and momentum grew through the first years of the Reagan administration, partly as a protest against Reagan's efforts to dismantle much of the federal civil rights enforcement initiatives of his predecessors. When the Senate again seriously took up the bill in the fall of 1983, there were fewer vocal opponents of the measure than there were in 1979, and those willing to attack the idea not just on the grounds of economy (an additional day off for federal workers was estimated to have a price tag of $200 million) but because King was undeserving of the honor were a lonely group indeed. Senator Jesse Helms, a Republican from North Carolina, probably embarrassed opponents of the measure by condemning King as an advocate of "action-oriented Marxism" and sued the National Archives for the immediate release of secret surveillance tapes that the FBI made of King that had been sealed for 50 years by court order in 1977. Helms introduced a series of amendments to derail the bill, including ones that would require creation of a federal holiday for Thomas Jefferson before that of King, create a federal holiday in honor of Hispanics, and hitch King to the black separatist Marcus Garvey by urging the president to posthumously pardon Garvey of his 1923 conviction for mail fraud. A dozen amendments attempting to water down the holiday bill were defeated before the final bill was brought to a vote on October 19. The galleries were packed for the final vote, and in attendance were Coretta Scott King and Stevie Wonder when the bill passed the Senate 78 to 22 (the House had already passed the measure by a vote of 338 to 90 on August 2).

To many observers, the popularity and perseverance of the King holiday movement was surprising and inexplicable. When the King holiday was first proposed, many refused to believe that a "symbolic" issue would take center stage in American politics over seemingly more pressing economic and legal issues. Even more puzzling to many pundits was why the holiday movement expanded over time even as the country as a whole seemed to move in a more conservative direction with the inauguration of Ronald Reagan.

On one level the King holiday proved politically important as a means of maintaining the unity of the African American community at a time when its leadership was relatively weak and fragmented. Although 96 percent of the African American vote went to Jimmy Carter in 1976, the proportion of this voting bloc given to Carter in 1980 was only between 85 and 91 percent. Even worse, more than a million fewer black voters turned out to the polls. Before Jesse Jackson's presidential run in 1984, no single galvanizing leader had emerged and so, in the breach, the memory of an old one had to serve the same purpose.[11]

On a deeper level, it was a mistake for anyone to believe that material issues should naturally trump symbolic ones. Sociologists since the great W.E.B. Du Bois have recognized that one of the deep characteristics of racism in America was what Du Bois termed the "psychological wage" that whites received by virtue of being allowed to consider themselves superior to those with darker complexions. Such privileges of rank and distinction, while contributing to the reservation of better education, housing, jobs, and legal protections for whites, degraded African Americans simply by making them feel at every turn that they did not belong, that there was something innately *wrong* with them. To demand that the Reverend Martin Luther King Jr. be honored equally with Christopher Columbus, Abraham Lincoln, and George Washington was not merely a way to honor a great leader, but was a means of cracking the presumed white privilege of possessing the most important national heroes.

The King holiday movement emerged not only with the assassination of King himself, but at the very moment when expressions of overt racism became increasingly unacceptable to the mainstream of American society. One of the greatest legacies of King and the Civil Rights movement generally was to make impolitic and impolite the casual racism that typified American society up to that time. The silencing of public racist expression had the ironic effect of making it more difficult to campaign against systemic racism and inequality, as the defenders of racial privileges now increasingly framed their arguments in ways that allowed them to deny their racist intentions. Economic and legal campaigns for racial equality, it was quickly realized by civil rights activists, were being increasingly stymied by race-neutral arguments. The King movement gained traction partly because race-neutral arguments for keeping King off the holiday calendar, such as the cost of providing a paid holiday, were obvious fig leaves concealing racist motives. The King holiday movement was politically and culturally powerful because it had the effect of "smoking out" racists at a time when racists were increasingly successful at disguising their motives.

JESSE JACKSON'S CAMPAIGN FOR PRESIDENT, 1984

For a moment in the early months of 1984, the American press corps seriously considered the possibility that a black man might win the Democratic party's nomination for president. The Reverend Jesse Jackson, a 42-year-old civil rights and community development activist, had announced his candidacy on October 30, 1983, to Mike Wallace on CBS television's *60 Minutes*. Although he was one of the last candidates to announce his bid, was already far behind in endorsements and campaign contributions, and had little support from established African American politicians, Jackson's campaign was taken seriously by both the media and political activists, not only because of the novelty of a black presidential candidate, but because of what the Jackson campaign revealed about the state of the Democratic Party and the traditional leadership of the African American community.

Jackson was not the first African American to run for president. In 1968, the comedian and activist Dick Gregory was nominated as the standard-bearer of the Freedom and Peace party. That same year Black Panther leader Eldridge Cleaver also announced his bid to win the highest office. Shirley Chisholm, a member of Congress representing New York, ran for the Democratic nomination in 1972 and won 152 votes (out of more than 3,000) at that summer's convention. But before Jackson, no black candidate was ever discussed by America's pundits as having a legitimate chance of winning the nomination.

Jackson's candidacy took on greater importance in 1984 than it would have in previous elections because it appeared to many experts that the African American vote was an especially crucial factor in that year's election. The election of 1980 had swept much of the formerly white Democratic vote of the South to the Republican column and dramatically reduced the share of northern urban ethnic white voters who traditionally turned out for the Democrats as well. These defections of white voters to the Republican party along with an expected drop in overall voter turnout made a unified and large turnout of African American voters more pivotal than ever before. Also, changes in the scheduling of primaries had created a "Super Tuesday," a single day when primaries would be held in 11 states, most of them in the South where more than half the nation's African Americans lived. Jackson, many Democratic insiders hoped, would mobilize the black electorate and, even if he didn't win the nomination himself, deliver them to whomever the party chose to run in November.

Even before Jackson threw his hat into the political ring, many of the leaders of mainline civil rights organizations publicly opposed his campaign. Coretta

Scott King, the widow of Martin Luther King, Detroit mayor Coleman Young, and Atlanta mayor Andrew Young all publicly endorsed Walter Mondale, the apparent frontrunner for the Democratic nomination. Benjamin Hooks, Executive Director of the National Association for the Advancement of Colored People (NAACP) expressed the common fears of many fellow leaders, saying "If the overwhelming number of black voters are voting for a black, we've lost our voice in selecting the white candidate."[12]

The opposition of the established black leadership to Jackson's campaign revealed the complexity and challenges of maintaining a Civil Rights movement in the face of both success in overcoming legal discrimination and failure in addressing the new social and economic problems of the black community. When combating segregation and legal discrimination, organizations like the NAACP advanced an agenda that promoted the interests and touched the lives of all oppressed racial minorities. But as these open and obvious forms of discrimination fell throughout the 1960s and 1970s, such organizations became seemingly less relevant to many former supporters for whom issues of jobs, income, health care, and safe neighborhoods were paramount. Indeed, by the 1980s, the civil rights agenda, by focusing on discrimination in higher education and corporate management, seemed to increasingly represent the interests of the middle class rather than the African American community as a whole. This impression was only reinforced as the mainline civil rights organizations acted as quasi-official institutions, becoming conduits for federal, state, and philanthropic foundation money for various projects and programs.

Part of Jackson's initial popularity seemed to be that he represented a break with a black leadership that many felt had lost touch with the problems of the day. Jackson had broken with his Southern Christian Leadership Conference in 1972 and formed his own organization dedicated to inner-city neighborhood development in Chicago. In 1983, he condemned the Democratic Party leadership for intervening on behalf of white candidates in Chicago's mayoral primary that Harold Washington, the city's first black mayor, narrowly won in a three-way contest. Later that year Jackson supported voter registration drives; criticized the Democratic Party's procedures for choosing delegates to its national convention, which reduced minority representation; and challenged the AFL-CIO to allow a greater voice for its minority members. Even though Jackson lacked a clear central program or platform to run on, his vocal criticism of establishment figures endeared him with those who felt increasingly unrepresented in Reagan's America.

Jackson's campaign received an early boost in January when he traveled to Syria and successfully secured the release of a U.S. Navy pilot, Lt. Robert O. Goodman, who had been captured in Lebanon. Arriving home to a hero's welcome. Jackson was appointed the primary frontrunner by some of the news media even though he had raised only $331,000 to Mondale's $9.4 million campaign chest. The coveted "frontrunner" title was short-lived, as a month later a reporter for the *Washington Post* revealed that Jackson had referred to Jews as "Hymies" and to New York City as "Hymie Town" in private conversations. The embarrassing

Jesse Jackson campaigning for president in Oakland,
California, 1984. AP Photo.

story only grew as Louis Farrakhan, leader of the Nation of Islam, made a cryptic
threat against this reporter's life and Jackson was condemned by the media for
not quickly denouncing Farrakhan. Accusations of anti-Semitism would hound
Jackson's campaign to its conclusion.

Along the way, ghosts of America's segregationist past appeared as the Louisiana legislature voted to cancel their primary election soon after Jackson announced his candidacy, claiming a lack of funds in the state budget. Jackson's
campaign successfully sued under the Voting Rights Act, and the U.S. District
Court for the Fifth Circuit ordered Louisiana to hold the primary, although it allowed it to move back the date by a month. Louisiana's legislature then refused
to appropriate money to print ballots, but state officials did so anyway. On April 7,
voters in Louisiana gave Jackson his first statewide primary victory with a nearly
two-to-one margin over Mondale.

Later victories in the District of Columbia and Puerto Rico and strong show-
ings in some urban districts had piled up more than 300 delegates pledged to the
Jackson campaign by the end of May, but this was far short of the nearly 2,000
needed to win the nomination. At the Democratic Party convention, Jackson

lent his support for Walter Mondale in exchange for party rules changes that promised to make the nomination process more representative of minority voices in the future.

As Mondale raced on to one of the largest electoral defeats in the modern history of presidential contests, many experts debated the impact of Jackson's historic campaign. Close analyses of voting patterns revealed that Jackson easily won a majority of African American votes in the 13 states where primaries were held. In contrast to the campaign's claims of representing the "underclass," however, Jackson actually attracted more support from higher income blacks than from those in the lowest income brackets. Overall, the Jackson campaign did seem to stimulate increased voter turnout in those states with substantial black populations. The wide historical gap between white and black voter turnout closed by half in that November's general election, but the weight of greater election-day voting by African Americans seemed to be balanced by a lower white turnout on election day. Indeed, a Gallup poll taken before the election revealed that 17 percent of whites admitted they were "less likely" to vote for a Democrat because of the Jackson campaign against only 10 percent who said they were "more likely" to do so.[13] Clearly, white America was not yet ready to accept a black man as President of the United States.

THE TAWANA BRAWLEY CASE

In early December 1986, stories began to appear in New York City newspapers and television news broadcasts of a teenage girl who had been discovered lying in a trash bag in the yard of a housing complex in the Hudson Valley town of Wappingers Falls. Fifteen-year-old Tawana Brawley had been missing from home for four days when she was found partially clothed and smeared with feces, with racial slurs scrawled across her chest and stomach. She was unresponsive when questioned by police officers and hospital staff. Her family told reporters that she had been abducted and gang raped by four or more white men, one of whom had a gun and a badge. When the county sheriff told the media that all evidence pointed to Tawana having faked her assault, it appeared to many people, long familiar with the tragic history of police abuse and racism in New York, that a cover-up was in progress.

What may have been just one more mysterious footnote in the history of race relations in New York exploded into one of the more famous racially charged incidents of the 1980s when attorneys Alton Maddox and C. Vernon Mason arranged to represent the Brawley family. Maddox was well known for taking cases aimed at exposing the racism of police and the biases of the legal system. Carrying into his law practice a lifetime of experience with racist abuse (he carried the scars of a childhood beating by a white mob in Newton, Georgia), Maddox followed a strategy of putting the justice system on trial in defending his clients. A few years earlier he had become locally famous for his handling of the case of Michael Stewart, a young graffiti artist strangled to death by police officers in

New York City and for representing one of the survivors of the Howard Beach attack on a group of black teens the year before. Maddox enlisted the help of the Reverend Al Sharpton, an activist who had successfully worked with him on the Howard Beach case and whose verbal talents, connections, and nose for publicity would be of immense value to him.

Maddox counseled the Brawley family not to cooperate with the police. Meanwhile, Sharpton addressed the media and accused the Dutchess County authorities of protecting the assailants. Such charges, made without any evidence, would normally not have lasted beyond that day's news cycle, but the apparent suicide of a part-time Dutchess County policeman was seized on by Maddox and Sharpton as evidence of a deeper plot. A large rally was held in Newburgh, New York that drew Louis Farrakhan, leader of the radical Nation of Islam, from his headquarters in Chicago to warn America, "You will not do to another black girl in America what you did to Tawana Brawley and get away with it!"[14] The political pressure mounted and within days New York Governor Mario Cuomo ordered a full state investigation of the Brawley case, and the county prosecutor, without having yet received the forensic evidence from a rape test, announced that he believed that Brawley had been sexually assaulted and that the Ku Klux Klan might be involved, a statement he retracted the next day.

On December 21, the one-year anniversary of the Howard Beach assault, 500 protesters led by Sharpton and Maddox disrupted Brooklyn's rush-hour traffic, leading to 70 arrests. In early January a grand jury began hearing testimony in the case, but before any of the principles had appeared, the investigation was suspended when the district attorney petitioned to be removed from the case and the prosecution was handed to a special prosecutor. No explanation was given for why this motion was requested or granted, which only reinforced the impression that guilty officials must be hiding something. A local lawyer appointed by the court to serve as a special prosecutor resigned within two days without explanation, adding yet more fuel to the arguments of those like Sharpton and Maddox who were screaming that this was evidence of a widespread whitewash of the investigation. Governor Cuomo then appointed his own attorney general, Robert Abrahms, special prosecutor in the case.

The media bandwagon that was rolling with the Brawley case gathered speed in early February when America's most popular television star, Bill Cosby, appeared alongside Al Sharpton and announced he was offering a $25,000 reward for information that could led to a conviction in the case. Not to be outdone, boxing champion Mike Tyson drove to the Brawley home with his promoter Don King and pledged to pay for Tawana's medical expenses and future college tuition.

On February 29, a second grand jury was empanelled on the same day the *New York Times* ran a story that cast serious doubts on the Brawley camp's story. Just as the grand jury began hearing evidence in the case, Maddox held a press conference and stated that he had information that Dutchess County Assistant Attorney Steven Pagones, was one of Tawana's assailants and was part of an "an officially sanctioned, conspiracy to obstruct and prevent justice in the case"[15]

These dramatic charges splashed across the front pages of America's daily newspapers.

While the press hounded Pagones, prosecutor Abrahms subpoenaed Brawley's mother, Glenda, to appear before the grand jury. Maintaining her family's long refusal to cooperate with officials, she refused to appear, prompting a state judge to cite her for contempt and ordering her arrest. Sharpton and Maddox rushed her away to a secret location and then to "sanctuary" at various churches around New York where supporters kept around-the-clock vigil to prevent authorities from seizing her. Phil Donahue hosted his daytime show from the Bethany Baptist church to interview Glenda and her advisors.

In the midst of this standoff, one of Sharpton's aides, Perry McKinnon, broke ranks and told reporters that the Brawley rape story was a "pack of lies."[16] McKinnon raised a suspicion that many had but that prominent whites were fearful of saying publicly lest they be branded as racists, that the Brawley case was a hoax. Indeed, the entire case had exposed several deep racial fracture lines in American society. Mainstream media outlets, although giving prominence to the Brawley story, maintained a skeptical posture throughout while the black press, led by the *Amsterdam News* and New York's independent WLIB radio, embraced the case as a celebrity cause in the tradition of other important civil rights struggles. Moreover, Brawley activists made no secret of their contempt for established civil rights leaders and organizations whom they referred to as "Uncle Toms" for taking a skeptical, "wait-and-see" attitude in the case.

After more than a month of living at Bethany Baptist church, Glenda emerged with her daughter and boarded a bus bound for the Democratic National Convention in Atlanta, Georgia. There they and their supporters protested outside the convention center, heckling members of the New York delegation. The Brawleys met Representative John Conyers of Michigan and discussed opening a congressional investigation.

While rumors, charges, and accusations had swirled around the case for months, the grand jury in Dutchess County had been steadily sifting through the evidence. Working for more than five months, the jurors had heard 180 witnesses, examined 250 exhibits and pieces of physical evidence, and taken 6,000 pages of testimony. In the end none of the physical evidence collected at the scene or from Brawley indicated that she had been raped or dragged through a woods. Steven Pagones, the man accused by Brawley's advisors of participation in the crime, had a solid alibi backed up by scores of witnesses and store receipts. Psychologists testified that Brawley did not display the typical symptoms of a trauma victim. The FBI crime lab concluded that feces smeared on her was from a dog that lived nearby where she was discovered, and the material used to scrawl the racist words on her body was the same as found under her own fingernails. In its final report, the grand jury completely exonerated Pagones and concluded that there was no evidence that a crime had been committed on Brawley.

In 1998, a jury awarded Pagones $345,000 for defamation from Sharpton, Maddox, and Mason. Brawley was ordered to pay $185,000 for her part in the hoax. Brawley never explained to either New York state authorities or to the public what exactly happened to her.

The Tawana Brawley case both captured the attention of Americans and demonstrated once again how differently white and black people view their society. Whites tended to condemn Brawley and view the case in isolation from history. They saw the increasingly shrill accusations made by her lawyers and advisors as evidence that minority communities were too eager to blame racism for all their problems. The black community viewed the Brawley case as just one in a long series of historical outrages and injustices and were more willing to look beyond the inconsistencies in the Brawley family's charges to the larger truth of a long pattern of police brutality and racism in the justice system. As the future first African American mayor of New York city, David Dinkins, wrote at the time, "more to blame are the New York City news media, which have chosen to make a circus of the case by focusing on ridiculous details without acknowledging the corrupt and sometimes racist criminal justice system."[17]

THE MURDER OF VINCENT CHIN, 1982

It was the summer of 1982, which was not a happy time for blue collar workers in the former manufacturing capital of the world, Detroit, Michigan. In addition to the continuing "white flight" and disinvestment from the city, the regional economy had slipped into recession. The American automobile industry had been losing market share to foreign competition since the early 1970s, especially after the oil shock of 1974 pushed the American consumer to consider economical alternatives to Detroit's offering of large, boxy, gas-hungry cars. Automobile executives did not complain when worker anger focused not on their disastrous strategic decisions but on foreign competitors—Japanese who they accused of "unfairly" flooding the market with cheap products calculated to "steal" market share and jobs from Americans and Arabs who conspired to raise gasoline prices. Many Detroit factories posted signs in their parking lots announcing that foreign-made cars would be towed away.

That June, Vincent Chin, a 27-year-old Detroiter was planning his wedding. Chin was born in China but was adopted and naturalized as a toddler by a Chinese American couple, Lily and David Bing Hing Chin. The Chin family personified the long and jagged history of Chinese American experience in an adopted land that desired their labor but not their presence. Vincent's great-grandfather was one of the Chinese laborers brought to America to build the transcontinental railroads during the nineteenth century and then was forced to return to China by racist immigration laws. Vincent's father, David Bing Hing Chin, was born in China, immigrated to Detroit in the 1920s, fought overseas as a soldier in the U.S. army during World War II, earning his citizenship, then met Lily in China and returned with her to Detroit. For Vincent, that summer was bittersweet, poised to begin a family of his own, beginning to establish his career as an industrial draftsman, but having just lost his father to kidney disease a few months earlier.

On June 19, two of Vincent's friends celebrated the end of his bachelorhood by taking him out to a strip club in the gritty Detroit suburb of Highland Park. There the trio was accosted by Ronald Ebens, a factory supervisor and his stepson, Michael Nitz, who was also an autoworker but had been laid off. One witness reported hearing Ebens shout at Chin, "It's because of you motherf——s that we're out of work," apparently mistaking Chin for Japanese and speaking on behalf of all white autoworkers because he had a good job at a Chrysler automobile plant. A scuffle ensued and all five men were thrown out of the club. Ebens and Nitz went back to their neighborhood and picked up a friend whom they hired to help them settle their scores with Chin and his friend. After cruising the area for half an hour, they spied Chin and his friends in front of a McDonalds and attacked. Chin was held down by Nitz while Ebens smashed his skull with four blows from a baseball bat. The attack was witnessed by a pair of off-duty police officers. Four days later, Chin died; his last words were, "It isn't fair."[18]

Ebens and Nitz were quickly arrested and their guilt was unequivocal, but prosecutors decided to bring only second-degree manslaughter chargers against the pair in return for their guilty pleas. At sentencing Judge Charles Kaufman shocked the packed court gallery by releasing the pair and placing them on probation for three years and fining them $3,780. Many observers wondered if Judge Charles Kaufman's experience as a Japanese prisoner of war for 18 months during World War II (in which he was reduced from an athletic 160 pounds to 90 pounds) may have colored his judgment. When Kaufman died in 2004, even his son admitted, "It embarrassed me that my dad erred in that case, but I'm very proud of the other 99 percent of his life."[19] Kaufman at least had the courage to declare his sentence and stick by it; the county prosecutors who offered the lenient plea bargain were nowhere to be found in the courtroom when Kaufman rendered his decision.

According to the census of 1980, there were only 1,213 people of Chinese descent living in Detroit, a city of 1.2 million people. As in many other Chinese American communities, there was a long tradition of staying out of the public eye and avoiding confrontation, political or otherwise, with the white majority and local government. But now many Chinese Americans viewed the Chin affair as an alarm bell they could not ignore. Frank Wu, who grew up in Detroit and went on to be the first person from a minority community to be appointed Dean of the Wayne State Law School, later recalled that Chin's death was what first turned his attention to the importance of criminal law: "I realized I had to care every bit as much about what it's like to be driving while black and what disparities there are in the legal justice system" Similarly, Harold Bong Leon, son of the owner of Detroit's Chinese Teapot restaurant, was first motivated to become active in the local Chinese American community by Chin's slaying and went on to found and lead the Asian American Bar Association of Michigan.[20]

Immediately after Judge Kaufman's decision was known, Detroit's Chinese American community began organizing for justice, forming the first Chinese American Civil Rights movement in Michigan, one that would become a catalyst for Chinese American activism nationwide. A core of organizers took the lead: Henry Yee, a well-known restaurateur and World War II navy veteran; Lily Chin, Vincent's mother; Liza Chan, one of the few Chinese women lawyers in the state; Helen Zia, a freelance journalist who later became editor of Ms. *Magazine*. They called their new organization, American Citizens for Justice, deemphasizing the ethnic qualification in Chinese American, and pursued the first-ever federal criminal civil rights prosecution for an assault on a person of Asian heritage.

Coordinating efforts with other Chinese advocacy organizations around the United States, American Citizens for Justice succeeded in prompting an F.B.I. investigation of the Chin case from the standpoint of federal civil rights laws in July 1983. Four months later, the U.S. Justice Department unsealed indictments against Ebens and Nitz, charging them with violations of Vincent Chin's civil rights. The next summer a jury found Ebens guilty but acquitted Nitz (mainly because in a civil rights trial, much hinged on determining the racist intent of an assailant's actions). Ebens was sentenced to 25 years in federal prison, although he later successfully petitioned an appeals court for a new trial. Ebens's new trial was moved to Cincinnati, a city with an even smaller Asian American population than Detroit, and there a jury decided it could not determine that his crime was racially motivated and freed him.

Upon Ebens's exoneration in 1987, Vincent's mother, Lily Chin, heartbroken and disgusted with her adopted country's lack of justice, returned to China, the country she had left 40 years before. In an interview before she left, she expressed her frustration: "I don't understand how this could happen in America...My husband fought for this country. We always paid our taxes and worked hard. We never had any trouble. Before I really loved America, but now this has made me very angry...Something is wrong with this country."[21]

In 1989, a documentary film shot by Christine Choy about the case, "Who Killed Vincent Chin?" was nominated for an Academy Award as Best Documentary Film.

"WILLIE" HORTON AND THE 1988 PRESIDENTIAL CAMPAIGN

Tough-on-crime rhetoric became a hallmark of Republican party strategy in the 1980s, reaching its pinnacle in President Reagan's declaration of a "War on Drugs." Its most obvious racial appeal actually came in the hard-fought election of 1988 that pitted a popular technocratic governor of Massachusetts, Michael Dukakis, against Vice President George Bush. At the outset of the campaign, as many seemed eager for a change after eight years of Reagan–Bush, Bush polled as many negative feelings as positive ones from likely voters and trailed Dukakis by double digits. Lee Atwater, Bush's brilliant campaign manager, hired dozens of researchers to pore over Dukakis's record as governor to find the one or two issues that could best portray him as a weak-kneed liberal disconnected from real Americans. Their digging quickly produced an issue embodied by a single man whose menacing image, in one gritty mug shot, evoked and symbolized white America's troubled confusion of race, crime, and liberalism.

William Horton was 22-years-old on October 26, 1974 when he and two bud-
dies robbed a gas station in Lawrence, Massachusetts. One of this trio, it was
never proven which, fatally stabbed the teenage attendant, Joey Fournier, 19 times
in the chest. Convicted of felony murder in the first degree and sentenced to
life without parole, Horton spent the next 11 years in various prisons in Massachusetts, earning a sufficiently good behavior record to eventually qualify for
short periods of release to visit his family. It was on the tenth of these furloughs
in April 1986 that Horton failed to return and fled the state. Nearly a year later
Horton broke into a suburban Washington, D.C. home, beating, robbing, and
tying up Cliff Barnes and raping Barnes's girlfriend, Angela Miller. Barnes and
Miller managed to escape in the midst of their ordeal, and Horton led police on
a high-speed chase in a stolen car that ended with his crashing and brandishing a
gun at police who responded by shooting him. Horton was convicted of burglary,
rape, and assault and sentenced to another life term in a Maryland prison.

Horton had been the beneficiary of a trend in prison administration beginning in the late 1960s that emphasized the readjustment of prisoners to life behind prison walls before their release. These "furlough" programs not only reduced
the rates at which ex-cons committed crimes after their release, they improved
discipline and control in prisons by providing a desirable incentive for good behavior, as well as a clear track record on which future decisions about parole
could be based. Such programs were designed with the average felon in mind, but
even those sentenced to life without parole were able to benefit from furlough
programs. The little-discussed fact of criminal justice in America was that few
inmates served their full sentences or spent their entire lives in prison. Even
a significant proportion of lifers had their sentences commuted and were paroled
as they approached old age (states had a large incentive in doing so—not only
because statistics indicated old men committed relatively few violent crimes,
but also because state budgets would not be burdened with the expense of their
geriatric medical and convalescent care).

Just a few years before William Horton participated in the murder of Joey
Fournier, a Republican legislature and a Republican governor in Massachusetts
enacted the Correctional Reform Act of 1972 that established the state's furlough system. It allowed for up to two weeks of furlough per year for any prisoner who had a good behavior record with the approval of state authorities, the
designation of a sponsor who would be responsible for the furloughed prisoners
conduct and the notification of local police, and a strict deadline beyond which a
convict would automatically be designated an escapee. A later ruling by the Massachusetts Supreme Court established that even those sentenced to life without
parole must be considered eligible for inclusion in the program. By the time the
Massachusetts furlough system was firmly established in the mid-1970s, 44 other
states and the District of Columbia had similar furlough programs. From the furlough program's beginning in 1972 to the year Horton escaped, Massachusetts
had furloughed 10,553 inmates, of whom 426, about one in 25, escaped. The

rate for those with life sentences was better: from 1981–1986, 112 lifers were furloughed and 3, one in 37, fled. By the cold logic of criminology, the marginal benefits of the program were measured by calculating the difference between the recidivism rate for furloughed convicts to that of those simply released on serving their sentences and then favorably comparing this "savings" to the number of crimes committed by escapees.

Michael Dukakis, a man who prided himself on his technical mastery of the arcane details of state administration, was well aware of these facts in the summer of 1988 when public outrage over William Horton's furlough, escape, and subsequent brutal crimes was whipped up by a small local newspaper, the *Lawrence Eagle Tribune* (which began to refer to "Willie" rather than William, in the racist tradition of infantilizing black men and spread false lurid rumors that Horton had sexually mutilated Joey Fournier before stabbing him). Grass roots protest against the furlough program grew with the establishment of Citizens Against Unsafe Society, which demanded Governor Dukakis meet with Horton's victims and that he support the ending of furloughs for lifers. Dukakis did neither until their campaign placed a referendum on a statewide ballot, and the state legislature overwhelmingly passed a bill to that effect. In the face of an incredibly emotional issue that played on base beliefs about family, race, and elitist liberalism, Dukakis appeared uncaring, academic, and removed. Reversing himself on the eve of the presidential spring primaries, Dukakis first suspended the furlough program and then signed legislation abolishing the privilege for lifers. The damage was done, however, and his opponents had a perfect symbolic issue with which to bludgeon him into defeat.

This club was first wielded by a fellow Democrat, Al Gore, who raised the furlough issue in a primary debate in New York City on April 12. Dukakis was again evasive and overly analytical on what was seen by most voters as a gut issue. In late June *Reader's Digest* appeared with a story written by a freelancer close to the Bush campaign entitled, "Getting Away with Murder," that recounted Horton's rape of a young white suburban woman after running away from his furlough. By then the Bush camp had latched onto Horton as the defining issue of its negative campaign—campaign manager Lee Atwater told a gathering of Republican organizers that when he was done, the voters would think Willie Horton was "Dukakis's running mate"[22] Although eager to use Horton to full effect (Roger Ailes, Bush's chief advertising man, told *Time* magazine that "the only question is whether we depict Willie Horton with a knife in his hand or without it"[23]), to avoid a possible backlash by playing such an obvious race card, the official Bush campaign released attack advertisements that focused on the "Dukakis Furlough Program" and refrained from mentioning Horton. A private political action committee, however, in close communication with the Bush campaign, released a scathing ad that featured a frightful mug shot of Horton in full beard and disheveled Afro (reportedly taken by police from his hospital bed soon after being shot) and placing the issue of race and crime at the center of the campaign.

The implication of the ad was obvious—decent white folks were being sacrificed to black criminals because of their coddling by soft liberal politicians like Dukakis. Another ad by the same group featured the sister of stabbing victim Joey Fournier and husband of rape victim Angela Miller, evoking the mythical fears of the black rape of white women that had been the excuse for more than a century of lynching and segregation. On the subterranean level of deep cultural and psychological symbolism, the campaign was now one of black "bestiality" versus the protection of white "purity."

Dukakis, to his credit, did not respond in kind and refused to pander to the base emotions whipped up by Horton images. This principled refusal, however, led directly to the Waterloo of the Dukakis campaign, the final debate where the first question he was asked by CNN anchor Bernard Shaw was, "Governor, if Kitty Dukakis were raped and murdered, would you favor an irrevocable death penalty for the killer?" Instead of saying he would prefer to strangle the killer with his own two hands, Dukakis launched into a dispassionate analysis of the deterrence value of the death penalty and crime rates. Dukakis also refused to denounce the Bush ads as being racist, calling them instead "lies." Other prominent Democrats, such as Jesse Jackson, however, were not so shy. Jackson called the ads "blatantly race-conscious signals, that have had the impact of instilling ungrounded fear in whites, in alienation from blacks... The use of the Willie Horton example is designed to create the most horrible psycho-sexual fears."[24] In the end, Bush sailed past Dukakis with a 7.8 percent margin of the popular vote, a three-to-one margin of the electoral vote, and four-to-one margin of states. Bush polled remarkably well in suburban areas and across the South, reflecting the tug of his crime and race appeal.

THE ANTIAPARTHEID MOVEMENT

Although many civil rights activists historically have been concerned with international issues—Marcus Garvey described himself as a "Pan-Africanist," W.E.B. Du Bois lived out his final years as a citizen of Ghana, and Martin Luther King Jr. raised the issue of war in Vietnam in the months before his assassination—rarely did international questions involving racial justice spark significant social movements in the United States. But in Reagan's first term, scattered voices calling for action against South Africa's racist system of apartheid grew loud and combined into a powerful social movement.

South Africa's apartheid system was constructed in 1948 at the very time that the United States was beginning to abandon its own long experiment in legal racial segregation. Although not entirely analogous because of South Africa's unique colonial history, apartheid was, nevertheless, a system of laws aimed at racial separation and preserving economic privileges and political power for whites that in many ways eerily mirrored the U.S. history of Jim Crow segregation. Indeed, many Americans felt that their own nation's guilty history of discrimination made action against South Africa a moral imperative.

Scattered protests in front of the South African embassy and at the United Nations in the 1970s and early 1980s soon spread to many states as activists demanded that American corporations, state governments, and universities divest themselves of all economic ties to the apartheid regime. The political movement, coordinated by a relatively new organization, Trans-Africa, led by Randall Robinson, a lawyer who advocated that African Americans become more activist in support of African issues and the African diaspora, proved just the tip of a protest iceberg. The antiapartheid movement caught on partly as a cultural movement, a means of clearly confronting racism at a time when racism in America had moved underground. When Stevie Van Zandt, guitarist for Bruce Springsteen's E-Street band, proposed doing a charity album for South Africa and having artists pledge to boycott the country, he thought he could enlist a handful of his musician friends in the effort. When the album "Sun City" was released, it featured the contributions of more than 50 leading musical artists mixing the worlds of hip-hop, rock, and pop. Unsurprisingly, the political album was banned in South Africa, although many observers were disturbed when about half the radio stations in America also refused to play it on the grounds that it was too "political," prompting Mayor Tom Bradley, the first African American mayor of Los Angeles, to urge California radio stations to give it more airplay. Other artists, such as Paul Simon, introduced American ears to South African township beats. South African groups and artists, such as Ladysmith Black Mambazo, Miriam Makeba, Hugh Masakela, Johnny Clegg, and Savuka, popularized a black South African cultural movement that integrated music, art, dance, and militant protest into one heady expression.

In the spring of 1985, the divestiture movement reached a crescendo, with hundreds of protests across the nation that included a two-week occupation of the state capital in Wisconsin by student activists. The next year scores of students at the University of California Berkeley were arrested when they protested their university's investments in South Africa by erecting a mock "shantytown" in front of Berkeley's administration building. With the vocal and impassioned support of civil rights organizations, churches, unions, and African American communities throughout America, dozens of local and state governments passed resolutions calling for divestment from South Africa by the end of the decade.

In the face of growing protests, President Reagan remained steadfast against any sanctions against South Africa, arguing that more progress could be made by "quiet diplomacy" and what he termed "constructive engagement." Reagan not only made clear that he believed economic sanctions were counterproductive, he seemed to believe that South Africa's apartheid laws did not extend to U.S. businesses operating there: "many people are critical and some of the protests and the demonstrations here have voiced disapproval of American investment in South Africa, of American companies that are in business there. Well, this is based on ignorance when they say this. The simple truth is that most black tribal leaders there have openly expressed their support in American business investment there because our American businesses go there and observe practices with regard to employees that are not observed by South African companies."

Congress took up a tough South African sanctions bill later that fall, which seemed assured of passage until Republican leaders in the Senate successfully outmaneuvered the Democratic majority, which included at one point Senator Robert Dole fleeing with the official copy of the bill and locking it in a safe and then invoking a rarely used technicality that no legislation could be debated that was not "physically present" in the Senate chamber. Nevertheless, the political momentum was all on the side of those wanting to isolate South Africa, and President Reagan was forced to announce a series of loophole-riddled economic restrictions in order to head off tougher legislation.[25]

Reagan's maneuver averted further action for nearly a year but could not hold against the unfolding backdrop of events in Africa itself. On May 19, South Africa launched cross-border attacks on three neighboring countries, Zimbabwe, Zambia, and Botswana, claiming it was rooting out "terrorists" poised to strike. Within days, new legislation was introduced in Congress that would prohibit all new bank loans and corporate investments in South Africa; ban the importation of South African coal, steel, and uranium to the United States; and revoke the American landing rights of South Africa's national airline. In a surprising indication of the level of frustration with administration policy toward South Africa in Congress, this bill was soon replaced by a far tougher measure that required all American business to leave South Africa within six months. The tough sanctions bill, introduced by Representative Ronald Dellums, whose home district encompassed most of Oakland, California, passed the House in June 1986 but failed in the Senate in favor of the original measure, which passed overwhelmingly, 84–14. Although many Republicans indicated that they voted for the bill to encourage Reagan not to make a political mistake and veto it, Reagan vetoed it anyway. In the end, only 21 Republicans, most notably including Senator Jesse Helms and Republican Robert Dole, stood with Reagan on the issue when the Senate voted to override his veto, handing Reagan the greatest political defeat on a foreign policy issue during his presidency.[26]

Scholars subsequently have debated the effect of Western economic sanctions on the apartheid regime, and most analysts say far more important was the military campaign of the African National Congress and other banned groups combined with the mass resistance of black South Africans who collectively made their townships and territories "ungovernable" through their refusal to pay taxes or obey racist authorities. Nevertheless, there can be little doubt that sanctions added pressure onto the government of South Africa to reform. By 1989, the South African president, P. W. Botha, opened secret negotiations with the African National Congress, a process that would lead to the legalization of several outlawed political parties, the release of African National Congress President Nelson Mandela, and the ultimate dismantling of apartheid in the early 1990s.

VOICES OF THE DECADE

JESSE JACKSON

Black civil rights leader Jesse Jackson was born in 1941 in South Carolina and distinguished himself as a scholar and athlete in high school. After graduating from North Carolina Agricultural and Technical State University, Jackson attended the prestigious Chicago Theological Seminary but withdrew to join the Civil Rights movement. Jackson rose quickly in Rev. Martin Luther King Jr.'s Southern Christian Leadership Conference (SCLC) and was working with King in his Memphis campaign when King was assassinated. In the 1970s, Jackson broke with SCLC and founded Operation PUSH in Chicago. In the 1980s, Jackson aimed to reorient the Democratic Party's agenda toward the multiracial constituency that was consistently its most reliable constituency but often its least attended to. Jackson's "Rainbow Coalition" was the vehicle for his presidential runs of 1984 and 1988. In the following extract from his keynote speech to the Democratic party in 1984, Jackson reiterates the class issues that unite the party across racial lines.

Thank you very much.

Tonight we come together bound by our faith in a mighty God, with genuine respect and love for our country, and inheriting the legacy of a great Party, the Democratic Party, which is the best hope for redirecting our nation on a more humane, just, and peaceful course.

This is not a perfect party. We are not a perfect people. Yet, we are called to a perfect mission. Our mission: to feed the hungry; to clothe the naked; to house the homeless; to teach the illiterate; to provide jobs for the jobless; and to choose the human race over the nuclear race.

We are gathered here this week to nominate a candidate and adopt a platform which will expand, unify, direct, and inspire our Party and the nation to fulfill this mission. My constituency is the desperate, the damned, the disinherited, the disrespected, and the despised. They are restless and seek relief. They have voted in record numbers. They have invested the faith, hope, and trust that they have in us. The Democratic Party must send them a signal that we care. I pledge my best not to let them down.

There is the call of conscience, redemption, expansion, healing, and unity. Leadership must heed the call of conscience, redemption, expansion, healing, and unity, for they are the key to achieving our mission. Time is neutral and does not change things. With courage and initiative, leaders change things.

No generation can choose the age or circumstance in which it is born, but through leadership it can choose to make the age in which it is born an age of enlightenment, an age of jobs, and peace, and justice. Only leadership—that intangible combination of gifts, the discipline, information, circumstance, courage, timing, will and divine inspiration—can lead us out of the crisis in which we find ourselves. Leadership can mitigate the misery of our nation. Leadership can part the waters and lead our nation in the direction of the Promised Land. Leadership can lift the boats stuck at the bottom.

I ask for your vote on the first ballot as a vote for a new direction for this Party and this nation—a vote of conviction, a vote of conscience. But I will be proud to support the nominee of this convention for the Presidency of the United States of America. Thank you.

America is not like a blanket—one piece of unbroken cloth, the same color, the same texture, the same size. America is more like a quilt: many patches, many pieces, many colors, many sizes, all woven and held together by a common thread. The white, the Hispanic, the black, the Arab, the Jew, the woman, the native American, the small farmer, the businessperson, the environmentalist, the peace activist, the young, the old, the lesbian, the gay, and the disabled make up the American quilt.

Even in our fractured state, all of us count and fit somewhere. We have proven that we can survive without each other. But we have not proven that we can win and make progress without each other. We must come together.

From Jesse Jackson, "Keep Hope Alive," Democratic National Convention, Atlanta, GA, July 19, 1988. (*Say It Plain: A Century of Great African American Speeches* available at http://americanradioworks.publicradio.org/features/sayitplain/jjackson.html.)

CÉSAR CHÁVEZ

United Farm Workers of America President César Chávez was born in Gila, Arizona to a semi-prosperous *mexicano* ranching family in 1927. When the family fell behind in their tax payments during the Great Depression, they were cheated out of their land by a white neighbor. Chávez's family was forced into joining the stream of migrant farm laborers seeking work in California. They settled in a neighborhood of farm workers in San Jose named *Sal Si Puedes* (or "get out if you can") where Chávez attended some school and worked in the surrounding fields. By the time he reached his teen years, Chávez had witnessed many union drives and strikes but was not yet interested in organizing, preferring the rebellious dress of the "Zoot Suiters" and the jazz music in local road houses. After Pearl Harbor was attacked in 1941, Chávez joined the Navy and served for two years as a deckhand before marrying his childhood sweetheart and returning to *Sal Si Puedes* and its surrounding fields and orchards. Tutored by a local priest, Chávez read widely and became an activist in his barrio and then a union organizer. By the early 1960s, Chávez had founded a farm workers association that would become the United Farm Workers (UFW). In 1965, Chávez's union supported a strike among grape pickers near Delano, California that soon expanded into a nationwide struggle that would propel Chávez and his young union to legendary status when they won a contract from growers a year later. Chávez distinguished himself as a compelling speaker and for his ardent adherence to the principles of nonviolence used to such dramatic effect in the American Civil Rights movement.

In 1984, the UFW launched a national boycott against grape growers that centered its public appeal on the danger to workers and consumers of the unregulated use of pesticides. UFW demanded limitations and regulations for the safe use of such chemicals written into its union contracts and hoped that an appeal to the environment might attract support from consumers in the otherwise rightward-leaning era of Ronald Reagan. In this extract from a speech, Chávez sketches the history of the UFW and argues for the sweeping social importance of its struggle.

Today, thousands of farm workers live under savage conditions—beneath trees and amid garbage and human excrement—near tomato fields in San Diego County, tomato fields which use the most modern farm technology. Vicious rats gnaw on them as they sleep. They walk miles to buy food at inflated prices. And they carry in water from irrigation pumps.

Child labor is still common in many farm areas. As much as 30 percent of Northern California's garlic harvesters are under-aged children. Kids as young as six years old have voted in state-conducted union elections since they qualified as workers. Some 800,000 under-aged children work with their families harvesting crops across America. Babies born to migrant workers suffer 25 percent higher infant mortality than the rest of the population. Malnutrition among migrant worker children is 10 times higher than the national rate. Farm workers' average life expectancy is still 49 years—compared to 73 years for the average American.

All my life, I have been driven by one dream, one goal, one vision: To overthrow a farm labor system in this nation which treats farm workers as if they were not important human beings....

I'm not very different from anyone else who has ever tried to accomplish something with his life. My motivation comes from my personal life—from watching what my mother and father went through when I was growing up; from what we experienced as migrant farm workers in California. That dream, that vision, grew from my own experience with racism, with hope, with the desire to be treated fairly and to see my people treated as human beings and not as chattel. It grew from anger and rage—emotions I felt 40 years ago when people of my color were denied the right to see a movie or eat at a restaurant in many parts of California. It grew from the frustration and humiliation I felt as a boy who couldn't understand how the growers could abuse and exploit farm workers when there were so many of us and so few of them....

I began to realize what other minority people had discovered: That the only answer—the only hope—was in organizing. More of us had to become citizens. We had to register to vote. And people like me had to develop the skills it would take to organize, to educate, to help empower the Chicano people....

History and inevitability are on our side. The farm workers and their children—and the Hispanics and their children—are the future in California.

And corporate growers are the past! Those politicians who ally themselves with the corporate growers and against the farm workers and the Hispanics are in for a big surprise. They want to make their careers in politics. They want to hold power 20 and 30 years from now.

But 20 and 30 years from now—in Modesto, in Salinas, in Fresno, in Bakersfield, in the Imperial Valley, and in many of the great cities of California—those communities will be dominated by farm workers and not by growers, by the children and grandchildren of farm workers and not by the children and grandchildren of growers.

From César Chávez, President of the United Farm Workers of America, AFL-CIO, speaking before the Commonwealth Club of California, in San Francisco on November 9, 1984. (Available at the United Farm Workers of America Web site http://www.ufw.org/common wealth.htm.)

MAYOR HAROLD WASHINGTON

Chicago Mayor Harold Washington was a Chicagoan through and through. Born at Cook County Hospital, son of a Chicago precinct captain, Washington attended the all-black DuSable High School (named for Jean Baptiste Pointe du Sable, the city's Afro-French founder). He took his bachelor's degree from Roosevelt College and his law degree from Northwestern University. Washington served as a combat engineer in the South Pacific during World War II and, after earning his law degree, went into city service as an assistant city prosecutor. He entered politics in 1965, winning election to the Illinois House of Representatives where he served for four terms before moving to the Illinois Senate and then, in 1981, to the U.S. Congress from the first district of Illinois on Chicago's South Side.

At the urging of a number of African American leaders fed up with Chicago's Democratic machine and its continuing refusal to equally reward its black supporters, Washington reluctantly agreed to stand for mayor again (he had done so in 1977 and failed badly, attracting just 11 percent of the vote) as long as activists could register 50,000 new voters. The prospect of a strong challenge to incumbent Jane Byrne energized the black neighborhoods of Chicago, and this goal was reached; Washington announced his candidacy in November 1982. The campaigning was vicious and racially –tinged, with one of the machine bosses, Council President Edward "Fast Eddie" Vrdolyak, telling precinct captains at a meeting that the election had become "a race thing" and that they had to support Byrne to "save your city" from Washington. Washington's old peccadilloes— a conviction for income tax evasion and suspension from the practice of law for not representing paying clients—were dredged up. In spite of being outspent 10 to 1, however, Washington went on to defeat Byrne and Richard M. Daley, son of the legendary Chicago mayor, in the Democratic primary, largely as a result of his brilliant performance in four televised debates where his wit, charm, plain talk, and honesty, distinguished him not only from the Democratic field but from politicians in general.

Winning the Democratic primary in Chicago was considered an assurance of winning the general election—Chicago had not elected a Republican mayor in 52 years—but with Washington, an African American who had fought the entrenched patronage system as the party's official choice, the election of a Democrat was suddenly in doubt. When the Cook County Democratic Party held a meeting to formally endorse the people's choice, one-third of the white delegates boycotted, and the party's leadership held a quick voice vote rather than go on record for Washington by the usual roll-call method. Republican candidate Bernard E. Epton appealed to the racial fears of white voters with his campaign slogan, "Epton now—Before It's Too Late!" "Bigots for Bernie" buttons were popular in some ethnic white neighborhoods. Polls showed that 90 percent of white Democrats were leaving the party rather than vote for Washington. On election day, 88 percent of the voters of Chicago turned out, the greatest percentage in the city's modern history and Washington became the city's first African American mayor. His years in office were contentious and difficult as he faced a hostile city council while attempting to distribute city services evenly and root out the privileges of an entrenched political machine. During his first term, his popularity grew in some swing white wards while, in his home district, it declined somewhat because Washington would not reward his supporters with the spoils of office in the usual way of doing business in the city. Nevertheless, he won reelection in a replay battle with Jane Byrne in the 1987 primary and his arch-enemy, Edward R. Vrdolyak in the general election. Just seven months into his second term, Washington suffered a heart attack at his desk in city hall and died.[27] His inaugural speech from April 29, 1983, is excerpted here:

This is a very serious vow that I've just taken before God and man, to do everything in my power to protect this city and every person who lives in it.

I do not take this duty lightly. I was up late last night thinking about this moment. It went through my head hundreds and hundreds of times, and words that I was reading put me in a reflective and a somber, somber mood.

On my right hand last night was a Bible, which is a very good book for a new mayor to pay attention to. And, in front of me was a report of the city's finances which my transition team had prepared, and it did not contain very good news. To my left there was no book because the one I wanted the most does not exist. It's the one I wish had been written by my tribesman, Jean Pointe Baptiste du Sable, who settled Chicago over 200 years ago.

And, as I reflected last night for a brief period of time, I wish he had written a book about how to be a mayor of a vast city like ours, a repository of wisdom that had been handed down from mayor to mayor for all these years.

Because, after reading the report about the actual state of the city's finances, I wanted some good, solid, sound advice. Then I realized that to solve the problems facing us, it will have to be decided between you and me, because every mayor begins anew, and there is no blueprint for the future course that these cities, these municipalities must follow.

So I made a list of some of the things you told me during the election campaign, and I found out that you had given me the best and most solid advice. The first thing you told me is to do no harm. You told me that the guiding principle of government is to do the greatest good. Your instructions which I heard from neighborhood after neighborhood, said to be patient and be fair, be candid and, in short, to continue to tell the truth....

All during the campaign I knew that the city had financial problems and I talked about them repeatedly, incessantly. A majority of the voters believed me and embarked on what can only be described as a great movement and revitalization labeled "reform."

My election was the result of the greatest grassroots effort in the history of the city of Chicago. It may have been equaled somewhere in this country, I know not where.

My election was made possible by thousands and thousands of people who demanded that the burdens of mismanagement, unfairness and inequity be lifted so that the city could be saved.

One of the ideas that held us all together said that neighborhood involvement has to take the place of the ancient, decrepit, and creaking machine. City government for once in our lifetime must be made equitable and fair. The people of Chicago have asked for more responsibility and more representation at every city level.

It's a good thing that your philosophy prevailed, because otherwise I'm not sure that the city could solve the financial crisis at hand.

Reluctantly, I must tell you that because of circumstances thrust upon us, each and everyone of us, we must immediately cut back on how much money the city can spend.

Monday, I will issue an order to freeze all city hiring and raises, in order to reduce the city expenses by millions of dollars. We will have no choice but to release several hundred new city employees who were added because of political considerations....

In the late hours last night, while contemplating the enormity of the challenge we face together, I remembered the great words of President John Fitzgerald Kennedy at his inaugural address in 1961. "Ask not for what your country can do for you" he said. "Ask what you can do for your country." In that same spirit, today I am asking all of you—particularly you who have taken the oath with me today—to respond to a great challenge: help me institute reforms and bring about the revival and renewal of this great city while there is still time....

Having said all this, I want you to know that the situation is serious but not desperate. I am optimistic about our future. I'm optimistic not just because I have a positive view of life, and I do, but because there is so much about this city that promises achievement.

We are a multi-ethnic, multi-racial, multi-language city and that is not a source to negate but really a source of pride, because it adds stability and strength to a metropolitan city as large as ours. Our minorities are ambitious, and that is a sign of a prosperous city on the move. Racial fears and divisiveness have hurt us in the past. But I believe that this is a situation that will and must be overcome....

In our ethnic and racial diversity, we are all brothers and sisters in a quest for greatness. Our creativity and energy are unequaled by any city anywhere in the world. We will not rest until the renewal of our city is done.

Today, I want to tell you how proud I am to be your mayor. There have been 41 Mayors before me and when I was growing up in this city and attending its public schools it never dawned upon me nor did I dream that the flame would pass my way. But it has....

It makes me humble, but it also makes me glad. I hope someday to be remembered by history as the mayor who cared about people and who was, above all, fair. A mayor who helped, who really helped, heal our wounds and stood the watch while the city and its people answered the greatest challenge in more than a century. Who saw that city renewed.

From the Inaugural Address of Mayor Harold Washington, April 29, 1983. (Chicago City Council Journal of the Proceedings, April 29, 1983, pp. 7–11. Available in the Municipal Reference Collection of the Chicago Public Library. This excerpt has been edited for both length and style.)

ROBERT T. MATSUI

Congressman Robert Matsui was six months old when his Japanese American family was ordered out of their home in Sacramento, California by government officials in 1942 and forcibly detained in a remote camp where persons of Japanese decent from around the West Coast of America were relocated. Thirty-six years later Matsui was sent to Congress by Sacramento voters, becoming only the second Japanese American born in the continental United States to be elected to the House of Representatives. In 1985, Matsui, his voice cracking with emotion, introduced legislation, the Japanese American Redress Act, to compensate the survivors of the mass violation of civil rights committed during the war and to issue a formal apology on the part of the American people. Three years later, this legislation would pass under President Reagan's signature.[28]

Mr. Speaker, it is with great pride that I join our esteemed majority leader, JIM WRIGHT and a number of our distinguished colleagues in introducing the Civil Liberties Act of 1985. This legislation addresses an issue of fundamental importance to our system of constitutional liberty....

I am particularly pleased by the number that has been chosen for the bill, H.R. 442. This number honors the famous 442d Regimental Combat Team of World War II. This unit was composed entirely of Americans of Japanese ancestry, many of whom had volunteered from this Nation's detention camps. Forced to leave their homes on the west coast with their families, these dedicated Americans volunteered for combat duty to protect and serve the United States. While they shed their blood in the service of this Nation, their families— parents, brothers, sisters, wives, and children—remained behind barbed wire and under armed military guard as prisoners of the country for which these men were willing to give their lives in combat.

The 442d fought in some of the fiercest and bloodiest campaigns of the European theater. It was the most highly decorated unit of its size in the military history of the United States. During five major campaigns, this unit earned over 18,000 decorations and had over 9,000 Purple Hearts. It is fitting that this historic legislation should be designated in honor of these fine men.

The civil rights abridgement which this legislation addresses began for Americans of Japanese ancestry on February 19, 1942 when President Franklin Roosevelt signed the infamous Executive Order 9066. This order authorized military commanders to exclude citizens and aliens from certain areas, supposedly to protect against acts of sabotage and espionage. The order was promulgated regardless of the fact that no documented cases of disloyalty by Japanese Americans existed and none has subsequently arisen.

Executive Order 9066 was the first step in an odyssey of deprivation, detention, and denial of civil rights. Soon after the order, all American citizens of Japanese ancestry and resident aliens were prohibited from living, working, or traveling on the west coast. Japanese Americans living in the area were removed to temporary assembly centers and then on to relocation camps where conditions ranged from passable to deplorable. The concept of habeas corpus was simply forgotten.

What was the experience of those camps? For my parents there was the discouraging loss of business, home, and other possessions. There are visions of barbed wire fences and sentry dogs, of loss of privacy and lack of adequate sanitation; and memories of the heart-wrenching divisions that occurred as families were separated by physical distance and the emotional distress of the camps. And there was the stigma of implied guilt as this Nation determined that we were a threat to national security, that because of our race, no matter how many generations passed, Americans of Japanese ancestry could never really be trustworthy Americans.

But what is most striking about all of these internment camp stories is the faith and hope that remained. Faith in the law of the land; pride in this country; and most of all, a sincere desire to prove loyalty to this great Nation and be allowed to serve its ideals and principles. All this, despite the fact that basic constitutional and civil rights were being denied.

It is the spirit of this faith that brings me before you today. For I firmly believe that our actions here are essential for giving credibility to our constitutional system and reinforcing our tradition of justice. More than half of the original internees have already died, but it is not too late to return the rightful honor to those who remain among us. It is certainly not too late to provide compensation for these living individuals. And it is never too late to send a message to future generations that such a tragic denial of constitutional rights cannot and will not be tolerated.

From a speech by Robert Matsui to the House of Representatives, January 3, 1985. (*Congressional Record*, archived at The Honorable Robert T. Matsui Legacy Project, http://www.digital.lib.csus.edu/mats/index.php, identifier no. 10226.)

RACE RELATIONS BY GROUP

AFRICAN AMERICANS

In the 1980s, a sudden increase in immigration from the Caribbean, especially from Haiti, changed the character of some urban neighborhoods, as well as the social, cultural, and political makeup of their African-American communities.

One of the unforeseen effects of a slight change in immigration law in 1976 that established a 20,000 ceiling for immigrants from any individual country was to favor those wishing to come to America from the smallest nations in the Western Hemisphere. Former British colonies in the Caribbean such as Dominique, Belize, St. Lucia, Grenada, and St. Vincent, once independent nations, suddenly had a far larger proportion of their population legally eligible to immigrate to the United States. Indeed, these small nations lost between 16 and 23 percent of their populations during the 1970s.

With a dramatic increase in the flow of non-Hispanic immigrants to the United States from Caribbean nations, the makeup of West Indian communities changed. Before the 1960s, immigrants from these areas tended to be more skilled and more affluent than they would be later. Although a larger proportion of West Indian immigrants were unskilled workers in the 1980s, many of whom were attracted to jobs in New York City's garment industry, many skilled workers, such as nurses and other medical professionals, continued to arrive. In fact, by the 1980s, a majority of West Indian immigrants were women.

The concentration of West Indian immigrants into just a few neighborhoods in Brooklyn, particularly in Crown Heights and Flatbush, had a large social and cultural impact. Indeed, the development of the musical and cultural style that would come to be known as "Hip Hop" was influenced by Caribbean "dance hall" rhythms and disc jockey techniques. One of the fathers of Hip Hop music, Clive Campbell (a.k.a. "Kool Herc") immigrated to the Bronx from Jamaica in the 1970s. West Indian immigrants tended to be more politically conservative than their African American neighbors, causing some friction and misunderstanding.

Among the most damaging developments of the decade was the mid-1980s epidemic of a new form of cocaine known as "crack." Whereas the previous decade's cocaine epidemic had been a mark of affluence and was primarily viewed as a "white" drug, the new drug problem unequally affected urban communities of color. The drug epidemic had the direct effect of fueling crime and gang violence, and it had the equally destructive indirect effect of provoking the passage of discriminatory criminal sentencing laws that threw a record number of America's racial minorities behind bars.

Drug use and poverty have been companions throughout the twentieth century, and in this light there was nothing novel about the introduction of a new form of smokeable cocaine known as "crack" in the 1980s. Cocaine was one of the most widely used drugs in America long before the so-called crack epidemic struck. It was commercially used in a variety of patent medicines, health tonics, and popular beverages in the nineteenth century and continued to be illegally used after its prohibition in 1914. Cocaine use skyrocketed in the 1960s along with many other drugs, especially among youth, although because of its relatively high cost, it was most frequently used by the sons and daughters of the wealthy and was considered to be a "white" drug. As cocaine use became ever more fashionable among young urban professionals in the 1970s, more coca was cultivated in South America, leading to a steady increase in purity and a decrease in price. By the early 1980s, some Caribbean cocaine middlemen developed a means of converting powdered cocaine into a conveniently transportable and smokeable solid called "crack" for the crackling sound produced when it was lit. Most significantly, this form was easily mass produced and therefore could be sold in smaller and cheaper doses, extending the market for the drug from the upper class to impoverished neighborhoods.

In a short time in the mid-1980s, because of its great supply and low cost, crack invaded urban neighborhoods throughout America and quickly became the drug of choice among the poor. At first, because it was a new drug without long-established supply syndicates and networks, it encouraged the proliferation of many small-time dealers and an initial spike of violence, as these pushers and gangs fought to consolidate their territories and markets. Because of the great number of street-corner dealers and the street-level turf battles that resulted, the introduction of crack was a much more public and obvious drug problem than those that came before making it seem in the mid-1980s that the drug problem had suddenly and dramatically worsened. Studies of patterns of drug abuse, however, have shown that most of the new users of crack were old users of other drugs, and the appearance of crack was less a new drug problem than a new form of an old one.

The rapid spread of crack was a fact in many urban communities, but its impact was often exaggerated. Hospitals began to report treating a large number of patients who had used cocaine and troubling growth in the number of babies born to crack-using mothers. Many inner-city residents identified crack as the cause of sharply increased levels of criminal activity. News media discovered that lurid stories about crack users and crack violence attracted viewers and sold publications. Politicians happily responded by campaigning on the need to get tough on crime and advocated a "war on drugs." It is clear from longer term statistics, however, that neither crack nor any other single drug problem significantly increased emergency room admission rates, birth abnormalities, or crime rates in the 1980s.

The rising incidence of violent crime in America has been shown by criminologists to have been a long-term trend of modern society, something more fundamental and more deeply rooted than the mere appearance of a new, cheaper drug. Crime rates began to rise after World War II, and the index of violent crimes more than doubled during the decade of the 1960s, increasing 126 percent. The 1970s saw a continuation of this trend, with crime rates continuing upward another 65 percent. Compared with these previous two decades, that of the 1980s was one in which the rates of increase began to slow, rising just 23 percent. Most of this increase came in the last half of the decade, contributing the contemporary perception of a crime wave rolling across America. In the context of the longer term trend of criminality, however, the 1980s were not nearly as unusual as they were then believed to be.[29]

Medical problems associated with crack use cannot be easily separated from the overall health problems associated with extreme poverty. Because the poor tend to use public hospital emergency rooms for their primary care providers, the high number of emergency room admissions of crack users did not necessarily indicate that crack was causing a medical crisis. Careful studies of the prenatal effects of crack abuse on infants showed that it was difficult to separate the negative consequences of drug use from the damaging effects of poor diets, lack of prenatal care, and exposure to violence, trauma, and stress that are all too common complements to poverty.

The specter of a new, allegedly instantly addicting drug spreading through America provoked an almost hysterical media reaction in the mid-1980s. Leading news magazines *Newsweek* and *Time* each featured the crack epidemic in cover stories five times in 1986 alone. In a single month (July 1986), the three major television broadcast networks had a total of 37 evening news reports on crack. Such a cacophony of alarmist reporting soon had the effect of raising the drug problem to the forefront of American's concerns. Just before the media blitz national polls showed that fewer than 1 percent of those surveyed believed drugs to be the nation's most important problem. Two years afterwards, an astonishing 64 percent identified drug use as America's most serious problem.[30]

When the danger of crack abuse was tragically illustrated with the death of rookie Celtics basketball star Len Bias, Washington politicians competed to see who could be tougher on drug users. President Reagan and Vice-President Bush both volunteered to have their urine tested for illicit drugs, and Reagan then issued an executive order requiring all federal workers to submit to drug tests. Congress responded in 1986 by passing the Anti-Drug Abuse Act (only 18 intrepid congressmen voted against this measure), which stiffened federal criminal penalties for nonviolent drug offenses. The Anti-Drug Abuse Act established mandatory minimum sentences for dozens of drug crimes, including a five-year minimum for anyone caught with more than 5 grams of crack. Notably, it required 100 times as much powdered cocaine, the form of the drug preferred by wealthier and whiter addicts, to trigger the same penalty. Many states followed suit and passed their own minimum sentencing acts, eliminating parole or probation for drug offenses and establishing long mandatory sentences for repeat offenses. In the wake of crime, in the menacing form of "Willie" Horton, being a centerpiece of the election of George Bush in 1988, Congress tightened the screws further. It passed another antidrug bill in 1988, this time loosening many restraints on police activities, providing greatly increased federal funding of drug enforcement efforts, and establishing a national "drug czar" at the cabinet level.

As a direct consequence of the racial disparity in the new drug laws that more harshly penalized users of crack and the tendency of law enforcers to show quick results by targeting the street-level dealers and users rather than higher-level kingpins, those caught in the nation's drug dragnet tended increasingly to be black. Although African Americans constituted at most one-fifth of the nation's drug abusers in many major cities, they accounted for more than half of all drug arrests. When caught, blacks were given more severe penalties: before 1986, the average sentence meted out for blacks was 6 percent higher than that for whites, but by 1990 the difference in white and black sentences had widened significantly. Blacks were being given average sentences that were 93 percent longer. No surprise then that the 1980s saw the largest expansion in the prison population in American history, more than doubling from 330,000 in 1981 to 804,000 in 1991, with most of this expansion being due to the "war on drugs," and by 1990 one in four of all young black men were under some sort of control by the nation's criminal justice system. By 1990, there were more African American men in prison than in college.[31]

The forces of black radicalism unleashed in the 1960s with the fiery emergence of the Black Panthers, Malcolm X, and the popular slogan of "Black Power" seemed to finally be exhausted in the decade of the 1980s. Several of the movement's most prominent leaders publicly repudiated their former commitments and embraced conservative politics. Eldridge Cleaver, former "Minister of Information" of the Black Panther Party and author of *Soul on Ice*, an early and influential black power manifesto, renounced his former radical ideas and became active in the Republican Party. Likewise, Nathan Wright, an organizer of the "Black Power Conference" of 1968 in Detroit, which demanded government reparations for slavery, endorsed Ronald Reagan's candidacy in the election of 1980. On August 22, 1989, the former leader of the Black Panther Party, Huey Newton, was gunned down in Oakland by a notorious drug dealer. Thus the 1980s seemingly ended one chapter in the history of black radicalism and social activism.

A more dramatic end to a radical black nationalist movement came in 1985. In a confrontation between Philadelphia's first African American mayor, W. Wilson Goode, and a separatist commune known as MOVE, Goode finally ordered the police to close down the MOVE headquarters and commune that had long been a thorn in the side of the city's police and administration. The police dropped a bomb on the structure located in a densely populated neighborhood, killing 11 members of the MOVE organization, including five children and leading to a conflagration that destroyed six city blocks of townhouses.

Police, firemen, and workers sort through the rubble resulting from a fire on May 13, 1985 that started at MOVE's headquarters after police dropped a bomb on the townhouse. AP Photo/ George Widman.

EUROPEAN AMERICANS

A new form of racial backlash gained power in working and middle class ethnic white communities, especially in the upper Midwest where the economic crisis of the 1970s was particularly deeply felt. These white voters, many of Eastern European and Catholic background and traditionally a core constituency of the Democratic Party and of the labor movement closely affiliated with it, responded enthusiastically to the "culture wars" appeal of Ronald Reagan. Their shift to the Republican Party proved decisive in ushering in an era of conservative political dominance.

White racial anxieties that were muted by the sweeping success of civil rights legislation in the mid-1960s were given voice in the 1970s in the form of two political issues that allowed racist feelings to be expressed in a form that was deniably racist. The first was opposition to school busing, which shifted white resistance to school integration from the schools themselves to the problems of long bus rides and the loss of community schooling. The other and more long-lived issue was crime. President Nixon pioneered use of the crime issue in the election of 1972 to appeal to white urban Democratic voters who felt that the party had lost touch with their day-to-day concerns, especially their racial fears heightened by the feeling that Democratic Party support for affirmative action, school integration, and welfare disadvantaged working-class whites and turned a blind eye to street crime, which was increasingly given a minority face by the news media.

On October 23, 1989, a crime was committed in Boston that rekindled the racial fears and tensions in a city still recovering from its racist antibusing riots of the 1970s. The crime had all the features of white America's worst fears. A white suburban couple driving home after their birthing class were reportedly hijacked by a black man hopped up on drugs. The assailant shot and killed the pregnant mother, Carol Stuart, and wounded her husband Charles before escaping. The initial description broadcast throughout the city by Boston police read "30 years old, 6 feet tall, and black." Public cries of outrage were quickly joined by Boston's Mayor Raymond Flynn who dispatched scores of extra officer to the area where the attack occurred. Governor Michael Dukakis pointedly attended Carol Stuart's funeral while the state legislature considered reinstating the death penalty in Massachusetts, a state that last executed a person in 1947. The media frenzy sparked by the crime kept it front-page news for nearly three months while other crimes—committed by whites on other whites or black on other blacks—were relegated to the fine print.

While Boston's citizens debated the relationship between race and crime in their city, the incident took a bizarre turn as one of Charles Stuart's brothers revealed to the police and the media that Stuart had asked him to help kill his wife weeks earlier because she had refused to get an abortion and so that he could collect $182,000 from life insurance. Soon after police issued a warrant for his arrest, Charles Stuart jumped to his death from Boston's Tobin bridge.

Stuart had been raised in the all-white working class neighborhood of Revere, a place where even its residents admit that "racism is a fact, good or bad," an upbringing that may well have suggested the idea of concealing his crime by playing on many whites' willingness to believe African Americans were capable of any depravity.

For many European Americans, the continuing demographic changes diversifying their communities was a growing source of anxiety. By the 1980s, 85 percent of immigrants to America came from countries commonly classified as "Third World," namely from places that were culturally, linguistically, and racially different from the America depicted in Norman Rockwell paintings. In the post-civil rights age where all respected political and community leaders endorsed Rev. King's goal of a "colorblind" society, however, these feelings of social unease had few legitimate outlets. Such anxiety contributed to the long-term demographic trends of so-called white flight from urban areas, which in many places accelerated over the decade of the 1980s, as the economic benefits of the Reagan "boom" were not felt equally, and many whites found the means and the opportunity to relocate to expanding suburban rings around the great cities of America. These inchoate racial fears also fueled the appeal of New Right groups such as the "Moral Majority" and the "Christian Coalition" who shunned outright racism but, by crusading against "welfare queens," "big government," and "affirmative action," ended up with mostly people of color on the other side of their line. At the far fringe of the conservative movement, white power, neo-Nazi, and Ku Klux Klan groups enjoyed a resurgence in new and more violent hate groups with names such as "The Order," "Posse Commitatus," and "National Alliance."

Besides the Reagan Revolution itself, the most open expression of the European American backlash against a more racially and culturally diverse society in America was in the meteoric appearance of a movement to make English the official, or even the only, language of the United States. The idea first surfaced in 1981, when Republican Senator S. I. Hayakawa, a Canadian immigrant of Japanese heritage himself, introduced legislation in Congress to make English the official language of the United States. Senator Hayakawa, an English professor, was moved to make English the official language because of what he perceived to be the creeping bilingualism of the federal government. Since passage of the Bilingual Education Act in 1968, schools that received federal funds had been required to offer bilingual education to its students who did not speak English. Federal ballots were permitted to be printed in multiple languages since the reauthorization of the Voting Rights Act in 1974. Use of multiple languages on federal forms had also become more common. Hayakawa argued that English was central to American identity and culture and urged that the government use its resources not to accommodate those who could not speak it, but to melt all newcomers into the same linguistic pot. No senators but Hayakawa thought it a problem needing correction in 1981, however, and his bill died in committee. (Indeed, the 1980 Census recorded that 98 percent of Americans over the age of four spoke English "well.")

Outside of Washington, the idea of making English an official language caught on, particularly in those communities where European Americans had experienced rapid growth in immigrant populations in the course of one generation. Southern California led the way, as a number of small towns with large Hispanic or Asian populations passed local ordinances demanding that outdoor signs include, and government business be conducted in, the English language. By the mid-1980s, more than one in four of all immigrants to America chose California as their destination. In the spring of 1986, with the support of U.S. English, Inc., an organization Senator Hayakawa founded three years before, more than 1 million signatures were gathered to place Proposition 63, a ballot initiative that would amend the state constitution to declare English the only official language of California, on the ballot. Proposition 63 passed that fall with 73 percent of the vote.

During the rest of the decade, no fewer than 37 states would consider bills declaring English an official language or amending their constitutions to so designate a national language. By 1990, three states besides California—Florida, Colorado, and Arizona—changed their constitutions to declare English official. Fourteen other states passed official English or even English-only bills. Congress considered a number of bills and constitutional amendments, but not enough politicians in Washington believed there was more to gain than lose by supporting these measures as part of a neo-nativist crusade, and none became law even though U.S. English Inc. raised $28 million to lobby the issue.

The movement sputtered in 1987 after a memo written for English-only activists by U.S. English co-founder, John Tanton, was leaked to the press. It warned darkly of a "Latin onslaught" and asked, "Will the present majority peaceably hand over its political power to a group that is simply more fertile?" Many of the most prominent members of U.S. English's board of directors, including broadcaster Walter Conkrite and Latino presidential aide, Linda Chavez, resigned. The movement retained sufficient power, however, to move the House of Representatives in 1996 to vote to approve a bill designating English as the only language to be used in federal government business, although it did not pass the Senate.

Of course, not all white Americans pretended that racism was a thing of the past and that the goals of the civil rights campaigns of the 1950s and 1960s had been completed. In the mid-1980s, a Danish vagabond, Jacob Holdt, who spent several years hitchhiking around America and documenting the poverty of many of the hundreds of families he befriended and stayed with and the lingering racism he observed, took his collection of photographs on tour in a presentation he called "American Pictures." His show struck a nerve among middle-class white youth as Holdt was invited to show his pictures at hundreds of colleges and universities.[32]

Jewish relations with the African American community took a turn for the worse when Jesse Jackson's campaign was dogged by ironic accusations of racial insensitivity as Jackson was quoted in the press as privately referring to New York City as "Hymie-Town," and he was generally denounced for not sufficiently distancing himself from Minister Louis Farrakhan after Farrakhan made several inflammatory anti-Semitic speeches.

NATIVE AMERICANS

The 1980s were an extremely significant period of change for native Americans. Federal support for tribal governments plummeted under President Ronald Reagan's redirection of the budget from social services to defense spending. On the other hand, changes in federal law stimulated economic development on tribal lands, especially in the areas of oil, gas, and mining, as well as gaming. The population of native peoples rapidly expanded from 1.4 million in 1980 to 1.9 million by decade's end, mostly as a result of a greater willingness of people with native ancestry to identify themselves as Native American.[33] Sovereignty, the right to govern oneself, a long unfulfilled promise of the federal government and of the treaties, finally came to be realized after a series of lawsuits demanding recognition of long ignored usufruct rights to use historical but ceded lands in traditional ways and in recognizing the ability of native nations to regulate their own gaming operations. In northern Wisconsin, Michigan, and Minnesota, native peoples won the right to hunt and fish on public lands in traditional ways that were not legally allowed under state game laws.

After a decade-long legal battle, a U.S. Appeals Court ruled in *Lac Courte Oreilles, etc. v. Voigt* that fishing and hunting rights granted in treaties made between the United States and the Chippewa (Ojibwe) of northern Wisconsin in the early nineteenth century must be respected. These riparian rights were preserved even though the millions of acres of land on which they were based were ceded and settled by generations of European Americans, meaning that the Chippewa now would enjoy the right to fish and hunt by traditional methods on both public and private lands in about one-third of the state of Wisconsin.[34]

Many local whites viewed this development both as a violation of basic ideals of equality in rights and as a direct threat to the single most important industry in the area, tourism. The battle would coalesce around one traditional practice, spear-fishing, used to harvest one particular fish, the Walleye Pike, the most coveted quarry of inland lake fishermen. Members of the Lac du Flambeau reservation (an area named for the torches held in front of canoes and used to lure the walleye near to the surface so they could be speared at night) embraced their legal victory as a means of reconnecting with their ancestral traditions and reclaiming a host of important social rituals and practices that strengthened their community ties. Non-Indian locals organized antitreaty rights organizations such as "Stop Treaty Abuse" and "Protect America's Rights and Resources" which held rallies and protests on boat landings and lobbied for laws that would overturn the court's decision.

In the last half of the 1980s, Wisconsin's northern lakes were the scenes of ugly and sometimes violent protests often with overtones of racism most often associated with the deep South of a generation earlier. Indeed, some wags began referring to the area as the "deep North." By openly displaying a racial hostility long suppressed beneath a veneer of Midwestern courteousness, local whites actually galvanized native communities into valuing these riparian rights more highly than they had ever been before. In 1989, the Lac du Flambeau tribe voted down an offer of $50 million from the State of Wisconsin in exchange for surrendering their rights. Instead, all the affected Indian tribes in a tristate area cooperated to regulate their natural resources rights through the Great Lakes Indian Fish and Wildlife Commission.

A similar victory eluded the Lakota Sioux who won a decisive battle in the courts but were unable to realize the prize they hoped for—the return of illegally seized lands in the Black Hills, a land sacred in both their religious life and their heritage. In 1980, the U.S. Supreme Court ruled in *United States v. Sioux Nation of Indians* that the land was illegally seized and the Sioux people were owed vast monetary damages (more than half a billion dollars).[35] Rebelling at the idea of selling their birthright and their traditions, Lakota citizens vote instead to reject the settlement and hold out for the return of their lands.

The same year the state of Maine settled the claims of the Passamaquoddy and Penobscot tribes for recovery of millions of acres of land illegally taken from them at the turn of the century for $81 million. The case had dragged through the courts since 1972 when the Maine tribes had first sued to recover lands seized by Maine in violation of the Indian Nonintercourse Acts of 1789–1790, which gave the federal government exclusive rights to negotiate Indian land cessations. Similar suits were entered by the Catawbas for land taken by South Carolina and by the Cayuga for 64,000 acres of land while the Oneida claim 5.5 million acres of New York. The Schaghticoke and the Wampanoag filed suit to recover pieces of Martha's Vineyard, and the Pequots sought 800 acres in Massachusetts. By 1982, there were 11 such pending land claims at the federal level; and it appeared that these pressing issues were beginning to be addressed when, in 1982, a federal judge ruled that the federal government had not fulfilled its legal obligation to resolve Indian land claims, either through the courts or negotiations, and ordered it to resolve 17,000 unaddressed claims. Congress then voted unanimously to pay the Pequots $900,000 to settle their claim to 800 acres stolen by local officials in 1856. President Reagan vetoed the bill, however, saying that since the land was stolen by the states, they should pay the bill. He also suggested that compensation should be only for the value of the land at the time of the original sale or theft—in the case of the Pequot land claim a total of $8,091.17. Curiously, less than a year later, the Reagan administration reversed itself and signed a second bill authorizing nearly the same compensation to the Pequots as the first. In 1987, Reagan signed a measure giving the Wampanoag tribe 400 acres on Martha's Vineyard.[36]

Ronald Reagan's administration had a long and contentious relationship with the Indian nations. Anger and resentment from native America began early in his term as president when Reagan successively slashed the budget for the Indian Health Service and other native social programs. It ended just as badly when, toward the end of his time as president, Reagan revealed his lack of knowledge of native peoples and their history when he said publicly: "Maybe we made a mistake. Maybe we should not have humored them in ... wanting to stay in that primitive lifestyle. Maybe we should have said: 'No, come join us. Be citizens along with the rest of us.' As I say, many have. Many have been very successful."[37]

In the fall of 1988, Congress passed the Indian Gaming Regulatory Act, which paved the way for greater native sovereignty by recognizing tribal right to establish and regulate gambling operations in their own nations. This law was the result of a decade of legal challenges on the part of a number of Indian nations to attempts by state governments to regulate bingo parlors on tribal lands. In 1979, the Seminole nation opened a bingo hall in South Florida, which the state of Florida attempted to restrict and regulate. The Seminoles sued claiming that the state's attempt to regulate the bingo parlor was a violation of their tribal sovereignty. A U.S. District Court, in *Seminoles v. Butterworth*, agreed with this interpretation and ruled that control of gaming was a civil and regulatory activity not surrendered to the state of Florida. The final word on the issue was handed down by the Supreme Court in 1987 in the case of *California v. Cabazon Band of*

Mission Indians, which established the principle that the only way for states to restrict gaming on Indian lands was to prohibit and criminalize all forms of commercial gambling, something that only the states of Utah and Hawaii did. This decision opened the door for Indian tribes throughout the rest of the states to vastly expand their gaming operations.

Fearing a sudden explosion of casino gambling throughout America, Congress acted at its very next session by passage of the Indian Gaming Regulatory Act, which required Indian nations to negotiate agreements with state governments in order to open casino-style gaming operations. Over the next seven years, 21 states would make such compacts and more than 120 Indian casinos would open across America. By 1995, 225 tribes, nearly half of the recognized Indian nations in America, would have some form of gaming facilities on their lands. Collectively, these operations generated approximately $5 billion in revenues each year, about one-tenth of the total revenue generated by legalized gambling of all sorts in the United States.

For some native peoples, the direct impact of legalized casino operations was swift and dramatic. The 11,000-member Wisconsin Oneida nation opened a large casino near Green Bay. Revenues from this casino allowed the tribe to diversify its economic base, opening a 183-acre business park and within four years becoming the largest employer in its county. Indian nations in upstate New York used gaming revenues to build new homes for tribal members, to repurchase lost tribal lands, and to expand programs to teach and preserve native languages.

Although the advent of widespread Indian gaming generally improved the economic standing of Native Americans, the benefits were very unequal. In the decade after the passage of the Indian Gaming Regulatory Act, the stubbornly high rates of poverty among Native Americans began to decline. In 1989, nearly one-third (31.2%) of Native Americans (excluding native Alaskans) lived below the federally established poverty line as compared with 13.1 percent of Americans generally. By 1999, the number of Indians living below the poverty line had dropped to one-quarter (25.8%); the total U.S. population of the impoverished was only slightly changed at 12.4 percent.[38] The economic disparities between different tribes, however, dramatically increased at the same time.

Because casino operations are most successful when located near large metropolitan areas, those Indian nations that had lands close to major cities stood to benefit the most from the opening of gambling operations. Some of the largest Indian nations, the Navajo, the Hopi, and the Sioux, were centered in areas with relatively low population density and little prospect of developing large gambling resorts. Indeed, in the early 1990s, both the Navajo and Hopi nations rejected proposals to build casinos on their reservation lands. On the other hand, some of the smallest tribes possessed tribal lands located in important metropolitan corridors. The most spectacular example of this was the tiny Mashantucket Pequot tribe of Connecticut composed of approximately 300 members in 1990, which opened the Foxwoods casino in 1992 located within an easy drive of both New York City and Boston, and which soon developed revenues in the hundreds of millions of dollars and employed thousands of workers. Because of these disparities, in spite of the overall windfall gambling has brought to Native America, three of the largest Indian nations, the Navajo, Pueblo, and Sioux, remain the poorest.

Whereas most of the increase in Indian-owned businesses during the 1980s were related in some way to the expansion of gaming, a significant boost to other economic activities was given by Congress. In 1982, passage of the Federal Oil and Gas Royalty Management Act and the Indian Mining Development Act allowed tribes to renegotiate old leases that had locked in exploitatively low royalties in long-term deals that had often been negotiated without proper tribal consultation. In renegotiating these leases, a number of tribes, such as Colorado's southern Ute tribe, established their own production and marketing companies to cut out the middlemen who had been siphoning away most of the profits. Another spark of economic development was passage in 1983 of the Indian Tribal Government Tax States Act, which reaffirmed that tribes could not be taxed by states and that tribal governments could enjoy the same right to issue bonds to finance their development that states and local governments did.

ASIAN AMERICANS

The subject of a new racial backlash partially prompted by the vast economic changes at foot in America, Asian Americans were also still separated and stigmatized by the lingering "model minority" myth. Since Japanese and Chinese immigrants were first proclaimed as having cultural advantages (family values, enterprise, discipline) that uniquely suited them to success in American society in a series of articles in 1966, the model minority idea had declined in the 1970s but was revived in the 1980s by the apparent economic miracles taking place in China and the "Little Tigers" of Taiwan, South Korea, and Singapore. Herman Kahn, founder of the Manhattan Institute, declared the competitive superiority of "Confucian cultures" at the dawn of the 1980s in a book provocatively titled, *The Japanese Challenge. Time* magazine reported on the superior academic abilities of Asian Americans in a cover story entitled "The New Whiz Kids" in 1987, locating the source of these advantages in "Confucian ethics" that supposedly governed Asian American families.

The 1980s saw a renewed surge of immigration from Asia as immigration restrictions were relaxed (Refugee Act of 1980). Hmong from Laos, South Vietnamese, and Cambodians continued to arrive from areas torn by U.S. military activities in Southeast Asia. Entire communities transplanted to New York City, Chicago, southern Louisiana, northern Wisconsin, and southern California. Overall, the Asian American population that had already doubled since 1970, doubled again in the 1980s. As growth by immigration remained the largest contributing factor to the overall Asian American population, the Asian American population, which had been overwhelmingly composed of those born in the United States before 1965, was increasingly composed of those born abroad. By the 1990s, two-thirds of all Asian Americans had been born in a foreign country and thereby constituted the most foreign-born of all major minority groups.

The perceived foreignness of Asian Americans, when combined with the economic recession that characterized Reagan's first term in office, made for a deadly brew, especially when combined with the proliferation of news stories explaining how factories in America closed and moved abroad. Many automobile assembly plants in the Midwest sported signs in the factory parking lots declaring the lots were closed to "foreign" cars. At union picnics, workers could take a whack at a foreign car with a sledgehammer for $1. And in June 1982, Chinese American Vincent Chin, mistaken for Japanese, was beaten to death by two auto workers in suburban Detroit, who blamed him as an Asian-looking man for the loss of jobs to Japan. Although found guilty of manslaughter, Chin's assailants were given probation and light fines and neither went to prison.

Politically, Asian Americans remained the "silent minority." Their voting rates remained the lowest among all minority groups through the 1980s. In San Francisco where the Asian American minority was equal to one-third of its population, only 1 in 20 were registered to vote. In 1989, however, the Chinese massacre of pro-democracy activists in Tiananmen Square seemed to mobilize many Chinese Americans into political action. Some recognition of their increasing political action came that same year when President George H. W. Bush appointed Elaine Chao Deputy Secretary of Transportation.

Forty-three years after the end of World War II, one of the greatest mass violation of civil liberties in American history was officially recognized and indemnified with passage of the Civil Rights Act of 1988, which compensated Japanese American families that had been confined to internment camps during the war years. The legislation was sponsored by California Congressmen Robert Matsui and Norman Mineta, both of whom had been sent to interment camps as children. Of interest, Senate support for the bill was rounded up by Wyoming Senator Alan Simpson who had first met Mineta during World War II while visiting the local Japanese internment camp with his boy scout troop. The 1988 law formally apologized for the grave injustice and violation of civil rights and offered a payment of $20,000 to each internment survivor. A compensation fund of $1.3 billion was allocated.

LATINOS

New waves of immigrants arrived in the United States in the 1980s, many driven to immigrate not by the usual factors of economic opportunity but as a consequence of growing geopolitical conflicts. Early in 1980, Fidel Castro's regime in Cuba announced a sudden relaxation in their otherwise total prohibition on emigration. Within weeks, more than 125,000 Cubans fled to Florida (more refugees than usually arrived in the United States in an entire year) in what became known as the Mariel Boatlift, named for the Cuban port from which most of the refugees embarked. President Carter's administration at first turned a blind eye to the widespread violation of U.S. immigration laws as Cuban Americans sailed a rag-tag armada of vessels to Cuba to assist in bringing the dissidents back. After several weeks and with news reports indicating that Castro was taking advantage of the situation to empty his asylums and prisons of their most incorrigible prisoners, public sympathy for the refugees cooled and Carter directed the Coast Guard to begin intercepting boats.

In the aftermath of the sudden influx of "Marielitos," the federal government expedited their processing through a brief detention and provided subsidies and grants to facilitate their entry into American society. In contrast, a similar attempt on the part of thousands of Haitians, derogatively referred to as "boat people," to enter the waters of south Florida in those years was carefully intercepted by the Navy and Coast Guard, who generally towed these refugees back to Haitian waters or detained them for long periods before releasing them without any federal assistance. Government officials defended the differential treatment of each group by saying that Cubans were fleeing political persecution, whereas Haitians were merely fleeing economic circumstances and the Refugee Act of 1980 allowed asylum only for political asylum-seekers.

Then, as Ronald Reagan's war against leftist regimes and movements in Central America intensified, refugees fleeing violence and repression streamed from Guatemala, El Salvador, and Nicaragua to America. The number of Central American refugees fleeing to "El Norte" could never be precisely counted because the vast majority of these immigrants arrived in the United States without legal permission or documentation. The 1986 Immigration Reform Act, which allowed for undocumented immigrants to apply for permanent residency, however, attracted 138,000 Salvadorans, 15,000 Nicaraguans, and 51,000 Guatemalans.[39]

During the 1980s, the political power of Hispanic Americans was increasingly registered, although much of this power remained potential and unrealized because of the low voter turnout. The number of Hispanics of voting age increased from 8.8 percent of the U.S. population to 12.9 percent between 1980 and 1988, but the percentage of registered Hispanic voters actually declined from 36.3 to 35.5 in the same period while overall voter registration rates remained steady.[40] The greatest disparity in voting rates between Hispanics and the overall population is a matter of class and not age, as it is for some other minority groups. While Hispanics making more than $50,000 per year voted at rates that were only 13 percent lower than all Americans in that upper income bracket, those making less than $10,000 voted only half as often as other equally poor Americans. Of course, much of this difference can be explained by the large number of Hispanics who lack the benefits of citizenship.

Many of those previously barred from voting were put on the road to citizenship by passage of the Immigration Reform and Control Act in 1986, which gave amnesty to those who entered the United States before January 1, 1982. Three million people, mostly from Mexico, Central America, and various Asian nations obtained permanent legal residency in the United States and a greater chance at becoming full citizens as a result. Other provisions, however, reflected the increasingly anti-immigrant mood of much of the country, such as those penalizing employers for hiring undocumented immigrants and another that for the first time required that anyone granted permanent residency in the United States first prove that he or she is proficient in English (a requirement that grew out of the fast-growing official English movement of the 1980s).

Although much of the power of the Hispanic vote remained latent, some new political muscles were flexed in the 1980s. The growing Cuban American community organized to pressure Washington's foreign policy toward its closest Caribbean neighbor, Cuba, by founding the Cuban American National Foundation in 1981, which was modeled on Jewish American success in lobbying on behalf of Israel with the American Israel Political Action Committee. That same year, Henry Cisneros was elected mayor of San Antonio, Texas, becoming the first Latino mayor of a large American city. In 1988, Lauro F. Cavazos was named secretary of education, the first Latino to hold a cabinet level post in the federal government. The next year, Ileana Ros-Lehtinen, a Florida Republican who was born in Havana, Cuba, became the first Latina elected to Congress.

LAW AND GOVERNMENT

Under the Reagan administration, the federal government steadily retreated from its historical role in enforcing desegregation and advancing remedies to past discrimination. For two decades before the 1980s, there was general bipartisan support for federal programs that aided those who had been the victims of racial oppression. As the prosperity of the 1960s turned into the "stagflation" of the 1970s (an economist's nightmare of a combination of economic stagnation and price inflation), however, those federal programs that aided the poor and oppressed came to be viewed by those in the middle class as unfair advantages handed out by the government to the least deserving. The tectonics of politics shifted and Reagan was swept into office by those who wished to believe that America had solved all of its racial problems and continued efforts at redress, especially those that took notice of the salience of race, were vilified as being "reverse discrimination." In these conditions Reagan was able to do what Nixon was unable to do—claim his belief in the Rev. Martin Luther King's dream of a colorblind nation while ending the programs that worked to overcome inequality. As Reagan said in various forms on many occasions, "If you happen to belong to an ethnic group not recognized by the federal government as entitled to special treatment you are the victim of reverse discrimination."[41]

In nearly every corner of the executive branch where racial discrimination was fought, the Reagan era brought a marked reduction in budgets, staffing, scope of action, or vigor of prosecution. Within a couple of years after Reagan took office, his Equal Employment Opportunity Commission budget had lost 12 percent of its staff.[42] The Justice Department filed no suits against businesses engaged in housing discrimination in Reagan's first year and just two his second. The previous three administrations had averaged 32 per year.[43] When he was harshly criticized by civil rights leaders, Reagan questioned their motives and sincerity. In a televised interview, President Reagan said: "Sometimes I wonder if they [civil rights leaders] really want what they say they want. Because some of those leaders are doing very well leading organizations based on keeping alive the feeling that they're victims of prejudice."[44]

Yet, in spite of its commitment to ending all forms of racial preferences aimed at redressing the legacy of discrimination, the Reagan administration found such initiatives deeply rooted in the federal bureaucracy, and as a result different bureaus and departments often battled over basic approaches to civil rights and even sometimes came into direct conflict. In 1983, the Justice Department took the unprecedented step of suing to prevent a federal court from implementing a remedy to employment discrimination and asked the Fifth Circuit Court of Appeals to overturn the city of New Orleans's plan requiring the promotion of one black officer for that of one white officer until the total force of higher ranked officers was half African American. Meanwhile the Equal Employment Opportunity Commission (EEOC) submitted an *amicus curia* (friend of the court brief) supporting New Orleans's affirmative action plan. The White House then exerted pressure on the EEOC to withdraw its brief, which it did by a vote of 4 to 1, the one holdout being the only member of the commission not nominated by President Reagan.[45] No one argued that New Orleans had not practiced racial discrimination in hiring in the past or that its police force was not deeply split by racial conflicts. New Orleans had not promoted a single black officer before 1966, and, at the time a black officer sued to force an affirmative action plan in 1973, only 5 of 247 higher officers on the force were black.[46] Indeed, the same week Attorney General William French Smith and top presidential adviser Edwin Meese III met with members of the EEOC to urge them to withdraw their appeal to the court, an all-white jury convicted three white New Orleans policemen of conspiracy and violating the civil rights of a black witness, one of several who had been beaten during police interrogations after the shooting of a white police officer. Adding yet another fault-line to the split, another federal agency, the U.S. Commission on Civil Rights, voted to support the EEOC over the Justice Department in the matter.

Reagan's primary tool with which he tried to undo federal affirmative action initiatives and soften enforcement of antidiscrimination laws was the power of appointment. Reagan appointed doctrinaire conservatives to each of the major civil rights agencies of the federal government. To head the Civil Rights Division of the Department of Justice, Reagan appointed William Bradford Reynolds, who stated soon after taking office that "there's a growing awareness that the agencies that enforce civil rights laws have been overly intrusive." Reynolds efforts at making these laws less "intrusive" prompted half the attorneys in his division to sign a petition opposing his policies. Reagan tapped Clarence Pendleton Jr., former coach at Howard University and director of the San Diego chapter of the National Urban League, to chair the U.S. Commission on Civil Rights. Pendleton famously defended his president's cuts in antipoverty programs by saying, "the best way to help poor folks is not to be one." Reagan's appointee to lead the EEOC, Clarence Thomas, also an opponent of racial quotas, implementation timetables, and remedies such as busing, was reminded on his nomination that he had been quoted as saying a few years earlier: "If I ever went to work for the EEOC or did anything directly connected with blacks, my career would be irreparably ruined. The monkey would be on my back again to prove that I didn't have the job because I'm black."[47]

This strategy often backfired, as the controversial activists that Reagan attempted to install left him feeling like President Warren Harding who once quipped, "I have no trouble with my enemies. I can take care of my enemies in a fight. But my friends, my goddamned friends, they're the ones who keep me walking the floor at nights!" Soon after Reagan nominated Rev. B. Sam Hart to head the U.S. Commission on Civil Rights, Rev. Hart held a press conference at which he expressed his opposition to an Equal Rights Amendment to the Constitution and to busing as one remedy to school segregation. One of Reagan's appointees to the Legal Services Corporation board, George E. Paras, was caught referring to Italians as "dagos" and denouncing some civil rights activists as "professional blacks." Reagan's appointee to head the U.S. Commission on Civil Rights, William Barclay Allen, eventually resigned under intense criticism for a speech he gave to an evangelical Christian group titled "Blacks?, Animals?, Homosexuals?, What Is a Minority?"[48]

The frontlines of the modern Civil Rights movement had been in the area of education. Just weeks after Reagan's landslide election, the House approved a bill that prohibited federal attorneys from seeking court-ordered busing plans to integrate schools by a vote of 240 to 59. The Senate quickly followed suit. President Carter, in that relatively powerless period between losing his election in November and leaving office on January 20, 1980, stood on principle and chose to veto the bill. Congress passed the same measure again the next June, but a handful of liberal senators led by Lowell Weicker of Connecticut managed to delay and filibuster the bill for eight months.[49] By September, Reagan's Justice Department intervened in three separate cases arguing that states had the right to prohibit busing altogether as a remedy for racial imbalances.[50] In November, near the anniversary of his presidential victory, Reagan fired the chairman of the U.S. Commission on Civil Rights, Arthur S. Flemming, who had been a strong advocate of busing and affirmative action and replaced him with Clarence M. Pendleton, a conservative opponent of such methods. Flemming characterized his firing as an indication that the Reagan administration was drifting back toward a theory of "separate but equal" in education.[51] Less than a week later, the Justice Department announced that it would no longer seek to desegregate school districts where segregation existed in only a portion of the district or where it was not the result of intentional state actions. William Bradford Reynolds, assistant attorney general for civil rights, in defending the new policy said, "We are not going to compel children who don't choose to have an integrated education to have one."[52]

The year 1988 was the watershed year in the history of school integration. Since the landmark decision of Brown v. Board of Education of Topeka Kansas in 1954, ending racial discrimination in schools had been a primary focus of the Civil Rights movement. Although integration plans did not begin to proliferate until the mid-1960s, progress since that time had been truly remarkable. In the year Brown was decided, only one-thousandth of 1 percent of African American schoolchildren in the South attended schools with a majority of white students. By the mid-1980s, more than 40 percent of black pupils attended integrated schools. In 1988, however, national statistics revealed a worrying trend— for the first time in 34 years these indices of racial integration reversed. From 1988 to 1998, the proportion of black children in integrated schools dropped to below one-third.[53]

The causes for this retreat extend far before the decade in which it occurred. Both public opinion and the direction of judicial interpretation soured in the 1970s as mandatory busing began in many school districts in both the North and South. Violent clashes over busing in Boston and an electoral shift of southern whites to the Republican party shifted the political context of integration efforts. The Supreme Court in Milliken v. Bradley (1974), led by the four recent appointees of President Nixon, limited all desegregation efforts to single districts, thus insulating white suburbs and urban enclaves from having to accept minority schoolchildren from the inner city. Two years later in Pasadena City Board of Education v. Spangler, the high court relieved school districts from having to respond to demographic changes that worsen racial disparities among their schools. Congress responded to the public's objections to forced busing by passing the Byrd Amendment in 1976, prohibiting the federal department of Heath, Education, and Welfare from requiring any district to adopt busing.

The historic electoral shift that the election of Ronald Reagan represented, the so-called, Reagan Revolution, accelerated these existing trends. Openly hostile to court oversight of integration efforts, the Reagan administration quickly moved to rein in the school desegregation activities of the Justice and Education departments by limiting their staffs and cutting their budgets. Reagan pushed for the discontinuation of the Emergency School Aid Act of 1972, which had long provided federal funding for school desegregation efforts. In 1984, the Reagan administration urged the Supreme Court to limit the ability of the federal government to withhold grants from colleges that discriminated, which the court did in Grove City College v. Bell. Congress later overturned this precedent over Reagan's veto with passage of the Civil Rights Restoration Act of 1988. In 1986, the Reagan administration successfully supported the Norfolk, Virginia, school board in its quest to end a desegregation plan inaugurated in 1972, even though the effect of doing so was to divide the district into 10 nearly all-black schools and three primarily white ones.

One of the many ironies in the manner in which school desegregation policies were developed by federal courts was that little notice was given to the trend toward the increasing segregation and isolation of Latino(a) students in American schools. As a consequence of the system of racial segregation being most concerned with keeping African Americans separate from whites, when the government took steps to break up that system, it naturally measured progress by the integration of black and white students. In spite of legal precedents, such as the Supreme Court ruling in the 1973 *Keyes v. Denver School District No. 1.*, which established that Hispanics were entitled to the same remedies as African Americans in cases where they were victims of segregation, during the 1980s and 1990s, as federal courts began to lift their supervision of historically segregated school districts, they largely did so based on the progress made in the integration of African Americans, not other minority groups. The actually increasing segregation of Hispanic students was left unaddressed.

Of course, no states or school districts in the 1980s passed laws ordering the separation of Hispanic students. Rather, the increasing concentration of Hispanic students into separate schools was a function of both historical patterns of housing discrimination and limited economic opportunities that concentrated Latino(a) populations into particular neighborhoods. Moreover, these residential patterns intensified with the rising numbers of Hispanic immigrants in the 1980s. The relatively younger average age of the Hispanic community compared to the overall population (which leads to having more school-age children) also contributed to raising the proportion of Hispanics in the American public school system nearly four times from 1968 to 1998.[54] Thus the issue of the educational isolation of Latino and Latina students worsened just as the government began to get out of the business of supervising the racial integration of school districts.

Such trends were allowed to continue by the abrupt shift in Washington politics with the inauguration of Ronald Reagan. Soon after Reagan took office, the Justice Department reversed its prior policies and advocated voluntary efforts at school desegregation, such as the creation of "magnet" schools rather than mandatory ones, such as busing. In 1981, the Justice Department permitted busing programs to end in Houston, Los Angeles, and Dallas, cities that had a large population of Hispanic students. Over the course of Reagan's administration, the Justice Department requested the dismissal of desegregation orders in 300 school districts that had long practiced racial discrimination.[55]

Supreme Court rulings on issues of civil rights proved increasingly inconsistent in the 1980s. The court was deeply divided between those believing, in the words of Justice Harry Blackmun, that "In order to get beyond racism, we must first take account of race" and those like Justice William Rehnquist who held that the Equal Protection Clause of the Fourteenth Amendment to the Constitution made all racial preferences, no matter how nobly intended, unconstitutional and illegal.[56] Over time the faction represented by Rehnquist prevailed.

Voting rights had long been an area of intense judicial supervision both because they were the focus of the last phase of the Civil Rights movement of the 1960s and because they are a powerful means of protecting other rights. Since the passage of the Voting Rights Act of 1965, courts had viewed any state or local government attempts to reduce or dilute the voting power of minorities with great suspicion. But in 1980, the Supreme Court weakened these protections by ruling in *Mobile v. Bolden* that a group of African Americans claiming that an at-large system of voting in Mobile, Alabama, was racially discriminatory must prove not only that this system weakened minority representation but was intentionally established to do so. In 1982, Congress amended the Voting Rights Act to close this loophole and force the courts to allow challenges to such voting systems based on their discriminatory results, not their intentions, which are difficult, if not impossible to prove.

Another area of active legal debate was that of employment law and the ability of governments to try to compensate for past racial discrimination through programs that helped minorities compete for government contracts, employment, or other benefits. The court ruled in *Fullilove v. Klutznick* (1980) that the Public Work Employment Act, with its minority hiring targets for federal contractors, was constitutional, just as it had the year before in *United Steelworkers v. Weber* in upholding a similar affirmative action program voluntarily adopted by a private employer. A similar affirmative action initiative by a public employer was ruled constitutional in 1987 in the case of *Johnson v. Transportation Agency, Santa Clara, California*. In all these cases the Court reasoned that the purpose of remedying and overcoming past discrimination (whose effects were still being felt by a later generation) was a justifiable and permissible reason to temporarily treat racial groups differently within certain limits.

Such race consciousness in the pursuit of goals of racial equity did not survive long as a constitutional principle. In 1986, a majority of justices chipped away at this principle by finding in *Wygant v. Jackson Board of Education* that government entities cannot implement such affirmative actions measures to remedy the general, societal discrimination that affected communities, but can legally attempt to redress only discrimination that these entities were themselves guilty of in the past. Then a pair of cases in 1989 marked the beginning of a retreat from the court's earlier acceptance of affirmative action programs. First, in *City of Richmond v. J. A. Croson Co.*, a case again questioning the constitutionality of a law requiring bidders for city contracts to subcontract 30 percent of work to qualified minority businesses, the court raised the legal standards of evidence applied to such cases. It required the use of a "strict scrutiny" standard that shifted the burden of proof from those affected by the law to the government, which now had to prove not only that there was a "rational relationship" between the law and its purpose, but that the law served a "compelling governmental interest" and was as narrowly constructed as possible.

The Court's decision in *City of Richmond v. J. A. Croson Co.* made it much easier for employers to challenge government programs that aimed to redress discrimination. A few months later, the decision made it far more difficult for employees who had been discriminated against to sue their employers under the Civil Right Act. Aleutian and Asian American cannery workers at a pair of companies in Alaska had long complained of the sort of overt discrimination most Americans thought had passed away with "colored only" signs in bus depots. Justice Blackmun characterized it this way in his dissenting opinion: "The salmon industry as described by this record takes us back to a kind of overt and institutionalized discrimination we have not dealt with in years: a total residential and work environment organized on principles of racial stratification and segregation, which, as Justice Stevens points out, resembles a plantation economy." The majority reversed a precedent set in 1971 and shifted the burden of proof on employers to defend business practices that had a discriminatory impact to their employees to prove, in the words of Justice White, "that it was 'because of such individual's race, color,' etc. that he was denied a desired employment opportunity."[57]

When former Vice-President George Herbert Walker Bush took office as president in 1989, it was not clear whether he would continue Reagan's attack on affirmative action policies and cuts in civil rights enforcement activities or whether he would chart a different course more in line with his pledge on the campaign trail to pursue a "kinder and gentler" conservatism. It did not take long for Bush to signal his intentions when he nominated William Lucas to succeed William Bradford Reynolds as the assistant attorney general in charge of the Civil Rights Division of the Justice Department, arguably the most important civil rights office in the federal government. William Lucas, a former social worker, FBI agent, sheriff, and one-time Republican candidate for governor in 1986, would have become the first African American to head the Civil Rights Division. Although Lucas was initially supported by many in the civil rights community, when more of his record and some his views, such as his statement during his nomination hearing that he did not think a recent string of Supreme Court decisions had weakened civil rights laws, were made known, opposition quickly built against him. At a time when charges of police racism and brutality were of increasing concern to minority communities and civil rights organizations, the fact that when William Lucas was sheriff of Wayne County, he was found guilty by an appeals court for failing to investigate charges of police brutality and by a state court of tolerating inhumane conditions in the county jail, sunk his candidacy.[58] Lucas's nomination was eventually rejected by the Senate Judiciary Committee.

MEDIA AND MASS COMMUNICATIONS

In fall 1984, a situation comedy premiered on television that not only came to dominate network programming for the next decade, but was hailed by many as a landmark in the history of racial stereotyping. *The Cosby Show*, whose namesake, comic Bill Cosby, not only acted in the central role, but participated

The Cosby Show cast. NBC/Photofest. © NBC.

in producing, writing, and directing the show, was the most popular show on television for its entire eight-year run. No sitcom in television history, not even *All in the Family*, proved as powerful a magnet for viewers. By 1985, every other television in America was tuned to *The Cosby Show* on Thursdays at eight o'clock eastern time. It single handedly catapulted its network, NBC, from last to first place in ratings and profits. It commanded the highest advertising fees ever charged for a network series. So popular was the show that game five of the World Series between the Oakland As and the Los Angeles Dodgers in 1988 was postponed until after *The Cosby Show*'s closing credits had rolled.

Cosby cannot be appreciated without reference to the lingering stereotypes that still dominated television's portrayals of black Americans. Just as the decade dawned, in 1979, two popular situation comedies premiered that rehashed the same tired stereotypes of African Americans that had predominated since the nineteenth century. In *Benson*, actor Robert Guillaume played a butler, surely a witty and wise one, but still very much a servant to the white head of the household as in the 1950s comedy, *Beulah*. A click of the tuner away, Gary Coleman, a precocious child actor, played the adopted son of a white widower on *Different Strokes* and did so with more than a hint of the bulging eyes, tom-foolery, and jive-talking derived from the minstrel stage.

The Cosby Show was not the first network series to challenge older racial stereotypes, but its complete and careful refusal to fall into any stereotypes was new.

Cliff was not the first wise and loving black father in a network sitcom. Clair Huxtable, Cliff's loving wife, as played by Phylicia Rashad, was not the first black mother character not to follow the Mamie stereotype, as Diahann Carroll broke this mold in her 1960s sitcom, *Julia.* The Cosby kids were not the first African American children to appear on the small screen who avoided black vernacular speech. But they were the first black family on television to have all these characteristics in one show.

Bill Cosby and his psychologist consultant, Alvin F. Poussaint, consciously constructed an image of a black family that ran counter to all the destructive stereotypes still pervasive in American society. At the same time they took care to scrub all hint of racial conflict from the scripts. Their studied refusal to deal with race as a social issue, certainly part of a tacit social contract struck with their white audience, was criticized at the time by academics and even some civil rights activists. Polling seemed to indicate, however, that many black viewers were relieved not to always see African Americans dealing with race as a "problem" but simply living their normal lives.

One key ingredient of *The Cosby Show*'s success was its positioning of the Huxtable family in the secure upper realms of the professional middle class where their blackness was accepted by white Americans as fitting within their understanding of what was "normal." In the mythically meritocratic America that remains the imagined reality in the minds of many white Americans, black working-class families on television, such as those on *Good Times, Amen,* and *227* were suspect because their lack of material success raised questions about their character. In avoiding this pothole at the crossroads of race and class, *The Cosby Show* was criticized by other critics for not being less real and therefore not "black enough." It is doubtful that the show would have been successful had NBC followed its original scripting plan and made Cliff and Claire both servants—he a chauffeur and she a maid.

What Bill Cosby did to the evening sitcom, Oprah Winfrey did for the daytime talk show. In the mid-1980s, Winfrey rose from being a local television personality in Chicago to being not only the most popular daytime television personality but a trendsetter in books, movies, food, and fashion. Winfrey began hosting her own show in 1978 at the age of 22 in Baltimore. In 1984, she moved to WLS in Chicago and hosted *AM Chicago,* which was quickly renamed *The Oprah Winfrey Show.* It took less than two years for *The Oprah Winfrey Show* to debut on national television and even less for her to exceed the viewership of the most successful daytime talk show to that point in history, *The Phil Donahue Show.*

Winfrey moved beyond daytime television by starring in Steven Spielberg's 1985 film adaptation of Alice Walker's *The Color Purple,* playing Sofia, a role for which she was nominated for an academy award, and by producing and starring in *The Women of Brewster Place,* a 1989 dramatic miniseries based on the novel by Gloria Naylor (1982). By the end of the century, she would not only be the nation's most popular television host, but its only African American female billionaire.

Minority broadcasting came into its own in the 1980s. First aired on January 8, 1980 and expanded in 1983 to a complete cable channel BET, or Black Entertainment Television, grew into a major outlet for African American programming. Likewise, the media visibility of Latinos in America grew steadily throughout the decade. In 1984, a number of independent Spanish-language stations combined to form NETSPAN, which changed its name two years later to Telemundo. That same year, the Univision television network was organized, creating an even larger national Spanish-language broadcasting network in the United States. Univisión would eventually become the fifth largest television network.

Trends in corporate marketing showed a new racial sensitivity: the restaurant chain "Sambos" changed its name to "Dennys." The century-old image of "Aunt Jemima" was updated to remove some of its "Mammy" connotations. And when the Colgate company purchased a small personal care products company in Hong Kong, Hawley & Hazel Chemical Co. and thereby acquired its "Darkie" brand toothpaste, which sported a picture of a grinning black minstrel on the tube, it quickly changed the name to "Darlie," although it kept the logo. Nevertheless, Cream of Wheat stuck with its "Rastus" logo, Uncle Ben continued to shuck and shuffle in selling rice, and the Chiquita Banana became the "Chiquita Girl," actually clarifying its stereotype of the dancing exotic Latina.[59]

CULTURAL SCENE

In July 1979, a small independent record company released a single with a new, beat-heavy, sound. The Sugar Hill Gang's *Rapper's Delight* caught on with listeners across America and brought to the nation the raw, urban sound that had been percolating through New York clubs for a few years. Artists such as Grandmaster Flash, KRS-One, and Public Enemy combined politically charged messages with heavy dance beats and rock rhythms to pioneer what would become the aural urban backdrop of the coming generation.

At the same time, Michael Jackson elevated his status as the king of pop by surpassing his 1979 sales of *Off the Wall*, which was the largest selling album by a male vocalist up to that time, with his album, *Thriller,* in 1982, which went on to become the best-selling album of all time.

In the 1980s, American readers showed an increasing curiosity and interest in literature and films by artists of color. The appearance of a new generation of race-conscious filmmakers including Spike Lee, John Singleton, Chris Eyre, Ramon Menendez, and Wayne Wang enjoyed popularity with a cross section of American audiences. Throughout the decade bestseller lists and award podiums were well represented by African American, Asian American, and Native American authors. In 1981, Maxine Hong Kingston became the first Asian-American woman to win the National Book Award for *China Men*. Kingston's success was quickly overshadowed by Amy Tan who brought the Chinese American experience into wider view with the publication of her first novel, *Joy Luck Club*, which quickly became the best-selling book by an Asian American author in U.S. history. *Joy Luck Club* sold millions of copies and was scripted into a blockbuster Hollywood movie in 1993. In 1984, Native American author Louise Erdrich published *Love Medicine*, which became one of the most popular books of that year.

Works by a number of African American women proved not only popular but critically acclaimed. In 1983, Alice Walker was awarded the Pulitzer Prize for Literature for *The Color Purple*. In 1988, Toni Morrison published *Beloved*, which earned both the Pulitzer in 1988 and the Nobel Prize for Literature in 1993. Gwendolyn Brooks, a poet who began publishing her work in 1930 at the age of 13 and whose poems appeared regularly in the *Chicago Defender* for many years, was named Poet Laureate of the United States in 1985.

Author Amy Tan. AP Photo.

Author Toni Morrison. Courtesy of
Photofest.

SPORTS

Even baseball, the pioneer in sport integration, continued to suffer embarrassments and setbacks in its progress toward racial equality. In 1987, Al Campanis, the general manager of the Los Angeles Dodgers (ironically, the team that had broken the color line in baseball by hiring Jackie Robinson in 1947), was forced to resign after giving a television interview marking the 40th anniversary of Robinson's first season. Campanis explained that the reason blacks were not more numerous in the management of the game was "that they may not have some of the necessities to be, let's say, a field manager, or perhaps a general manager. So it just might be—why are black men, or black people, not good swimmers? They just don't have the buoyancy." At the time Campanis made his on-air remarks, no baseball team had a black team manager or general manager (although there had been two as recently as 1980). According to one study published at the time, of 879 administrative positions, baseball employed just 17 African Americans. The situation was not much better in other sports, as just four coaches in the National Basketball Association were black, and no professional football team had employed a black coach since Fritz Pollard led the Akron Pros in 1921 and the Milwaukee Badgers in 1922.[60]

Campanis's insensitive remarks prompted the California State Assembly to pass a resolution censuring him. It pushed Jesse Jackson to threaten a national boycott of baseball stadiums beginning on the Fourth of July, a move he later called off when Campanis resigned and baseball Commissioner Peter Ueberroth pledged more attention to the issue. Likewise, it provoked Benjamin Hooks, director of the NAACP, to visit dozens of baseball team owners to stress the importance and justice of opening up their front offices to minority executives. Hooks's campaign seemed something of a success when Commissioner Ueberroth attended the NAACP national convention and pledged to require that all teams develop affirmative action hiring plans and that baseball would work to lead all other professional sports in the hiring and advancement of minorities in executive positions.[61] Likewise NBA Commissioner David Stern pledged to ensure that there was equal opportunity in basketball's administrative positions and boasted that nearly one-third of the NBA's front-office positions were held by minorities.[62]

Sports also demonstrated that racial insensitivity could cut both ways. Detroit basketball rebounding star Dennis Rodman, who was African American, criticized Celtic Larry Bird after a championship game in which Bird scored 37 points. According to Rodman, "the only reason he [Bird] won all those MVPs is because he's white." Fellow Piston's great Isiah Thomas chimed in, "If he was black, he'd be just another good player."[63]

INFLUENTIAL THEORIES AND VIEWS OF RACE RELATIONS

Thinking and writing about racial relations in the 1980s was dominated by the conservative shift in American politics and culture brought about by the election of Ronald Reagan. By advocating fundamental changes in the nation's social insurance, welfare, medical, and affirmative action programs, Reagan and his partisans provoked a fresh round of debate over the causes of poverty and the character of race in America.

Charles Murray, a sociologist with the conservative think-tank, the Manhattan Institute, provided a key rationale to the Reagan administration's desire to eliminate federal welfare programs in his 1984 book, *Losing Ground: American Social Policy, 1950–1980. Loosing Ground* was hailed by conservatives as the definitive retort to Michael Harrington's classic *The Other America*, the 1962 study that built support for President Lyndon Johnson's famed "War on Poverty." So influential was Murray at the time that when a federal program was cut, it was commonly referred to as having been "Murrayed" by Washington insiders.

In *Losing Ground* Murray argued that not only were the welfare programs initiated in the 1960s wasteful, but they were actually counterproductive in that they created a system of social incentives that rewarded the poor for doing the very things—avoiding work, having children out of wedlock, and committing crimes—that kept them in poverty. Even worse, Murray argued, striking a note that seemed at times to be based as much on racial stereotypes as on statistical evidence, that the expansion of welfare programs had changed cultural attitudes, especially among the nation's blacks, to the point where welfare was no longer viewed as shameful but as ordinary, even a customary right. Critics quickly pointed out that Murray's statistics misrepresented both the scope of poverty before the 1960s and the impact of government programs since. They particularly criticized his tendency to disbelieve that downward shifts in the economy in the 1970s had a significant impact on overall poverty rates.

Of all experts who crossed swords with Murray, perhaps the most successful was William Julius Wilson who laid out his most compelling case for understanding the worsening condition of the black "underclass" not in terms of a "culture of poverty" but more directly as a consequence of joblessness and deindustrialization in his 1987 work, *The Truly Disadvantaged: The Inner City, the Underclass, and Public Policy.* The "War on Poverty" failed to achieve its goals not because it rewarded bad behavior, as Murray would have us believe, but because it focused only on providing a basis from which the disadvantaged could enter the economic mainstream without changing the rules of the economic system to favor the poor. As it turned out, white flight to the suburbs, a shift from factory to service jobs, and the widening class divide within the black community stacked the deck against the inner-city underclass.

Whereas both Wilson and Murray, for opposite reasons, downplayed the importance of race, other scholars made the case for the continuing power and relevance of race. Michael Omi and Howard Winant in their 1987 book, *Racial Formation in the United States from the 1960s to the 1980s,* argued that race cannot be conceived as a simple category but must be viewed as a shifting set of meanings, a system of racial ideology that is a deep-seated part of the culture, that subtly changes in response to larger institutional and historical contexts. In their analysis, race is such a central force in American life that even when seemingly overcome by a successful civil rights mobilization, race re-forms itself with a new vocabulary and system of coded meanings that preserve its relevance and power. Likewise, Werner Sollors, in *Beyond Ethnicity* (1986), called on literary scholars to focus more on the ways in which ethnicity was a product of the construction and definition of group boundaries than on an accumulation of specific group characteristics constituting identity.

Almost as if to confirm theories of how the established structures of the legal system in America, although no longer resting on racist legal statutes, still operate to exclude minority voices, early advocates of critical legal studies provoked sweeping condemnation from the scholarly legal establishment. Randall Kennedy, professor at Harvard Law School, led the backlash in early 1989 in an article entitled, "Racial Critiques of Legal Academia," which caricatured critical race theory as simply holding that scholars who had experienced racial oppression were uniquely situated to understand racist legal structures and relying on a methodology of personal testimony and story-telling.[64]

Enough time had passed by the 1980s that historians could begin to look at the actions of civil rights leaders and the dramatic protests of the 1950s and 1960s that ended the regime of segregation in America as a single complete era. A number of books offered new perspectives on the Civil Rights movement and its leaders and a landmark public television series reminded Americans of the difficulty and the many individual sacrifices it took to end Jim Crow. Three of the decade's Pulitzer Prizes for nonfiction works were awarded to books that explored the civil rights movement. David J. Garrow won a Pulitzer in 1987 for his study of Rev. Martin Luther King Jr. and his leading organization in the struggle, *Bearing the Cross: Martin Luther King Jr. and the Southern Christian Leadership Conference*. The next year Taylor Branch won the same honor for his *Parting the Waters: America in the King Years, 1954–1963*, the first volume of what would be a magisterial three-volume study of the Civil Rights movement. The 1985 Pulitzer went to J. Anthony Lukas's best-selling *Common Ground: A Turbulent Decade in the Lives of Three American Families*. Lucas intricately traced the course of the integration of public schools in Boston, Massachusetts and its deeply personal consequences on a trio of families that represented various sides of the racial fault-lines in that city. Public broadcasting aired *Eyes on the Prize: America's Civil Rights Movement, 1954–1965* in 1987, a 14-hour documentary that earned 23 filmmaking awards and was proclaimed by *T.V. Guide* as the best documentary of all time.

RESOURCE GUIDE

SUGGESTED READING

Alba, Richard D. *Ethnic Identity: The Transformation of White America*. New Haven, CT: Yale University Press, 1990.

Amaker, Norman C., ed. *Civil Rights and the Reagan Administration*. Washington, D.C.: Urban Institute Press, 1988.

Anderson, Elijah. *Streetwise: Race, Class, and Change in an Urban Community*. Chicago, IL: University of Chicago Press, 1990.

Brownstein, Harry H. *The Rise and Fall of a Violent Crime Wave: Crack Cocaine and the Social Construction of a Crime Problem*. Guilderland, NY: Harrow and Heston, 1996.

Colburn, David R. and Jeffrey S. Adler, eds. *African-American Mayors: Race, Politics, and the American City*. Urbana: University of Illinois Press, 2001.

Crawford, James. *Hold Your Tongue: Bilingualism and the Politics of "English Only."* Reading, MA: Addison-Wesley Publishing Co., 1992.

Hostetter, David L. *Movement Matters: American Antiapartheid Activism and the Rise of Multicultural Politics*. New York: Routledge, 2006.

La Botz, Dan. *César Chávez and la Causa*. New York: Pearson Longman, 2006.

Laham, Nicholas. *The Reagan Presidency and the Politics of Race: In Pursuit of Colorblind Justice and Limited Government.* Westport, CT: Praeger, 1998.

Marable, Manning. *Race, Reform, and Rebellion: The Second Reconstruction and Beyond in Black America, 1945–2006.* Jackson: University Press of Mississippi, 3rd ed., 2007.

McFadden, Robert D., et al., *Outrage: The Story behind the Tawana Brawley Hoax.* New York: Bantam Books, 1990.

Nelson, George, *Post-Soul Nation: The Explosive, Contradictory, Triumphant, and Tragic 1980s as Experienced by African Americans* (previously known as *Blacks and before That Negroes*). New York: Viking, 2004.

Nesbitt, Francis Njubi. *Race for Sanctions: African Americans Against Apartheid, 1946–1994.* Bloomington: Indiana University Press, 2004.

Parenti, Christian. *Lockdown America: Police and Prisons in the Age of Crisis.* New York: Verso Press, 1999.

Perea, Juan F., ed. *Immigrants Out!: The New Nativism and the Anti-Immigrant Impulse in the United States.* New York: New York University Press, 1997.

Porter, Bruce and Marvin Dunn. *The Miami Riot of 1980: Crossing the Bounds.* Lexington, MA: D.C. Heath, 1984.

Reed, Adolph L. Jr. *The Jesse Jackson Phenomenon: The Crisis of Purpose in Afro-American Politics.* New Haven, CT: Yale University Press, 1986.

Reinarman Craig and Harry G. Levine, eds. *Crack in America: Demon Drugs and Social Justice.* Berkeley: University of California Press, 1997.

Rivlin, Gary. *Fire on the Prairie: Chicago's Harold Washington and the Politics of Race.* Henry Holt & Company, 1992.

Shull, Steven A. *A Kinder, Gentler Racism?: The Reagan-Bush Civil Rights Legacy.* Armonk, NY: M. E. Sharpe, 1993.

Smith, Robert C. *Racism in the Post-Civil Rights Era: Now You See It, Now You Don't.* Albany: State University of New York Press, 1995.

Tatalovich, Raymond. *Nativism Reborn?: The Official English Language Movement in the American States.* Lexington: University Press of Kentucky, 1995.

Wilson, William Julius. *The Truly Disadvantaged: The Inner City, The Underclass, and Public Policy.* Chicago: University of Chicago Press, 1987.

FILMS AND VIDEOS

America Becoming (1991). Dai Sil Kim-Gibson, producer. Charles Burnett, director. WETA.

Eat a Bowl of Tea (1989). Wayne Wang, director. Columbia Pictures, Burbank, CA: Columbia TriStar Home Video.

El Norte (1983). Gregory Nava, director. Independent Productions: CBS/Fox, Distributed by Madera Cinevideo.

Eyes on the Prize (1986). Henry Hampton, director. Blackside, PBS Video.

Glory (1989). Edward Zwick, director. TriStar Pictures.

Hollywood Shuffle (1987). Robert Townshend, director. Samuel Goldwyn Co.

The Milagro Beanfield War (1988). Robert Redford, director. Universal City Studios, MCA Home Video.

She's Gotta Have It (1986). Spike Lee, director. Island Pictures, Key Video.

Who Killed Vincent Chin? (1988). Christine Choy and Renee Tajima-Pena, directors. Film News Now Foundation & WTVS Detroit; Filmakers Library, 1988.

WEB SITES

Applied Research Center ("Advancing racial justice through research, advocacy, and journalism") http://www.arc.org/content/view/23/43/.

Asian and Pacific Islander Population of the United States, United States Census, http://www.census.gov/population/www/socdemo/race/api.html.

Black Los Angeles Project, Ralph J. Bunche Center for African American Studies at UCLA, http://www.bunche.ucla.edu/frames/index.html.

The Black Population of the United States, United States Census, http://www.census.gov/population/www/socdemo/race/black.html.

Environmental Justice Center, Clark Atlanta University, http://www.ejrc.cau.edu/Welcome.html.

Federal Bureau of Investigation Hate Crime Statistics, http://www.fbi.gov/hq/cid/civil rights/hate.htm.

Interracial Population of the United States, United States Census, http://www.census.gov/population/www/socdemo/interrace.html.

The Native American Population of the United States, United States Census, http://www.census.gov/population/www/socdemo/race/indian.html.

Race the Power of Illusion, PBS Television, http://www.pbs.org/race/000_General/000_00-Home.htm.

U.S. Commission on Civil Rights, http://www.usccr.gov/.

NOTES

1. *New York Times*, September 21, 1980, 34.

2. *New York Times*, September 27, 1980, 8.

3. Marvin Dunn, *Black Miami in the Twentieth Century* (Gainesville: University Press of Florida, 1997); Issues of the *New York Times*, *Washington Post*, for May 19–23, June 10, 1980.

4. Bruce Porter and Marvin Dunn, *The Miami Riot of 1980: Crossing the Bounds* (Lexington, MA: Lexington Books, D.C. Heath & Co., 1984).

5. Porter and Dunn, *Miami Herald*, May 17–22, 1990.

6. *New York Times*, October 26, 1983, 24.

7. *New York Times*, October 22, 1983, 7.

8. *Washington Post*, April 3, 1977; January 13, 1978.

9. William P. Jones, "Working-Class Hero," *The Nation*, January 30, 2006.

10. *New York Times*, January 13, 1979.

11. Manning Marable, *Race, Reform, and Rebellion: The Second Reconstruction and Beyond in Black America, 1945–2006* (Jackson: University Press of Mississippi, 3rd. ed., 2007), 177.

12. *New York Times*, July 31, 1983, E4.

13. Adolph L. Reed, Jr., *The Jesse Jackson Phenomenon: The Crisis of Purpose in Afro-American Politics* (New Haven, CT: Yale University Press, 1986), 25.

14. *New York Times*, December 14, 1987, B1.

15. Robert D. McFadden, et al., *Outrage: The Story Behind the Tawana Brawley Hoax* (New York: Bantam Books, 1990), 254.

16. *New York Times*, June 16, 1988, A1.

17. *New York Times,* July 19, 1988, A30.

18. *Detroit Free Press,* June 19, 1992, 1A; Helen Zia, *Asian American Dreams: The Emergence of an American People* (New York: Farrar, Straus, and Giroux, 2000).

19. *Detroit Free Press,* July 1, 2004, 5B; July 8, 2004, 8A.

20. *Detroit Free Press,* July 27, 2004, 1B; April 5, 2003, 10A.

21. *Detroit Free Press,* June 13, 2002, 6B.

22. *Washington Post,* July 31, 1988.

23. *Time,* November 14, 1988.

24. *Chicago Tribune,* October 24, 1988.

25. Steven Pressman, "Climate of Violence, Crackdown: House Panels Prepare the Way for South Africa Sanctions Bill." CQ Weekly Online (June 14, 1986): 1317–1319; "Reagan Holds Q and A Session with the Press: December 7, 1984." CQ Weekly Online (December 15, 1984): 3110–3112; John Felton, "Reagan Averts a Confrontation on South Africa." CQ Weekly Online (September 14, 1985): 1800–1804.

26. "Bill Filed Imposing New South Africa Sanctions." CQ Weekly Online (May 24, 1986): 1211–1211; Steven Pressman, "Stunner in House: Tough Anti-Apartheid Bill." CQ Weekly Online (June 21, 1986): 1384–1385; John Felton, "A Welter of Amendments: Senate Votes a Bill to Impose New Sanctions on South Africa." CQ Weekly Online (August 16, 1986): 1860–1862; John Felton, "Republicans Divided: Bucking Strong Hill Sentiment, Reagan Vetoes South Africa Bill." CQ Weekly Online (September 27, 1986): 2268–2268; John Felton, "Hill Overrides Veto of South Africa Sanctions." CQ Weekly Online (October 4, 1986): 2338–2342.

27. *Washington Post,* February 24, 1983, A1; March 25, 1983, A3; April 10, 1983, A1.

28. The Honorable Robert T. Matsui Legacy Project, California State University, Sacramento, http://digital.lib.csus.edu/u?/mats,185.

29. Harry Brownstein, *The Rise and Fall of a Violent Crime Wave: Crack Cocaine and the Social Construction of a Crime Problem* (Guilderland, NY: Harrow & Heston, 1996), 6.

30. *Crack in America: Demon Drugs and Social Justice,* Craig Reinarman & Harry G. Levine, eds. (Berkeley: University of California Press, 1997), 20–24.

31. *Crack in America,* 240, 264.

32. *Lexington Herald-Leader* (Kentucky), March 8, 1985, D9; *New York Times,* September 5, 1984, C16.

33. Dan Frost, "American Indians in the 1990s," *American Demographics* (December 1991), 26–34.

34. Larry Nesper, *The Walleye War: The Struggle for Ojibwe Spearfishing and Treaty Rights* (Lincoln: University of Nebraska Press, 2002).

35. *United States v. Sioux Nation of Indians,* 448 U.S. 371 (1980).

36. *New York Times,* May 1, 1983, E9; *Washington Post,* November 18, 1982, A2; *New York Times,* October 20, 1983, B2, August 23, 1987, 54.

37. *Washington Post,* June 1, 1988, A30.

38. Statistics from Stella Ogunwole, *We the People: American Indians and Alaska Natives in the United States* (U.S. Census Bureau, 2006); *1990 Census—Selected Social and Economic Characteristics from the 25 Largest American Indian Tribes* (U.S. Census Bureau, 1993).

39. Roger Daniels, *Coming to America: A History of Immigration and Ethnicity in American Life* (New York: HarperCollins, 1990), 382.

40. *Hispanic Americans: A Statistical Sourcebook: 1992 Edition*, Alfred N. Garwood, ed., (Boulder, CO: Numbers & Concepts, 1992), 110, 114–115.

41. Linda F. Williams, *The Constraint of Race: Legacies of White Skin Privilege* (University Park: Pennsylvania State University Press, 2003), 189.

42. Williams, 197.

43. Williams, 196.

44. *St. Louis Post-Dispatch*, January 14, 1989.

45. *New York Times*, April 8, 1983.

46. *New York Times*, June 7, 1983.

47. Robert R. Detlefson, *Civil Rights under Reagan* (San Francisco: ICS Press, 1991), 61; *Washington Post*, November 14, 1982; February 13, 1982.

48. *New York Times*, February 13, 1982; *Washington Post*, April 22, 1982, A4; *New York Times*, October 17, 1989, A26.

49. *New York Times*, November 22, 1980, 17; December 6, 1980, 10; June 14, 1980, E4; February 26, 1982, A14.

50. *New York Times*, September 19, 1980, 22.

51. *New York Times*, November 17, 1981, A1. Vice chairman Stephen Horn was also fired and replaced by Mary Louise Smith, chairman of the Republican National Committee during the second Nixon administration.

52. *New York Times*, November 20, 1981, A14.

53. John Charles Boger and Gary Oldfield, eds., *School Resegregation: Must the South Turn Back?* (Chapel Hill: University of North Carolina Press, 2005).

54. Boger and Oldfield, *School Resegregation* (2005), 13.

55. *New York Times*, March 12, 1989.

56. *Regents of the University of California v. Bakke*, 438 U.S. 265 (1977).

57. *Ward's Cove Packing Co., Inc. v. Antonio*, 490 U.S. 642 (1989).

58. *New York Times*, March 31, 1989, A10; July 21, 1989, B9.

59. *Chicago Defender*, February 1, 1989, 9; *Philadelphia Inquirer*, May 13, 1984, E1.

60. *Washington Post*, April 8, 1987, b2; *San Francisco Chronicle*, April 14, 1987, 43.

61. *Philadelphia Inquirer*, July 10, 1987.

62. *Washington Post*, April 10, 1987, d7; *Chicago Tribune*, July 1, 1987; *Washington Post*, July 9, 1987.

63. *Washington Post*, June 3, 1987, c1.

64. Randall Kennedy, "Racial Critiques of Legal Academia," *Harvard Law Review*, 102:8, June 1989, 1745–1820.

1990s

Timeline

1990

January   Washington, D.C. Mayor Marion Barry is arrested in a Washington hotel for possession of cocaine. He is later convicted and serves six months in prison but wins a fourth term as mayor in 1994.

An altercation between a Haitian American shopper and a Korean grocery store owner in New York city escalates into a boycott that lasts more than nine months and sets apart black and Korean New Yorkers.

April   Mohawk activists occupy disputed territory around Miner Lake, New York, set up roadblocks, and prevent federal authorities from entering on the grounds of native sovereignty. A compromise is later worked out for a two-hour visit by federal agents.

June 28   South Africa's most famous black leader and recently released political prisoner, Nelson Mandela, is snubbed by Miami city officials who refuse to honor his visit with the usual commendations and key to the city because of remarks Mandela made in support of Fidel Castro. National civil rights and African American organizations declare a national boycott of Miami for its treatment of Nelson Mandela and its poor record of treatment of its African American communities and the federal government's double standard of turning away Haitian refugees while welcoming those from Cuba. Over the next two years, at least two dozen conventions with expected economic impact of $40 million to the local economy were canceled.[1]

President George H. W. Bush signs the Hate Crime Statistics Act into law. The law requires that the Justice Department collect statistics of crimes committed against people targeted because of their "race, religion, disability, sexual orientation, or ethnicity." In addition to being the first step toward a national hate crimes criminal statute, it was also the first federal crime law to recognize sexual orientation as a protected category.

July 6

A peaceful group of 50 Haitian Americans and their supporters protesting against the discrimination at a local clothing store are beaten by 100 club-wielding police officers in Miami, Florida. Two years later the city offered some of protesters compensation for this violation of their civil rights.

Congress passes the Native American Graves and Protection and Repatriation Act, which requires all museums, libraries, and other federally funded repositories holding Native American remains and sacred cultural items to return them to the appropriate tribes.

November

The Immigration Act of 1990 steadily increases the annual quota of immigrants allowed into the United States, setting the stage for a large jump in the number of immigrants from the Middle East and from South Asian nations, primarily India and Pakistan.

Arizona voters reject a proposal to allow state employees paid time off in observance of Martin Luther King Jr. day. Many conventions scheduled to meet in the state cancelled in protest and both college teams scheduled to meet in that state's Fiesta Bowl pulled out. Arizona remains only one of three states that do not provide time off for state employees on King Day (along with New Hampshire and Montana) and is the only state to have considered the question in a state referendum. Arizona reversed itself in 1992, but not in time to prevent the National Football League from relocating the Superbowl from Phoenix to Pasadena, California in protest.

1991

January

Dolores Huerta, a founder of the United Farm Workers union, is given an apology and an $825,000 settlement from the city of San Francisco in compensation for the injuries she sustained during a protest against a visit by President Bush in 1988. Huerta, a 58-year-old grandmother, 5 feet, 2 inches tall and 110 pounds at the time, was distributing leaflets in front of the hotel at which Bush was speaking and was clubbed by a police officer when she did not move aside quickly enough, breaking two of her ribs and rupturing her spleen.

February 20   The United States Supreme Court ruled 7–2 that refugees and undocumented immigrants have the right to have their challenges to Immigration and Naturalization Service (INS) rulings heard in federal courts. The Bush administration had followed a policy of not allowing appeals to the courts until after the INS had ordered individuals to be deported and had denied the right of groups of undocumented immigrants to file class action suits, which the high court also ruled was within their rights.

March 3   Rodney King, a 26-year-old African American parolee is pulled over after a high-speed chase in Los Angeles and beaten by more than a dozen Los Angeles police officers. The beating was captured on videotape by a curious neighbor and broadcast around the world, setting the stage for severe riots the following year when the principal police officers involved were acquitted by a jury.

March 16   Latasha Harlins, a 15-year-old African American, is shot in the back and killed as she leaves the Empire Liquor Mart in Los Angeles by Soon Ja Du, who suspected her of shoplifting. Although Du was found guilty of voluntary manslaughter by a jury, Judge Joyce Karlin released her on probation, further adding to the tensions in Los Angeles between the African American and Korean communities.

August 19   A car that was part of a motorcade transporting the Grand Rebbe of the Lubavitcher Hassidic Jewish Congregation of New York jumps a curb, killing a seven-year-old Haitian American child, Gavin Cato, and severely injuring his cousin, Angela Cato. The incident sparks three nights of rioting in the Crown Heights section of Brooklyn between Jews and African Americans.

October   The Supreme Court hears the first Civil Rights case, *Freeman v. Pitts*, since the retirement of its pillar of civil rights, Justice Thurgood Marshall. The ruling reduces the ability of federal courts to supervise school desegregation orders.

October 11   Anita Hill, a former employee of Supreme Court nominee Clarence Thomas, testifies before a Senate committee that Thomas sexually harassed her. Her charges deeply divide the country but do not derail Thomas's confirmation as the successor to Justice Thurgood Marshall.

October 29   A jury issues a verdict of "not guilty" in the case of Lemrick Nelson Jr., a black teenager accused of knifing and killing

Yankel Rosenbaum, a Hasidic Jewish scholar from Australia, during the Crown Heights riots in August.

November   The Civil Rights Act of 1991 passes, which restores many of the employment provisions of the Civil Rights Act of 1964 that had been weakened by a series of Supreme Court rulings.

1992

January   Arkansas Governor William Jefferson Clinton, locked in a tight field of hopefuls vying for the Democratic Party's presidential nomination, permits the execution of Ricky Ray Rector, a brain-damaged African American man. The fact that Rector did not have the mental ability to recognize what was happening to him was evident when he was given his last meal and he asked his guard to save his dessert "for later."

April 29   Riots erupt across a wide area of South Central Los Angeles, leaving 44 people dead and more than $1 billion in property damage when a jury, which included no African Americans, acquitted four Los Angeles police officers in the beating of Rodney King the year before.

July   The Supreme Court, in *R.A.V. v. St. Paul*, strikes down a local "hate crimes" ordinance of St. Paul, Minnesota because, they said, by criminalizing some hateful words and actions (such as burning crosses or scrawling swastikas on property) and not others, it selectively suppressed speech and therefore violated the First Amendment.

1993

January   Carol Mosely Braun (Dem. Illinois) becomes the first African American woman to be elected to the U.S. Senate.

February   Arthur Robert Ashe Jr., the African American tennis star and political activist, dies of AIDS at the age of 49.

April 23   César Chávez, the founder and president of the United Farm Workers (UFW) union, dies in Yuma, Arizona, while staying with the family of farm workers and preparing to testify in a lawsuit against a grower. Forty thousand people marched in his funeral procession behind the plain pine coffin made by Chávez's son and adorned with the black eagle symbol of the UFW and a small-handle hoe, the tool of the farm workers.

May   President Clinton signs into law the National Voter Registration Act, known as the "Motor-Voter" bill because it required all states to allow citizens to register to vote at motor vehicle and other state offices. When the law went into effect in 1995, a record 11.2 million new voters registered to vote.

June   The Supreme Court, in *Wisconsin v. Mitchell*, upholds Wisconsin's hate crime statute that enhanced the penalties for crimes committed against victims selected for their "race, religion, color, disability, sexual orientation, national origin or ancestry."

June 1   Connie Chung signs on and introduces the CBS Evening News. Chung is the first Asian American and only the second woman to anchor a network news broadcast.

June 20   The *Golden Venture*, a small tramp steamer, runs aground on Long Island, disgorging its smuggled cargo of 286 Chinese immigrants into the sea. Ten men and women drowned within sight of the city lights of America while the rest were arrested and detained. The Clinton administration, under pressure to crack down on immigrant smuggling, made an example of the *Golden Venture* immigrants and vigorously sought their deportation. In the end, one-third of the *Golden Venture's* passengers were deported back to China, and most of the rest endured years of detention, some being jailed for nearly four years.

October   The Swedish Academy announces that Toni Morrison, the famed African American novelist, is the winner of that year's Nobel Prize in Literature.

November   Congress passes a joint resolution apologizing for the American-sponsored coup that overthrew the government of Hawaii in the nineteenth century.

              President Clinton signs into law the North American Free Trade Agreement (NAFTA), which lowers tariffs on goods imported into the United States from Canada and Mexico. This law vastly increases the economic ties between the United States and Mexico but also stimulates increased cross-border movement of people, which in turn provokes an anti-immigrant political backlash.

1994

February 11   President Bill Clinton issues Executive Order 12898, the first presidential directive requiring all federal agencies to uphold a policy of "environmental justice," which was defined as "identifying and addressing, as appropriate, disproportionately high and adverse human health or environmental effects of its programs, policies, and activities on minority populations and low-income populations in the United States."

March 21	Raoul Lowery Contreras became the first Mexican American to host his own nationally syndicated radio talk show in the United States. Contreras, an ex-Marine, opened each show with the "Guadalcanal March" and promoted a hard-line conservative ideology.
April	The Florida legislature votes to allocate $150,000 to each surviving victim of the January 1923 Rosewood massacre. The Florida State Rosewood Claims Act was part of a $2.1 million-apology from the state for the mass lynching of as many as eight residents of the small town of Rosewood, which was completely razed after a white woman claimed she was raped by black man from the town.
	Congress passes legislation permitting the use of peyote, a strong hallucinogenic drug, for the ceremonial and religious purposes of recognized Native American tribes.
August	President Clinton's "Anti-Crime Bill" clears the Senate and is sent for his signature. This bill provided more than $30 billion for the hiring of 100,000 additional police officers, the construction of new prisons, and set higher minimum sentencing standards for many crimes.
October	President Clinton signs into law the Hate Crime Enhancement Act of 1994, a federal statute that increases the penalties for crimes committed against individuals who were singled out because of their because of the actual or perceived race, color, religion, national origin, ethnicity, gender, disability, or sexual orientation of any person.
	The 850-page book, *The Bell Curve: Intelligence and Class Structure in American Life*, by psychologist Richard J. Herrnstein and political scientist Charles Murray attempts to revive largely discredited theories that race and intelligence are linked. The book attracts a frenzy of media attention in spite of its rather unoriginal and out-of-date claims.
November	California voters pass Proposition 187, a law that bans the distribution of any state services, including medical care and schooling to anyone who is not a citizen or legal resident, by an overwhelming margin.
	National elections result in Republicans gaining control of both houses of Congress for the first time in 40 years.

1995

January–May	A rash of mysterious arsons destroy African American church buildings, mostly in the deep South. In all, 36 churches are burned in half as many months. In June 1996, President Clinton

established a National Churches Arson Task Force to investigate the attacks. Although suspects were never apprehended, the arsons tailed off the next year. Thousands of college students from around the nation volunteer to help rebuild black churches.

April   The United States Sentencing Commission recommends that existing disparities between the prison terms given to those caught with cocaine, who were mostly white and given lighter sentences, and those caught with crack, who were mostly black and given longer sentences, be reduced. Later that year, however, Congress votes to overturn these recommendations and keep the disparities in place.

April 19   White supremacists blow up the Alfred Murrah Federal Building in Oklahoma City, killing 168 people in what was the worst act of domestic terrorism in American history up to that point.

June 12   The United States Supreme Court, in *Adarand Constructors v. Pena*, rule that federal affirmative action programs must meet the narrow "strict scrutiny" standard in order to be legal, a ruling that made it difficult for such programs to be continued.

October 13   A jury composed of both blacks and whites declared former football pro O. J. Simpson not guilty in the slashing murders of Simpson's former wife, Nicole Brown Simpson and her friend Ronald Goldman. The trial had taken nine months, the longest in California history. The defense reputedly required the services of 36 full-time lawyers. In all, about 2,000 reporters covered the proceedings and 142 million people watched on television as the verdict was read.

October 16   Between 400,000 and 800,000 African American men fill the Capitol Mall as part of the "Million Man March." The "Million Man March" fills the same area of Washington, D.C. where the famed "March on Washington" in 1963 was held, although this time, in place of the Reverend Martin Luther King Jr., the keynote speaker was the Minister Louis Farrakhan of the Nation of Islam, and instead of demands for federal antidiscrimination laws, the speakers demanded responsibility of their listeners and respect for the African American community from the rest of the nation.

1996

August 22   President Clinton signs the "Personal Responsibility and Work Opportunity Act," a law overhauling the nation's 30-year-old welfare system, limiting the time any person can obtain benefits to five years and ceding more control over the system to the states.

November

California voters narrowly approve Proposition 209, the "California Civil Rights Initiative" that banned the state from using racial preferences in jobs, contracts, or college admissions. Other states follow suit and consider legal bans on the use of affirmative action by their governments.

In a stunning reversal, the chairman of the Texaco Oil company agrees to compensate black employees whose race discrimination suit had been fought by the company for years. Texaco agreed to pay $176 million, the largest settlement of its kind in history, to compensate 1,400 former and current black workers for pay raises they were not given, jobs they were not promoted to, and franchises they were not awarded.

1997

Alexis Herman is appointed as Secretary of Labor, the first African American woman to hold this cabinet post. Herman had been a feature of the Clinton administration from the beginning, starting out as a personal assistant to the president and working her way up through a number of posts.

March

Thirteen-year-old Lenard Clark, an African American boy conspicuous as he rode his bike through the predominately white Bridgeport neighborhood of Chicago, is set upon and beaten into a coma by teenagers objecting to his presence.

April

More than 600 African American farmers, mostly from southern states, file a $2.5 billion class action suit against the U.S. Department of Agriculture (USDA), charging discrimination in the allocation of farm loans and subsidies. In 1999, a federal judge ruled for the farmers and ordered the USDA to pay compensation to 18,000 farmers who had been discriminated against.

June 14

President Clinton announces his new initiative to address continuing racial problems in America. The initiative will consist of the creation of a panel of experts to survey the issue and a series of "town-hall" meetings to freely discuss issues of race and racism in America.

August 9

Abner Louima, a 31-year-old Haitian immigrant, is arrested by New York City police officers and taken to a station house in Brooklyn where he is beaten and sodomized with a toilet plunger. More than 5,000 people protest at city hall after Police Chief Howard Safir claims that race was not a factor in Louima's brutalization.

October 30	The Clinton administration accepts the recommendations of an advisory task force and orders that all federal forms that gather information on race allow individuals to choose multiple races to describe themselves.

1998

February	Two Texas men, saying they were looking for "an adrenaline rush," kidnap a disabled 19-year-old co-worker who they picked because she "wasn't white," and use her for target practice outside of Fort Worth. Michael Hall and Robert Neville later admitted they both "burst out in laughter" when she died.[2]
April–May	President Clinton visits 18 African nations and formally apologizes for the United States' role in the transatlantic slave trade.
May	President Clinton gives a formal apology on behalf of the U.S. government for syphilis experiments, conducted on black men in Tuskegee Alabama beginning in 1932, in which hundreds of African Americans were allowed to suffer and die by being given sham medications so that the progression of the disease could be carefully documented.
	At a large Memorial Day party in Santee, California, a fight breaks out in which at least five whites beat an African American Marine, Lance Cpl. Carlos Colbert, while shouting racial epithets and "white power." The beating broke Cpl. Colbert's neck leaving him paralyzed. One of the assailants later admitted that his participation in the attack was motivated by racism, and he was given a heavier sentence under California's hate-crimes law.[3]
June	James Byrd, Jr., a middle-age, disabled black man is seized by three white supremacists who chained him to their truck and dragged him through Jasper County, Texas until his body was scattered in pieces. When one of the killers, a white supremacist named John William King, is sentenced to death and asked if he had anything to say to Byrd's grieving relatives, he said in effect that they could all perform a sexual act on him.

1999

January	The Department of Housing and Urban Development (HUD) announces that it has reached a settlement with one of the nation's largest home mortgage companies, Columbia Mortgage Company, whereby it would address decades of refusing to underwrite mortgages in minority areas by providing $6.5 billion in

loans to minorities in 28 states. HUD had also forced another large mortgage company, AccuBanc Mortgage to fulfill the terms of the 1968 Fair Housing Act by providing $2.1 billion in mortgage loans to underserved minority communities in 1998.[4]

January   A sharply divided Supreme Court in the case of *Department of Commerce v. House of Representatives* rules that the Census Bureau may not use statistical sampling methods for the purpose of apportioning representatives in the House of Representatives. Sampling had been advocated as a means of adjusting for the large undercounting of population in minority and low-income communities as a result of the difficulty of finding those who move often, are homeless, or are recent immigrants, as well as poor children. The Census Bureau estimated that at least 5 million people would not be counted in the upcoming 2000 census, with large consequences for the representation of these constituencies in the Congress.

January 21   In a gesture of racial reconciliation on Martin Luther King Jr. day, white and black volunteers tear down an iron fence that had separated the white and black sections of the local graveyard in Jasper, Texas, for 160 years. Jasper was the site of the murder of African American James Byrd Jr., one year before, the racist brutality of which was reminiscent of the days of lynching.[5]

February 4   Amadou Diallo, a 23-year-old Guinean immigrant, was confronted in the foyer to his Bronx apartment building by four plainclothes police officers from the New York police department's special "street crimes unit." The officers open fire on the unarmed Diallo, firing 41 bullets, 19 of which hit Diallo, killing him on the spot. In response, a thousand protesters demanding a change in police policies at city hall are arrested including the former mayor David Dinkins and Congressman Charles Rangel. The next year the four officers were acquitted of second-degree murder charges.

September   When the fall lineup of new television programs is announced, many observe that none of the new series on any of the four major television networks have any leading roles for minority characters. The National Association for the Advancement of Colored People protest and meet with network executives who claim this is just an "anomaly" and promise to include more people of color in major roles in the future.[6]

December   A group of nine technical workers of Asian heritage sue their employer, the Lawrence Livermore National Laboratory, claiming they were discriminated against by being passed over for promotions and given lower salaries than white co-workers. In 2000, the workers' expanded their suit into a class-action encompassing other workers at the national laboratory. In 2002, the General Accounting Office, an arm of Congress, issued a report evaluating hiring and employment practices among 22,000 workers at three national laboratories and found statistical evidence of discrimination against minorities.[7]

The State of New Jersey reach an agreement with the Justice Department to appoint an independent monitor to ensure that its state police stop racial profiling of motorists on its highways. This action was taken nine months after the chief of the New Jersey State Police was fired after he defended his police officers' actions by saying: "Today with this drug problem, the drug problem is cocaine or marijuana. It is most likely a minority group that's involved with that."[8]

December 24   President Clinton issues a Presidential pardon to 88-year-old Freddie Meeks, one of the last two survivors of the Port Chicago Naval Magazine mutiny of 1944, when 50 black sailors refused to load ammunition under oppressive and unsafe conditions after an explosion at the facility killed 300 men. All 50 men were sent to prison for their actions and dishonorably discharged. In 1994, the Navy reviewed the case and declared the men victims of racial discrimination but did not reverse their convictions.

New Hampshire renames its Civil Rights Day in honor of Martin Luther King.

2000

January   The State of New York agrees to compensate victims of the Attica Prison Uprising of 1971 for $8 million.

March   Preston King, who fled to England in 1961 after being sentenced to 18 months in prison for draft dodging, is pardoned by President Clinton. King, an African American from Albany, Georgia, refused to answer his draft boards letters unless they addressed him as "Mister," as they did for white inductees. The Georgia draft board refused to do this.

April   Richard Baumhammers, a 34-year-old lawyer and son of Latvian immigrants, went on a 20-mile killing spree across southern Pennsylvania, singling out Jews, African Americans, and immigrants. Baumhammers shot and killed five people before being apprehended, beginning with a 63-year-old Jewish woman who lived next door in his wealthy Virginia Manor neighborhood, two Chinese American restaurant workers who he murdered in front of diners, a young African American shot through the front window of a karate school, and a man of South Asian descent, shot at an Indian grocery store. After shooting his Jewish neighbor, Baumhammer drove to the local synagogue, shot out its windows, and painted a red swastika on the door.[9]

June 6   Missouri becomes the fifth state in the union to pass a law banning the police practice of racial profiling. The law requires police agencies to collect statistics on the race, gender, and age of individuals stopped by police, and these statistics are later used to determine whether the police are biased against some groups.

Utah becomes the last state in the nation to adopt a holiday in honor of Martin Luther King Jr. Previously, it had designated the same day as "Human Rights Day."

OVERVIEW

The atmosphere in Atlanta was electric as some of the largest crowds in the city's history gathered under the Georgia sun (which some said felt just like it did in South Africa) to catch a glimpse of the South African antiapartheid leader Nelson Mandela. Mandela had been recently released from Robbin Island prison and was visiting the United States for the first time. To many, Mandela's appearance was confirmation of the importance of the broad movement of organizations that had pushed for sanctions against South Africa for the past decade. It was one of the few victories and one of the most hopeful moments in the movement for civil rights and international solidarity in a generation. On that afternoon of June 27, 1990, in the city that became the national headquarters of civil rights activism, everything seemed possible and a new world seemed to dawn.

While Mandela would go on to be elected president of the government that once put him in jail to silence him, America seemed to move in the opposite direction. Less than a year after Mandela's visit to Atlanta, a different sort of drama, all too typical many would say, played out in Los Angeles, a city that was fast becoming the nation's cauldron of racial conflicts. Rodney King, an African American motorist, had run from police after the red lights flashed in his rearview mirror and, when finally cornered, was brutally beaten with nightsticks by a group of Los Angeles police officers. The incident was surreptitiously videotaped by a concerned neighbor. Four officers were indicted for assault and after a year of procedural maneuvers on all sides, including the relocation of the entire trial to the affluent white suburb of Simi Valley, an all-white jury found all defendants innocent. Los Angeles then erupted into the worst urban rioting in its history, eclipsing even the famed Watts riot of 1964.

Against this checkered backdrop of progress and decay, Americans by a plurality of votes ended 12 years of Republican control of the White House and elected William Jefferson Clinton to be their president. Bill Clinton had campaigned as a "New Democrat" by which he attempted to distance himself from the Democratic Party's liberalism in matters fiscal and economic while retaining, even embracing, most of its traditional social and cultural agenda. The political strategy of the "New Democrat" wing of the party was to woo back significant blocks of voters—northern ethnic blue-collar whites and southern whites of all classes—who had been poached by the Republican party since the early 1970s while holding on to the party's base of suburban women, bicoastal liberals, and African Americans. The problem was that many of these groups had conflicting interests: working-class whites favored trade protectionism whereas Democrat-allied business interests favored free trade; many whites opposed affirmative action and welfare programs that blacks saw not as handouts but as steps toward equality and justice; culture wars raged between liberal urban professionals and a growing evangelicalism in the heartland. The political answer to these intractable tradeoffs was to use symbolism to counterbalance opposition to policy.

This strategy was most evident during the campaign in the uncharacteristic way that Clinton treated a popular African American rap artist, Sister Souljah. As blocks of Los Angeles continued to smolder, Sister Souljah, a popular up-and-coming Bronx rapper, appeared on numerous news talk shows and defended the violent actions of the rioters. "I mean, if black people kill black people every day, why not have a week and kill white people? You understand what I'm saying? In other words, white people, this government and that mayor were well aware of the fact that black people were dying every day in Los Angeles under gang violence. So if you're a gang member and you would normally be killing somebody, why not kill a white person? Do you think that somebody thinks that white people are better, or above dying, when they would kill their own kind?"[10]

One month later, Democratic candidate Clinton chose to denounce Sister Souljah's comments in a speech before the Rainbow Coalition, a predominately African American organization led by Jesse Jackson. At the end of his otherwise standard speech, up to then notable only for his public apology for having accepted an invitation to golf at an all-white country club in Arkansas, Clinton noted that the Rainbow Coalition had heard a speech by Souljah the night before and said: "If you took the words 'white' and 'black' and reversed them, you might think [Klansman] David Duke was giving that speech." Jackson, who had earlier boasted that Souljah had appeared, was seated on the dais just to Clinton's right, and later admitted he had been shaken by Clinton's unexpected attack. Political analysts at the time speculated that Clinton made his remarks in an attempt to demonstrate his independence from black "special interest" groups and appeal to white voters.[11]

Once in office, President Clinton deftly used the same balancing act but in reverse—symbolically appointing the most racially diverse cabinet in American history while deploying policies, such as dismantling welfare while increasing federal funding for police and prisons, that disproportionately impacted minority communities. This began on Clinton's first day on the job: on Jan. 20, 1993, African American poet Maya Angelou read her poem, "On the Pulse of Morning," on the steps of the Capitol in Washington, D.C. during Clinton's inauguration. Angelou was more than the first poet to take part in inaugural ceremonies since Robert Frost honored President John F. Kennedy in 1961: As an African American woman she was a visible symbol of the new administration's desire to be more racially inclusive than its predecessors.

Clinton's determination to use his appointment powers to bring to Washington more people of color became a major battleground of the nations "culture wars." Throughout his first term in office, a fiercely partisan and Republican-controlled Congress combined with a new beltway journalism that seemed unusually eager to doggedly pursue more minor and unproven allegations than they had in the past to skewer Clinton's appointments. Joycelyn Elders, a fellow native of Arkansas, was appointed by President Clinton to be surgeon general, the nation's first African American woman to ever hold the post of America's top physician. Elders distinguished herself as a strong advocate of sexual education for youth in the face of rising rates of teen pregnancy and sexually transmitted diseases. Her blunt support of a common-sense approach to sex education eventually led to her being attacked by conservatives who pounced on a few comments she made at press conferences about the merits of masturbation to force her to resign after less than a year-and-a-half in her post.

Lani Guinier, a graduate of Yale Law School and a leading civil rights attorney, was nominated by President Clinton to lead the Justice Department's Civil Rights Division. Like the other nonwhite Clinton nominees, Guinier was subject to an unusual degree of scrutiny by administration's critics who dubbed her the "quota queen" for her scholarship on alternative voting methods to enhance the legislative power of minority communities. In response to the unexpectedly harsh response of the announcement of her appointment, Guinier withdrew before Congress had an opportunity to consider her nomination.

Clinton appointed Henry Cisneros as secretary of Housing and Urban Development (HUD). Cisneros became one of the first Hispanics to join the president's cabinet. HUD was an agency founded during the peak of liberal reform in the Johnson administration and was much maligned and neglected during the Reagan era. Cisneros attempted to reinvigorate the moribund national housing program and break long-established concentration (and de facto segregation) of public housing projects in inner cities by providing vouchers to poor renters to move to the suburbs. Cisneros resigned early in Clinton's second term under a cloud of scandal involving lying to federal investigators about payments to a former lover.

Hazel R. O'Leary was tapped to be secretary of energy, the first African American woman to hold that office. Although she managed to serve out her full term, she was later hounded by accusations of lavish junkets on taxpayer expense and soliciting of illegal campaign contributions. Although none of these charges were found to have substance, she stepped down in favor of Federico Peña, who also resigned within a year. The position finally stabilized with the appointment of former New Mexico congressman, ambassador to the United Nations, and rising star in the Democratic Party, Bill Richardson, continuing Clinton's tradition of having at least one Hispanic in his cabinet.

KEY EVENTS

CONFEDERATE FLAG ISSUE

History shows that symbols can, from time to time, become flash points for tensions that have accumulated throughout a society but have had no outlet for release. The Confederate battle flag, the blue St. Andrews cross (or "saltire") across a red field, was never an official symbol of the Confederate States of America but gradually became popular as a symbol of the "lost cause" of the South after its defeat. Its popularity among whites jumped suddenly as a means of voicing opposition to the Civil Rights movement in the 1950s. It was then that several southern states adopted the Confederate standard into their state flags and seals and mandated that these flags flap from their statehouses.

There were some scattered protests and petitions against the use of the Confederate flag during the 1960s and early 1970s, but the work of tearing down Jim Crow institutions seemed a far more pressing priority, and little organized work was done to root out this symbol of white supremacy. By the later 1970s, as the struggle against openly discriminatory laws was receding into the past, some activists turned their attention to calling for the ending of all state endorsement, all "official" display of the Confederate flag. One of the earliest protests broke out on January 5, 1978, when a group of several dozen students at Fairfax High School in Virginia walked out of classes in protest of their schools' "Johnny Reb" mascot who was depicted waving a Confederate battle flag. School administrators, responding to both the publicity raised by the walkout and the trouble the flag had been causing in school for some time—flag-waving having provoked numerous fistfights between black and white students in the past—announced they would retire "Johnny Reb" and organized a student design contest for a new mascot.[12]

In 1983, when John Hawkins became the first African American varsity cheerleader at the University of Mississippi, there was one routine he would not perform—he refused to wave the Confederate "stars and bars" flag. After Hawkins called attention to the issue, black students at the university petitioned the administration to end the display of Confederate symbols, which were insensitively featured in the school yearbook, provoking counter protests from the Ku Klux Klan. Events escalated into a march by a group of several hundred white students who waved the "stars and bars" flag and sang the southern anthem, "Dixie," in front of the home of a black fraternity. A university spokesman later downplayed the racial intent of the white students and compared their behavior to "a pep rally." A few days later more than 100 African American students protested their university's continued display of the Confederate flag in front of the administration building, singing "We Shall Overcome." University chancellor Porter L. Fortune responded to these escalating events by announcing the banning of all official uses of the Confederate flag at the university.[13]

The growing grass roots movement against the flag took more organized form when the southeastern regional conference of the National Association for the Advancement of Colored People (NAACP) declared that the flag was "a symbol of divisiveness, racial animosity and an insult to black people" and made resistance to the display of the flag a priority. The NAACP specifically called on Alabama and South Carolina to take down the flags flying over the state capitals and for Georgia and Mississippi to redesign their state flags with designs incorporating the "stars and bars." Taking this call literally, Representative Thomas Reed, an African American member of the state house and president of the state chapter of the NAACP, vowed to personally climb the dome of the state capitol building and remove the Confederate flag flying there unless Republican Governor Guy Hunt

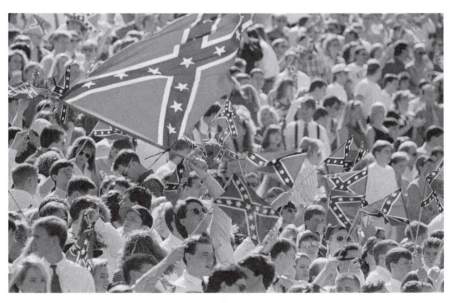

The "Rebel" flag being waved at a 1995 football game at the University of Mississippi. AP Photo/Tannen Maury.

ordered its removal by the opening of the legislative session. On February 3, 1988, the day after the legislative session began, Reed made good on his promise and arrived at the capitol with 13 other state legislators and a crowd of supporters, and all 14 legislators were arrested while symbolically attempting to scale a fence into the closed building. After the legislators took their complaint to court, a federal appeals court later ruled that display of the Confederate banner did not violate anyone's constitutional rights. A few months later, someone successfully scaled the state capitol building in Montgomery in the middle of the night and stole the official Confederate flag.[14]

Momentum against official display of the Confederate flag accelerated in the 1990s. In 1991, Robert E. Lee high school in San Antonio, Texas announced it would abandon display of the Confederate flag. City officials in Hollywood, Florida agreed in 1991 to remove a Confederate flag that was part of a city war memorial. Later that summer, the Boy Scouts of America announced it was banning the use of all Confederate flag symbols from its insignia and official activities. Southern scouts had long incorporated the Confederate flag into their regalia and ceremonies. The all-white Kappa Alpha fraternity at Jacksonville State University voted to put away the Confederate uniforms and flags they had traditionally used in their springtime marches celebrating "Old South Week." An advisory committee at the Citadel military academy recommended that the Confederate flag be banned from all academy events in 1992. Governor L. Douglas Wilder of Virginia ordered the state's Air National Guard to strip the Confederate flag from all its fighter planes and pilot suits. In 1993, an Alabama state judge ruled that an obscure 1895 law banned the display of any flag other than the United States flag over the capitol and ordered the removal of the rebel flag, providing just enough political cover for a newly elected governor to order the flags removed.[15]

Still, in some places white public opinion remained staunchly behind the anachronistic flag. In Georgia competing petition drives to retire or retain the Confederate flag revealed about a three-to-one margin in favor of keeping the symbol. Conscious that the eyes of the world would be on Georgia when the Olympics came to town in 1996, Governor Zell Miller gave an impassioned speech to the Georgia legislature urging them to pass a law ending the official display of the Confederate flag in their state.[16]

As the weight of public opinion was swinging against the defenders of the Confederate flag, they were forced to use more subtlety and subterfuge than they may have had to use in the past. Senator Jesse Helms, a four-term senator from South Carolina and the staunchest defender of the Confederate flag in Congress, attempted to retain the official United Daughters of the Confederacy design patent for a symbol that incorporated the Confederate battle flag by sneaking such a provision into an unrelated bill. Although a Congressional design patent is a mostly honorific law, it did confer some cache to an organization's symbol. Moreover, such patents are rarely awarded, fewer than two dozen private organizations currently having their symbols recognized. As senators were voting, mostly unaware that they were endorsing the Confederate flag in addition to passing an educational bill, Senator Carol Mosely Braun, the only African American and one of the few women in the Senate, called attention to what the senators were voting on, calling Helms's tactic "an outrage" and "an insult." Braun expressed the feelings of many African Americans when she declared, "it is absolutely unacceptable to me...that we would put the imprimatur of the United States Senate on a symbol of this kind of idea."[17] In reaction to Braun's impassioned speech, 27 senators changed their votes and defeated the Helms amendment.

Six years later Senator Helms was still eager to repay Braun for upending his Confederacy bill. Since defeated for reelection to the Senate, Braun was nominated to be ambassador to New Zealand by President Clinton. Helms used his senatorial privileges to hold up her nomination—no senator appointed to an ambassadorship had been turned down by the Senate since 1835. Helms made his intentions very clear, telling a reporter that "At a very minimum, she [Braun] has got to apologize for the display that she provoked over a little symbol for a wonderful group of little old ladies." A month later, under considerable criticism from his colleagues, Helms relented and Braun received her ambassadorship.[18]

By the end of the decade, in July 2000, the last Confederate flag still flying over a southern capitol was removed when South Carolina's legislature voted to relocate it from the peak of the capitol dome to a pole next to a veteran's memorial on the capitol grounds.

CLARENCE THOMAS/ANITA HILL HEARINGS

In 1991, Supreme Court Justice Thurgood Marshall announced that he was retiring from the court he had served for 24 years. Marshall was the first African American to be appointed to the highest court, a man whose entire legal career had been focused on breaking Jim Crow and legal inequality, first as legal counsel to the NAACP where he argued dozens of cases before the Supreme Court (including the landmark *Brown v. Board of Education of Topeka, Kansas* case of 1954 that broke the back of segregation) and then as a member of the court he had so often addressed. Marshall had been a pillar of the liberal majority throughout the 1960s and 1970s that were supportive of government affirmative action programs, struck down the vestiges of legal racial discrimination, expanded the rights of criminal defendants, shielded many aspects of personal privacy, and widened the latitude of the free press.

President George H. W. Bush, faced with his second opportunity to appoint a new member of the court, turned to a man long groomed for the bench by Republican leaders but also someone who would maintain the African American presence on the court, as Marshall had been the court's only black member. Bush named Clarence Thomas, a 43-year-old graduate of Yale law school, a longtime aide and confidant of powerful Missouri Senator John C. Danforth, and a rising bureaucrat in the Reagan administration, swiftly moving from assistant secretary in the Office of Civil Rights to chair of the Equal Employment Opportunity Commission.

From the moment President Bush named Thomas as his choice, the selection was controversial, primarily because Thomas was obviously politically and ideologically opposite to the justice he was replacing. Thomas was a self-proclaimed "black conservative" and an outspoken opponent of affirmative action, describing all such programs in 1987 as creating a "a narcotic of dependency" and denouncing their advocates: "Those who insist on arguing that the principle of equal opportunity, the cornerstone of civil rights, means preferences for certain groups, have relinquished their roles as moral and ethical leaders in this area." Because Thomas had only recently been appointed to the U.S. Court of Appeals the year before, however, there was not much of a specific track record of his judicial philosophy for his critics to use against his nomination.[19]

Opposition to Thomas's nomination was significant—the Congressional Black Caucus quickly voted 19 to 1 to reject his nomination and other civil rights organizations followed suit—but other than a small bump in the road when Thomas admitted to having smoked marijuana in college (a revelation that had sunk the chances of an earlier Reagan appointee, Douglas H. Ginsberg, in 1987), the nomination seemed assured of success as the Senate prepared to vote in early October. But two days before the scheduled confirmation vote, New York's *Newsday* and National Public Radio reported that a former employee of Thomas had secretly revealed to the Senate Judiciary Committee that she had been the victim of repeated acts of sexual harassment by Thomas. The Senate quickly postponed its confirmation by a week and the Judiciary Committee opened hearings into the matter that drew intense interest from the American public.[20]

The woman who had been asked by Senate staffers to come forward and share her experiences with the Senate committee on the condition of confidentially was Anita Hill, an African American law professor at the University of Oklahoma and a former employee of Thomas's at both the Education Department and the Equal Employment Opportunity Commission. Hill was forced into the media spotlight as she was called to publicly testify and repeat her embarrassing allegations in front of television cameras. The hearings transfixed the nation not only because of the titillating details of Thomas's alleged advances, but also because of the way in which these allegations played into historically created stereotypes of black male sexual aggressiveness.

Hill detailed a long pattern of Thomas's unwanted and persistent efforts to date her. She recounted the salacious language he allegedly used toward her, boasting of his sexual prowess and details of porn actors and videos he liked. Hill was the subject of intense media scrutiny and debate as the whole hearing seemed to hinge on her word versus his. Conservative media outlets let loose a widespread attack on her character and loudly charged her with having made up her story out of a partisan desire to sink Thomas's nomination.

Once Hill had presented her charges, Thomas was recalled to the committee and given the opportunity to defend himself. Thomas denied all of Hill's claims and implied she was unstable. The pivotal moment in his testimony came when Thomas, in a voice charged with emotion, accused the committee of conducting

University of Oklahoma law professor Anita Hill testifies before the Senate Judiciary Committee on the nomination of Clarence Thomas to the Supreme Court in Washington, D.C., October 11, 1991. Hill testified that she was "embarrassed and humiliated" by unwanted, sexually explicit comments by Thomas a decade before. AP Photo/Greg Gibson.

a "high-tech lynching" of him. "Mr. Chairman, I am a victim of this process. My name has been harmed...I will not provide the rope for my own lynching, or for further humiliation. I am not going to engage in discussions, nor will I submit to roving questions, of what goes on in the most intimate parts of my private life"[21]

Democrats on the committee were taken aback, evidently sensitive to such charges, as they were an all-white committee facing a black nominee. Thomas's injection of race into the debate in such a poignant fashion disarmed his leading critics, although many noted that he had a history of playing the race card when attacked (such as when, as director of the Equal Employment Opportunity Commission, he responded to the criticisms of civil rights leaders by bringing up his sharecropping grandfather and saying they should "call him from the grave and indict him"[22]). Only Senator Robert C. Byrd of West Virginia challenged his colleagues not to be cowed by Thomas's use of the race card. "A black American woman was making a charge against a black American male. Where's the racism? Nonsense."[23]

The public was deeply divided. A number of critics noted that Thomas avoided questions of his racial identity throughout his confirmation hearings but then stressed his southern black roots once he had been accused of sexual harassment by Anita Hill. Other observers faulted Hill for her lack of racial solidarity and raising personal issues with another member of the African American community.[24]

Even after a second woman, Angela Wright, who was Thomas's public relations assistant at the EEOC, came forward to recount being harassed by Thomas (remembering that he had hounded her for a date, asked her what her breast size was, and even showed up unexpectedly at her apartment), the Senate seemed intent on sweeping the whole messy issue under a rug and proceeded to confirm Thomas.[25]

1992 RODNEY KING BEATING AND LOS ANGELES RIOTS

It was nearly one in the morning on March 3, 1991, when Los Angeles police officers finally pulled over motorist Rodney King after an eight-mile chase in which King pushed his Hyundai to 115 miles per hour. More than a dozen officers encircled King and his two companions; King lunged toward Officer Laurence Powell, and Powell and two other officers pummeled King with their metal batons. The beating continued for more than a minute. Fifty-six blows were captured by a video camera trained on the incident from a nearby apartment building. King's injuries were extensive: his skull was shattered in nine places, his leg was broken, and he had serious injuries to both knees. Within days, images of a crowd of police beating and kicking a face-down black man would flash on televisions around the world.[26]

The anger these images stirred in minority communities throughout Los Angeles had been brewing for many years. Throughout the 1980s, a statewide property tax freeze forced police budgets and force levels to decline in the face of growing populations and crime rates that were trending upward. In just two years before the night King was beaten, the number of police in Los Angeles dropped from 8,400 to 7,800. Short-handed, poorly equipped, and burdened by a siege mentality, the Los Angeles police department's (LAPD) relations with the communities they policed were typified by mutual mistrust and anger. The LAPD's reputation for callousness and brutality was well established long before the world had ever heard of Rodney King. From 1986 to 1990, the LAPD received more than 2,000 public complaints that their officers had used excessive force against citizens. In the 1980s, 16 African Americans had died after being held in chokeholds by police. Police Chief Daryl Gates described all these deaths as being accidents caused partially by the "abnormal anatomy of black necks."[27] Although people of color around the nation recognized the King beating as emblematic of a problem plaguing minority communities generally, Congresswoman Maxine Waters, whose district included South Central L.A., could not get her resolution condemning King's attack and the problem of police brutality in general out of committee and onto the floor of the House for a vote.[28]

Less than two weeks after King's pummeling, a 15-year-old African American girl, Latasha Harlins, walked into the Empire Liquor Mart and Deli, a convenience store in her South Central Los Angeles neighborhood owned by a Korean family that lived on the other side of the city. Since the 1960s, the population and prominence of Koreans and other East Asian immigrants had grown dramatically in Los Angeles. By the day Harlins stopped at the Empire Liquor Mart, Koreans owned 3,300 retail stores in the city. Harlins picked a bottle of juice from the cooler, put it in her backpack, and dropped some bills on the store counter as Soon Ja Du, the 51-year-old proprietress, grabbed her sweater and accused her of shoplifting. Harlins punched Du and Du threw a stool at Harlins. The young girl turned to leave and Du pulled a .38 pistol from underneath the counter, braced herself with both hands and fired into the back of Harlin's head. Like the beating of Rodney King, Du's shooting of Harlins was captured by the store's surveillance camera and later broadcast on the evening news.

Such violent encounters were not unusual in Los Angeles. Since the Empire Liquor Mart and Deli opened, it had been robbed more than 30 times. In the previous two years, 25 Korean merchants had been killed in South Central Los Angeles. In the same month Du shot and killed Harlins, two other African Americans and two Korean businessmen had been shot in stores in Los Angeles.[29]

No one could have expected at the time that these two events, related only by the coincidence of their timing, would catapult the city of Los Angeles toward the worst episode of rioting in 25 years and by some measures the costliest in American history. On the surface, race relations seemed to have improved in the city; the city was administered by its first African American mayor, Tom Bradley, and many of the city's minority communities were represented on its city council. A city that had once been both white-dominated and intolerant of people of color was noted in the census of 1990 as becoming a population with a majority of minorities composed of Latinos, African Americans, and Asians. But just below this seeming interracial amity, great resentments and rivalries were building. Since the 1970s and vastly accelerating in the 1980s, the city had witnessed both a jump in immigration, especially from Latin America, and a steady deindustrialization as factories were relocated south of the border. Between 1982 and 1989, 131 plants closed in Los Angeles eliminating 124,000 jobs. At the same time the Hispanic population rose 62 percent, the size of the smaller Asian community more than doubled while the black population held steady, scarcely registering any change at less than 1 percent growth. The combination of ethnic succession, deindustrialization, and an erosion of public services proved a toxic brew that caused many ordinary people to vent their frustrations in extraordinary ways once a breakdown in routine public order occurred.[30]

The focal point for community rage was the seeming confirmation that the justice system, long proclaimed as impartial and colorblind, was simply unwilling or incapable of providing justice for black victims. First, the killer of Latasha Harlins was convicted by a jury of voluntary manslaughter, a crime carrying a potential sentence of up to 11 years in prison. But at her sentencing, Soon Ja Du, facing a young judge, Joyce Karlin, who had never before presided over a criminal case, was released on probation rather than sent to prison. At the time it was common for nonviolent drug offenders to be given lengthy jail terms, and few of the city's legal insiders could recall a similar case where the perpetrator was not locked up. Los Angeles District Attorney Ira Reiner ordered his assistant to refuse to try any cases before Judge Karlin, and she was transferred to juvenile court duties soon afterward, but the damage had been done. Outraged residents of South Central Los Angeles organized a boycott of all Korean businesses. The family of Latasha Harlins was awarded $300,000 in a subsequent civil wrongful death suit and the Empire Liquor Mart was shuttered for good.[31]

For a time it seemed as though justice might be carried out in the case of Rodney King. Mayor Bradley empanelled a special commission headed by former Assistant Secretary of State Warren Christopher to investigate police conduct. The U.S. Attorney General's office began an investigation of police brutality in the LAPD. The Police Commission suspended Chief of Police Daryl Gates who later resigned and was replaced by Willie L. Williams, the first black chief of police in Philadelphia. Four white police officers, Sergeant Stacy Koon, Officers Laurence Powell, Timothy Wind, and Theodore Briseno, were suspended and indicted under charges of assault with a deadly weapon. Koon and Powell were also charged with submitting a false report.

Using claims of undue publicity as grounds, the police officers' lawyers succeeded in moving the trial from Los Angeles to largely white and suburban Simi Valley. There they were able to seat a jury that had no black members (of the 12 jurors, 10 were white, 1 was Asian-American, and 1 was Hispanic.) Focusing on the circumstances of the high-speed chase and King's generally belligerent attitude, defense lawyers succeeded in deflecting attention away from the incriminating video images of King's beating and to the actions of the victim, which contributed to his being in that place at that time. In spite of strong evidence including the powerful images of baton-blows, the testimony of one of the four officers who turned state's evidence, and even radio communication between the police officers (Powell and Wind sent a message to other officers boasting, "I haven't beaten anyone this bad in a long time"), the jury acquitted the four officers on all charges (although the jury could not agree on one charge of brutality against Powell).

Within hours of the jury's verdict, the center of Los Angeles erupted in rioting. A crowd gathered at the corner of W. 67th and 11th avenues, in the stable middle-class black neighborhood of Hyde Park and began throwing bricks and stones at passing motorists. When a white pedestrian happened by, the mob beat him and tossed him into a dumpster before moving on to loot nearby Korean-owned stores. A mile or so away in the heart of South Central, Normandie and Florence streets, another group pelted cars with rocks and bottles and dragged white-looking drivers from their cars and beat them on the street. Police responding to reports of violence were turned away by large stone-throwing crowds. An hour or so later, television crews capturing the rioting live from a helicopter hovering over the area beamed images around the world of the beating of white truck driver Reginald Denny. Denny was pulled from his truck and beaten nearly to death, including what seemed at the time as a coup de grace delivered by a young man smashing his skull with a fire extinguisher. Denny was rescued by other African American men who lived nearby. They had seen the horror unfolding

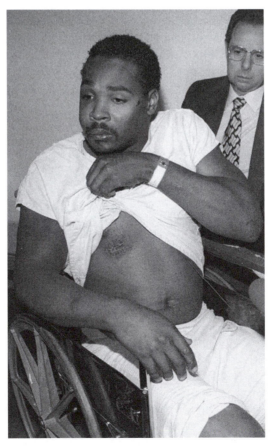

Rodney King shows his bruises in Los Angeles, March 1991. AP Photo/Kevork Djansezian.

on their television and rushed to the scene, bundled Denny into a car, and drove him to the hospital. An organized protest outside the city police headquarters at the Parker Center to demand the resignation of Chief of Police Gates escalated into a riot with street-fighting between police and protesters, smashing of windows, and overturning of cars.

By nightfall, 60 square miles of Los Angeles had descended into anarchy, looting, and riot. Unable to quell the anger of black and Hispanic residents, police merely tried to contain it and prevent others from becoming entangled in it. Police sealed off all the Harbor freeway exits leading to affected areas while Mayor Tom Bradley declared a state of emergency and Governor Wilson dispatched 2,000 National Guardsman to the city. Korean businessmen formed armed patrols to keep looters and arsonists from their stores, but with little success. A thousand fires lit the area overnight—so many that the Los Angeles International Airport was forced to close all but one runway because of the smoke. Of the 403 buildings totally destroyed, nearly half were owned by Koreans. Three days later when the rioters went home, the fires burned down, and the rubble-strewn streets were patrolled by rifle-wielding soldiers, the tally was 44 dead, more than 1,000 injured, and well over $1 billion in property damage.

In Washington, politicians added their own spin to the riots as President George H. W. Bush and his chief spokesman Marlin Fitzwater described the Los Angeles riots as being caused by the failed liberal social welfare policies of the previous quarter century. "We believe that many of the root problems that have resulted in inner-city difficulties were started in the 60's and 70's," Mr. Fitzwater told reporters, adding such welfare programs "have failed."[32]

A week after the acquittal of the Los Angeles police officers and the riots that followed, a four-foot tall sign planted on a well-manicured lawn at the entrance to a south central LA neighborhood read simply, "Guilty."[33]

The next year four of the officers who beat Rodney King, Officers Wind, Briseno, Koon, and Powell, were tried again under federal statutes criminalizing the violation of someone's civil rights. Although the second trial was controversial as many alleged it amounted to the sort of double jeopardy prohibited by the U.S. Constitution (which was the position of the American Civil Liberties Union), to many it was a late but welcome expression of justice. Officers Koon and Powell were found guilty and sentenced to two-and-a-half years in federal prison.

THE VOYAGE OF THE GOLDEN VENTURE

It was two hours past midnight when the 286 Chinese men and women who had endured more than 100 days at sea in the crowded hold of the 147 foot tramp steamer, the *Golden Venture,* felt the ship lurch to a halt and heard the shouts from crewmen above for them to jump off the ship and swim to shore. Each of these hopeful immigrants had paid between $20,000 and $35,000 for their illegal transportation from the South China Sea, west to Africa and around the Cape of Good Hope (where a sudden storm and 50-foot waves nearly sank them) to this sand bar within sight of the lights of Long Island, New York. Only five people made it to shore and fled to begin their new lives in America with nothing but the wet clothes on their bodies. Ten others drowned, their bodies being discovered one by one along the coast during the next four weeks. The rest were scooped up by the Coast Guard and local police and taken into detention while their immigration status was determined by Immigration and Naturalization Service officials and federal judges.

Beyond the torturous journey itself, the huge debts the men and women incurred to the Chinese gangs that ran the operation, and the chaotic ending of their voyage, the greatest misfortune of these hopeful immigrants was that their arrival occurred just at the moment when the question of illegal entry into the United States was becoming a hot political issue. A threatened flood of immigrants fleeing political chaos in Haiti, alongside a renewed stream from Cuba, reignited immigration as a partisan issue fraught with racial implications.

Into the midst of this debate arrived a succession of boats crammed with human cargo from Asia. In the six weeks leading up to the beaching of the *Golden Venture*, officials seized boats off the coasts of Jacksonville, Florida; San Diego, California; and three vessels near San Francisco, all smuggling Asian immigrants. As some Congressmen accused the Clinton administration of not doing enough to protect America's borders, the President responded to the public's sensitivity to the issue and pursued a tough policy toward the passengers of the *Golden Venture* in the hopes of discouraging other would-be illegal immigrants from China.[34]

In the year before the arrival of the *Golden Venture*, the Immigration and Naturalization Service had released, with some sort of regularized residency status, about one-third of all the Chinese people caught entering the country illegally. The treatment of the *Golden Venture* passengers was different: after three months of waiting in jail, only 14 of more than 250 had been granted asylum. As their wait stretched from months to years, half of the *Golden Venture* refugees were sent to a county jail in York, Pennsylvania, and another group was sent to a detention center in California. At the one-year anniversary of their incarceration, 224 *Golden Venture* immigrants remained locked up. In August 1993, the 114 *Golden Venture* inmates at the York County jail staged a short hunger strike in protest of their treatment and against the possibility of being sent back to China, where many feared government reprisals. After two years of detention, two dozen of the *Golden Venture* detainees gave up and voluntarily accepted deportation back to China. By the third anniversary of their landing in America, there were still 175 *Golden Venture* passengers in American jails.

An interesting unintended consequence of the *Golden Venture* immigrants' long detention in a small community in Pennsylvania was that they quickly forged strong friendships and relationships with local people who had had no connection to immigration issues. Local York county residents sent food and homemade quilts to the jail while detainees returned the favor with intricate origami sculptures. Locals began holding weekly candlelight vigils to protest the continuing detention of the *Golden Venture* passengers.

The Clinton administration's harsh treatment of the *Golden Venture* immigrants was hailed by some observers as having had the desired effect—the number of ships caught smuggling Chinese immigrants into the United States declined from 15 in 1993 to 6 in 1994. While the *Golden Venture* detainees languished in jail, Congress enacted several pieces of legislation to crack down on illegal entry and human smuggling including the Illegal Immigration Reform and Immigrant Responsibilities Act of 1996 that expedited deportation procedures (now renamed "removal" actions) and made it more difficult for undocumented immigrants or their advocates to challenge their detentions or deportations in court.[35]

Supporters of the *Golden Venture* detainees observed their 182nd weekly candlelight vigil before it became clear that the passengers of that sorry boat would eventually take a free step on American soil. In September 1996, Congress ordered the Immigration and Naturalization Service to recognize those who resisted China's policy of punishing families who have more than one child as being eligible for political asylum. This prompted the Clinton administration to order the release of the last 53 *Golden Venture* detainees, three years and eight months after their ship ran aground off the coast of Long Island. In 2000, Congress took a step to ensure that in the future victims of human smugglers would not languish in American jails by passing the Victims of Trafficking and Violence Protection Act, which allocated special "T-visas" to victims of "severe" human smuggling.[36]

THE O. J. SIMPSON TRIAL

Around midnight on June 12, 1994, a neighbor of Nicole Brown Simpson in the Brentwood section of Los Angeles heard her dog wailing and walked over to Nicole's condominium to investigate. There the neighbor discovered the slashed bodies of Nicole and her friend Ronald Goldman sprawled in a small courtyard outside the door. At that moment Nicole's ex-husband, hall-of-fame football player, O. J. Simpson, was on board a red-eye flight to Chicago that took off from Los Angeles at 11:45. The next morning Simpson was called and informed of his ex-wife's death, and he flew back to L.A. the same day to find police technicians and detectives combing over his home.

While Simpson clearly was a suspect from the moment police began investigating the case, his celebrity seemed to stymie early police efforts. Officers who interviewed him for half an hour on the day he arrived back home avoided difficult lines of questioning and failed to pursue obvious leads, not even pressing Simpson about how he had suffered a deep cut on his right hand. Nevertheless, the police accumulated what they thought was sufficient evidence of Simpson's guilt and notified his attorney a few days later to arrange his surrender. Simpson promised that he would turn himself in the morning after Nicole's funeral, June 17; instead he fled, leaving behind a rambling note that denied his involvement in Nicole's murder but also implied he was soon to die: "Don't feel sorry for me. I've had a great life, great friends. Please think of the real O. J. and not this lost person." That evening, on a tip from a passing motorist who recognized the wanted celebrity, police found Simpson being driven in a white Ford Bronco by his friend A. C. Cowlings through Orange County. A swarm of police cars and news helicopters followed at a distance behind the Bronco, kept back by the knowledge that there was a pistol in the car and Simpson's threats that he was going to kill himself. Cowlings eventually pulled into Simpson's driveway where he surrendered to police, and one of the most publicized trials of the century began.

From the inception of the trial, racial issues dictated the directions and decisions that would ultimately lead to its complicated and contentious outcome. Prosecutors, fearful of a replay of the Rodney King riots in 1992, chose not to file the case in Santa Monica County where the crime occurred (which would have been standard practice), but instead filed in Los Angeles County, knowing that a Santa Monica jury pool would be predominately white, and a decision by a nearly all-white jury would inflame racial tensions downtown. Similar considerations led the prosecution team neither to seek the death penalty nor to use all their peremptory challenges to influence the selection of a more sympathetic jury, another standard legal maneuver. Simpson was arraigned on July 22, but the trial did not begin until January 24, and then continued for another nine months.

As the trial dragged on, racial allegations and tensions mounted. In mid-April, one of the jurors, Jeanette Harris, who was African American, was removed from the jury when prosecutors discovered that she had been the victim of domestic abuse herself but had not revealed this during her juror's examination. Harris quickly appeared on the top-rated television news magazine, *20/20* and said that racial tensions were mounting among the jurors. She said she was kicked by a white juror and that there had been shouting matches between the whites and blacks in the jury room. She charged that the sheriffs assigned to guard them on outings from the courthouse treated the white and black jurors differently. Harris said that based on the evidence she had heard, she would have voted to acquit Simpson.[37]

It was clear midway through the trial that the defense was increasingly successful at turning the tables and putting the Los Angeles Police Department on trial. Given the sordid and troubled history of the department, the rampant racial profiling that many of its officers engaged in—even Christopher Darden, the county prosecutor who helped lead the prosecution later admitted that he was used to being stopped at least five times per year himself because he was a black man driving a Mercedes—it was easy to appeal to the jury in this way.[38] More damaging was the fact that one of the lead detectives in the case, Mark Fuhrman, denied on the witness stand using the "N-word" in the recent past, a testimony contradicted when it was revealed that Fuhrman had tape recorded an interview with a screenwriter that had captured some racist remarks.

As the trial proceeded, Simpson's defense managed to cast doubt on all the forensic evidence introduced by the prosecution by implying it was planted by racist police officers. Most damning of all circumstantial evidence were blood stains found inside Simpson's home and car that contained the DNA of Nicole

O. J. Simpson, right, confers with his attorney Johnnie L. Cochran Jr., center, as attorney Robert Blasier, left, listens to the defense's closing arguments in Simpson's double-murder trial in Los Angeles, September 28, 1995. AP Photo/Sam Mircovich, pool.

Simpson and a bloody glove found on the grounds of his property that matched a similarly cast off glove found at the crime scene. In a particularly dramatic moment of the trial, prosecutor Darden instructed Simpson to try on the gloves to show the court they were his, but Simpson struggled to pull them on saying, "See, they don't fit!" Later in the most famous line from his summation to the jury, Simpson's fiery lawyer, Johnnie Cochran, declared, "If it doesn't fit, you must acquit!" And that is what the jury did after just three hours of deliberation.

Beyond the media circus, the voyeuristic fascination of celebrity lives, and the horrifying details of murder, the Simpson trial attracted attention as no other courtroom drama of the late twentieth century had largely because it highlighted the stark divisions between the perceptions of black and white America. Every aspect of the Simpson case seemed racially charged and laden with metaphorical meanings. *Time* magazine came under fire for publishing a cover portrait of Simpson that it had doctored to darken his skin. James R. Gaines, managing editor at the time, apologized to those who saw racism in the way Simpson was portrayed, saying "it seems to me you could argue that it's racist to say that blacker is more sinister," and explained that his magazine aimed to create covers that were "in some way iconographic."[39]

From the moment Simpson was charged with the murders of Nicole Brown Simpson and Ron Goldman, national polls revealed that black and white Americans held nearly opposite views of it. One of the first polls conducted just three weeks after the murders, before much of the evidence gathered by detectives had been revealed publicly, showed that more than two-thirds of all whites believed that Simpson was guilty, whereas fewer than one-quarter of African Americans thought he was guilty. These initial impressions proved extremely durable, unmoved by the thousands of hours of courtroom testimony and public commentary on the case over the coming years. A poll taken two-and-a-half years later showed that nearly three-quarters of whites believed Simpson was guilty (73%), but only one-fifth of blacks thought him a murderer. The passage of a decade did slowly allow an increasing element of doubt to spread in the black community. In a 2007 poll, slightly more than a third of African Americans (34%) said Simpson was guilty, and the number of those unsure of his guilty or innocence rose from one-fifth (22%) to more than one-third (36%). Time could not erase the racial disparities in opinion, however, as whites were even more sure of their conclusion that Simpson was guilty (80%).[40]

VOICES OF THE DECADE

PRESIDENT BILL CLINTON

On June 14, 1997, President Clinton delivered the keynote commencement address to the graduates of the University of California San Diego and used the occasion to announce a new initiative aimed at overcoming racial divisions still evident throughout the country. Clinton's plan, officially called "One America in the Twenty-first Century: The President's Initiative on Race," consisted of the appointment of a blue-ribbon advisory panel chaired by distinguished African American historian, John Hope Franklin, and a series of three "town hall" meetings intended to provide a venue for the frank discussion of racial issues.

> Today we celebrate your achievements at a truly golden moment for America. The cold war is over and freedom has now ascended around the globe....
>
> Of course, there are still challenges for you out there. Beyond our borders, we must battle terrorism, organized crime and drug trafficking, the spread of weapons of mass destruction, the prospect of new diseases and environmental disaster.... But I believe the greatest challenge we face... is also our greatest opportunity. Of all the questions of discrimination and prejudice that still exist in our society, the most perplexing one is the oldest, and in some ways today,

the newest: the problem of race. Can we fulfill the promise of America by embracing all our citizens of all races, not just at a university where people have
the benefit of enlightened teachers and the time to think and grow and get to
know each other within the daily life of every American community? In short,
can we become one America in the 21st century?

I know, and I've said before, that money cannot buy this goal, power cannot
compel it, technology cannot create it. This is something that can come only
from the human spirit....

Though minorities have more opportunities than ever today, we still see
evidence of bigotry, from the desecration of houses of worship, whether they
be churches, synagogues, or mosques, to demeaning talk in corporate suites.
There is still much work to be done by you, members of the class of 1997. But
those who say we cannot transform the problem of prejudice into the promise
of unity forget how far we have come, and I cannot believe they have ever seen
a crowd like you...

To be sure, there is old, unfinished business between black and white Americans, but the classic American dilemma has now become many dilemmas of
race and ethnicity. We see it in the tension between black and Hispanic customers and their Korean or Arab grocers; in a resurgent anti-Semitism even
on some college campuses; in a hostility toward new immigrants from Asia to
the Middle East to the former communist countries to Latin America and the
Caribbean—even those whose hard work and strong families have brought
them success in the American way....

Remember too, in spite of the persistence of prejudice, we are more integrated than ever. More of us share neighborhoods and work and school and
social activities, religious life, even love and marriage across racial lines than
ever before. More of us enjoy each other's company and distinctive cultures
than ever before. And more than ever, we understand the benefits of our racial,
linguistic, and cultural diversity in a global society, where networks of commerce and communications draw us closer and bring rich rewards to those who
truly understand life beyond their nation's borders.

...I have come here today to ask the American people to join me in a great
national effort to perfect the promise of America for this new time as we seek
to build our more perfect Union...

Let me say that I know that for many white Americans, this conversation
may seem to exclude them or threaten them. That must not be so. I believe
white Americans have just as much to gain as anybody else from being a part
of this endeavor—much to gain from an America where we finally take responsibility for all our children so that they, at last, can be judged as Martin
Luther King hoped, not by the color of their skin but by the content of their
character.

What is it that we must do? For four and one-half years now, I have worked
to prepare America for the 21st century with a strategy of opportunity for all,
responsibility from all, and an American community of all our citizens. To succeed in each of these areas, we must deal with the realities and the perceptions
affecting all racial groups in America.

First, we must continue to expand opportunity. Full participation in our strong and growing economy is the best antidote to envy, despair, and racism. We must press forward to move millions more from poverty and welfare to work, to bring the spark of enterprise to inner cities, to redouble our efforts to reach those rural communities prosperity has passed by. And most important of all, we simply must give our young people the finest education in the world.... In our efforts to extend economic and educational opportunity to all our citizens, we must consider the role of affirmative action. I know affirmative action has not been perfect in America—that's why 2 years ago we began an effort to fix the things that are wrong with it—but when used in the right way, it has worked...

To those who oppose affirmative action, I ask you to come up with an alternative. I would embrace it if I could find a better way. And to those of us who still support it, I say we should continue to stand for it, we should reach out to those who disagree or are uncertain and talk about the practical impact of these issues, and we should never be unwilling to work with those who disagree with us to find new ways to lift people up and bring people together...

We must build one American community based on respect for one another and our shared values. We must begin with a candid conversation on the state of race relations today and the implications of Americans of so many different races living and working together as we approach a new century. We must be honest with each other. We have talked at each other and about each other for a long time. It's high time we all began talking with each other.

Over the coming year, I want to lead the American people in a great and unprecedented conversation about race. In community efforts from Lima, Ohio, to Billings, Montana, in remarkable experiments in cross-racial communications like the uniquely named ERACISM, I have seen what Americans can do if they let down their guards and reach out their hands.

I have asked one of America's greatest scholars, Dr. John Hope Franklin, to chair an advisory panel of seven distinguished Americans to help me in this endeavor... I want this panel to help educate Americans about the facts surrounding issues of race, to promote a dialog in every community of the land to confront and work through these issues, to recruit and encourage leadership at all levels to help breach racial divides, and to find, develop, and recommend how to implement concrete solutions to our problems—solutions that will involve all of us in Government, business, communities, and as individual citizens...

Honest dialog will not be easy at first. We'll all have to get past defensiveness and fear and political correctness and other barriers to honesty. Emotions may be rubbed raw, but we must begin.

What do I really hope we will achieve as a country? If we do nothing more than talk, it will be interesting, but it won't be enough. If we do nothing more than propose disconnected acts of policy, it will be helpful, but it won't be enough. But if 10 years from now people can look back and see that this year of honest dialog and concerted action helped to lift the heavy burden of race from our children's future, we will have given a precious gift to America.

From "Remarks at the University of California San Diego Commencement Ceremony, June 14, 1997," Weekly Compilation of Presidential Documents (1997), 33:25, 871–915.

THURGOOD MARSHALL

On July 4, 1992, Thurgood Marshall accepted the Medal of Liberty, an award established by the National Constitution Center in 1989 to celebrate the bicentennial of the U.S. Constitution. Marshall had, just the year before, retired from the Supreme Court he joined in 1967. Standing in Independence Hall on the nation's Independence Day, Justice Marshall delivered what would be one of his last speeches before his death six months later.

Marshall's tone here is both hopeful and dark. He notes the sacrifices that have made possible the tremendous progress he witnessed in America over his lifetime, but he also emphasized the grave problems still facing the nation, especially the lingering force of racism. Marshall specifically called upon his listeners to work to overcome these problems through "building bridges" and through "dissent"—a strategy harkening back to his younger days in the Civil Rights movement.

Who would have thought that in the wake of Smith against Allright, and Shelley against Karma, and Brown against the Board of Education, that I would be giving a talk now on the anniversary of our nation's independence? I would have predicted that I would have spoken with much pride and optimism of the enormous progress this nation has already made . . . I wish I could say that racism and prejudice were only distant memories. I wish I could say that this nation had traveled far along the road to social justice and that liberty and equality were just around the corner. I wish I could say that America had come to appreciate diversity and to see and accept similarities.

But as I look around, I see not a nation of unity, but a nation of division: Afro and White, indigenous and immigrant, rich and poor, educated and illiterate. Even many educated white people and successful Negroes have given up on integration, and lost hope in equality. They see nothing in common, except the need to flee, as fast as they can, farther from our inner cities.

A Pullman porter once told me when I was a kid that he had been in almost every city in the country. He said he never was in a city where he had to put his hand in front of his face to know he was a Negro. Well, I'm afraid that I've been in every city in this country, and it's thirty or forty years after what he said. And I hate to tell you, what he said is still true.

But there's a price to be paid for division and isolation as the recent events in California indicate. Look around. Can't you see the tension in Watts, California? Can't you feel the fear in Scarsdale? Can't you sense the alienation in Simi Valley? The despair in the South Bronx and Brooklyn? It's all around you. We cannot play hostage. Democracy just cannot flourish amid fear. Liberty cannot bloom with hate. Justice cannot take root amid fear.

America must get to work. In the chilled climate in which we live, we must go against the prevailing winds. We must dissent from the indifference. We must dissent from the apathy. We must dissent from the fear, the hatred, and the mistrust. We must dissent from a nation that buried its head in the sand waiting in vain for the needs of its poor, its elderly, and its sick to disappear and just blow away. We must dissent from a government that has left its young without jobs, education, or hope. We must dissent from the poverty of vision and timeless absence of moral leadership. We must dissent, because America can do better, because America has no choice but to do better.

The legal system can force open doors, and sometimes-even knock down walls, but it cannot build bridges. That job belongs to you and me. The country can't do it. Afro and White, rich and poor, educated and illiterate, our fates are bound together. We can run from each other, but we cannot escape each other. We will only attain freedom if we learn to appreciate what is different, and muster the courage to discover what is fundamentally the same. America's diversity offers so much richness and opportunity. Take a chance, won't you? Knock down the fences, which divide. Tear apart the walls that imprison you. Reach out. Freedom lies just on the other side. We shall have liberty for all. Thank you.

From "We Must Dissent," [excerpted] from Supreme Justice Speeches and Writings Thurgood Marshall, J. Clay Smith, Jr., ed. (University of Pennsylvania Press, 2002).

TONI MORRISON

Author Toni Morrison was awarded the Nobel Prize for Literature in 1993, the eighth woman and the first African American woman so honored. She had previously won the Pulitzer Prize for her novel *Beloved* (1987). Morrison grew up in Lorain, Ohio, in a working-class neighborhood where a love of stories, lore, and folktales ran deep and where she discovered her love for the richness of language. After earning a graduate degree from Cornell, she taught at Texas Southern in the mid-1950s and then at Howard University, where one of her students was the future "Black Power" pioneer, Stokely Carmichael. In the 1960s, Morrison left academia to be an editor for Random House, a position that offered her a unique vantage point from which to survey the trends of American literature. In 1970, after editing and publishing dozens of other writers' work, she published the first novel of her own, *The Bluest Eye*, which was adored by critics but ignored by the public. Over the next decade, she produced a stream of acclaimed and award-winning novels: *Sula* (1973), *Song of Solomon* (1977), *Tar Baby* (1981), as well as the trilogy of *Beloved* (1987), *Jazz* (1992), and *Paradise* (1998).

Morrison's fascination and serious appreciation for language is evident in her Nobel speech. She understands language to be a more than a system of meaning or of symbolic importance but she finds it to be also a system of power. She warns against blind acquiescence to what she terms the "policing languages of mastery" and instead urges people to love words for their sublime ability to construct meaning, which, she finds, is what makes us human.

Once upon a time there was an old woman. Blind but wise." Or was it an old man? A guru, perhaps. Or a griot soothing restless children. I have heard this story, or one exactly like it, in the lore of several cultures....

In the version I know the woman is the daughter of slaves, black, American, and lives alone in a small house outside of town. Her reputation for wisdom is without peer and without question...

One day the woman is visited by some young people who seem to be bent on disproving her clairvoyance and showing her up for the fraud they believe she is. Their plan is simple: they enter her house and ask the one question the answer to which rides solely on her difference from them, a difference they regard as a profound disability: her blindness. They stand before her, and one of them says, "Old woman, I hold in my hand a bird. Tell me whether it is living or dead."

She does not answer, and the question is repeated. "Is the bird I am holding living or dead?"

Still she doesn't answer. She is blind and cannot see her visitors, let alone what is in their hands. She does not know their color, gender or homeland. She only knows their motive.

The old woman's silence is so long, the young people have trouble holding their laughter.

Finally she speaks and her voice is soft but stern. "I don't know," she says. "I don't know whether the bird you are holding is dead or alive, but what I do know is that it is in your hands. It is in your hands."

Her answer can be taken to mean: if it is dead, you have either found it that way or you have killed it. If it is alive, you can still kill it. Whether it is to stay alive, it is your decision. Whatever the case, it is your responsibility.

For parading their power and her helplessness, the young visitors are reprimanded, told they are responsible not only for the act of mockery but also for the small bundle of life sacrificed to achieve its aims. The blind woman shifts attention away from assertions of power to the instrument through which that power is exercised.

Speculation on what (other than its own frail body) that bird-in-the-hand might signify has always been attractive to me, but especially so now thinking, as I have been, about the work I do that has brought me to this company. So I choose to read the bird as language and the woman as a practiced writer. She is worried about how the language she dreams in, given to her at birth, is handled, put into service, even withheld from her for certain nefarious purposes. Being a writer she thinks of language partly as a system, partly as a living thing over which one has control, but mostly as agency—as an act with consequences. So the question the children put to her: "Is it living or dead?" is not unreal because she thinks of language as susceptible to death, erasure; certainly imperiled and salvageable only by an effort of the will. She believes that if the bird in the hands of her visitors is dead the custodians are responsible for the corpse. For her a dead language is not only one no longer spoken or written, it is unyielding language content to admire its own paralysis. Like statist language, censored and censoring. Ruthless in its policing duties, it has no desire or purpose other than maintaining the free range of its own narcotic narcissism, its own exclusivity and dominance. However moribund, it is not without effect for it actively thwarts the intellect, stalls conscience, suppresses human potential. Unreceptive to interrogation, it cannot form or tolerate new ideas, shape other thoughts, tell another story, fill baffling silences. Official language smitheryed to sanction ignorance and preserve privilege is a suit of armor polished to shocking glitter, a husk from which the knight departed long ago. Yet there it is: dumb, predatory, sentimental. Exciting reverence in schoolchildren, providing shelter for despots, summoning false memories of stability, harmony among the public....

Word-work is sublime, she thinks, because it is generative; it makes meaning that secures our difference, our human difference—the way in which we are like no other life.

We die. That may be the meaning of life. But we do language. That may be the measure of our lives

From *Nobel Lectures, Literature 1991–1995,* Sture Allén, ed. (Nobel Foundation, World Scientific Publishing Co., Singapore, 1997).

LOUIS FARRAKHAN

On October 16, 1995, hundreds of thousands of African American men gathered on the Washington Mall to demonstrate their commitment to personal and social transformation. The actual number of those who turned out that day was disputed. Organizers claimed that at least a million men were present; the National Park Service, which is charged by Congress with estimating the size of all such events, counted less than half that; the Center for Remote Sensing at Boston University arrived at a figure of 870,000.[41] Whatever the precise number, all agreed it was one of the largest gatherings of African Americans in American history.

The mass gathering in Washington, D.C. of hundreds of thousands of African American men on October 16, 1995 was the brainchild of Louis Farrakhan, leader of the Nation of Islam and one of the most controversial figures in American society. Farrakhan delivered a speech that rambled widely across politics, religion, history, numerology, and ethics, and stretched for more than two-and-a-half hours—a speech that even one of his supporters and a member of the organizing committee of the event said "should have been shortened by, at the minimum an hour and a half."[42] Farrakhan urged his listeners to focus on supporting their families and their churches, mosques, or other religious organizations; to vote; to contribute money to a fund for national black economic development; and to respect themselves and the women in their lives.

So, we stand here today at this historic moment. We are standing in the place of those who couldn't make it here today. We are standing on the blood of our ancestors. We are standing on the blood of those who died in the middle passage, who died in the fields and swamps of America, who died hanging from trees in the South, who died in the cells of their jailers, who died on the highways and who died in the fratricidal conflict that rages within our community. We are standing on the sacrifice of the lives of those heroes, our great men and women that we today may accept the responsibility that life imposes upon each traveler who comes this way.

We must accept the responsibility that God has put upon us, not only to be good husbands and fathers and builders of our community, but God is now calling upon the despised and the rejected to become the cornerstone and the builders of a new world

....we as a people now have been fractured, divided and destroyed, filled with fear, distrust and envy. Therefore, because of fear, envy and distrust of one another, many of us as leaders, teachers, educators, pastors and persons are still under the control mechanism of our former slave masters and their children....

Oh, but you better look again...There's a new Black man in America today. A new Black woman in America today. Now Brothers, there's a social benefit of our gathering here today. That is, that from this day forward, we can never again see ourselves through the narrow eyes of the limitation of the boundaries of our own fraternal, civic, political, religious, street organization or professional organization. We are forced by the magnitude of what we see here today, that whenever you return to your cities and you see a Black man, a Black woman, don't ask him what is your social, political or religious affiliation, or what is your status? Know that he is your brother.

You must live beyond the narrow restrictions of the divisions that have been imposed upon us. Well, some of us are here because it's history making. Some of us are here because it's a march through which we ca express anger and rage with America for what she has and is doing to us. So, we're here for many reasons but the basic reason while this was called was for atonement and reconciliation....

And as we leave this place, let us be resolved to go home to work out this Atonement and make our communities a decent, whole, and safe place to live. And oh, Allah, we beg your blessings on all who participated, all who came that presented their bodies as a living sacrifice, wholly and acceptable as their reasonable service.

Now, let us not be conformed to this world, but let us go home transformed by the renewing of our minds and let the idea of atonement ring throughout America.

That America may see that the slave has come up with power. The slave is been restored, delivered, and redeemed. And now call this nation to repentance. To acknowledge her wrongs. To confess, not in secret documents, called classified, but to come before the world and the American people as the Japanese prime minister did and confess her faults before the world because her sins have affected the whole world. And perhaps, she may do some act of atonement, that you may forgive and those ill-affected may forgive, that reconciliation and restoration may lead us to the perfect union with thee and with each other. We ask all of this in your Holy and Righteous Name, Allah,....[Now] Turn to your brother and hug your brother and tell your brother you love him and let's carry this love all the way back to our cities and towns and never let it die, brothers. Never let it die.

From transcript of Minister Louis Farrakhan's remarks at the Million Man March October 17, 1995, Web posted at: 1:25 A.M. EDT. (CNN http://www.cgi.cnn.com/US/9510/mega march/10–16/transcript/.)

ANITA HILL

Anita Hill was a dramatic witness during the Clarence Thomas confirmation hearings for Supreme Court Justice in 1991, not only because of the explosive charges of sexual harassment against Thomas that she related, but for the dignified and sophisticated manner in which she presented herself. Hill was a quiet, unassuming 35-year-old professor of contract law whose musical tastes ran to opera and who, like Thomas, overcame many obstacles to climb professionally. She was the youngest in a farm family of 13 children who had picked cotton and peanuts in eastern Oklahoma. Class valedictorian in high school, honor student in psychology at Oklahoma State, and, like Thomas, a standout student at Yale law, Hill was one of four aids hired by Thomas when he was first appointed as an assistant secretary in the Education Department. Hill followed Thomas when he made his move to chair of the Equal Employment Opportunity Commission until she accepted an offer to teach at Oral Roberts University back in her home state.

MS. HILL: In 1981, I was introduced to now Judge Thomas by a mutual friend. Judge Thomas told me that he was anticipating a political appointment, and he asked if I would be interested in working with him....

During this period at the Department of Education, my working relationship with Judge Thomas was positive. I had a good deal of responsibility and independence. I thought he respected my work and that he trusted my judgment. After approximately three months of working there, he asked me to go out socially with him.

What happened next and telling the world about it are the two most difficult things—experiences of my life. It is only after a great deal of agonizing consideration and sleepless number—a great number of sleepless nights that I am able to talk of these unpleasant matters to anyone but my close friends. I declined the invitation to go out socially with him and explained to him that I thought it would jeopardize what at the time I considered to be a very good working relationship. I had a normal social life with other men outside of the office. I believed then, as now, that having a social relationship with a person who was supervising my work would be ill-advised. I was very uncomfortable with the idea and told him so.

I thought that by saying no and explaining my reasons my employer would abandon his social suggestions. However, to my regret, in the following few weeks, he continued to ask me out on several occasions. He pressed me to justify my reasons for saying no to him. These incidents took place in his office or mine. They were in the form of private conversations which would not have been overheard by anyone else.

My working relationship became even more strained when Judge Thomas began to use work situations to discuss sex. On these occasions, he would call me into his office for reports on education issues and projects, or he might suggest that, because of the time pressures of his schedule, we go to lunch to a government cafeteria. After a brief discussion of work, he would turn the conversation to a discussion of sexual matters.

His conversations were very vivid. He spoke about acts that he had seen in pornographic films involving such matters as women having sex with animals and films showing group sex or rape scenes. He talked about pornographic materials depicting individuals with large penises or large breasts involved in various sex acts. On several occasions, Thomas told me graphically of his own sexual prowess.

Because I was extremely uncomfortable talking about sex with him at all and particularly in such a graphic way, I told him that I did not want to talk about these subjects. I would also try to change the subject to education matters or to nonsexual personal matters such as his background or his beliefs. My efforts to change the subject were rarely successful.

Throughout the period of these conversations, he also from time to time asked me for social engagements. My reaction to these conversations was to avoid them by eliminating opportunities for us to engage in extended conversations. This was difficult because at the time I was his only assistant at the Office of Education—or Office for Civil Rights.

During the latter part of my time at the Department of Education, the social pressures and any conversation of his offensive behavior ended. I began both to believe and hope that our working relationship could be a proper, cordial, and professional one.

When Judge Thomas was made chair of the EEOC, I needed to face the question of whether to go with him. I was asked to do so, and I did. The work itself was interesting, and at that time it appeared that the sexual overtures which had so troubled me had ended. I also faced the realistic fact that I had no alternative job. While I might have gone back to private practice, perhaps in my old firm or at another, I was dedicated to civil rights work, and my first choice was to be in that field. Moreover, the Department of Education itself was a dubious venture. President Reagan was seeking to abolish the entire department.

For my first months at the EEOC, where I continued to be an assistant to Judge Thomas, there were no sexual conversations or overtures. However, during the fall and winter of 1982, these began again. The comments were random and ranged from pressing me about why I didn't go out with him to remarks about my personal appearance. I remember his saying that some day I would have to tell him the real reason that I wouldn't go out with him.

He began to show displeasure in his tone and voice and his demeanor and his continued pressure for an explanation. He commented on what I was wearing in terms of whether it made me more or less sexually attractive. The incidents occurred in his inner office at the EEOC.

One of the oddest episodes I remember was an occasion in which Thomas was drinking a Coke in his office. He got up from the table at which we were working, went over to his desk to get the Coke, looked at the can and asked, "Who has pubic hair on my Coke?" On other occasions, he referred to the size of his own penis as being larger than normal, and he also spoke on some occasions of the pleasures he had given to women with oral sex.

At this point, late 1982, I began to feel severe stress on the job. I began to be concerned that Clarence Thomas might take out his anger with me by degrading me or not giving me important assignments. I also thought that he might find an excuse for dismissing me.

In January of 1983, I began looking for another job....

In the spring of 1983, an opportunity to teach at Oral Roberts University opened up...I agreed to take the job in large part because of my desire to escape the pressures I felt at the EEOC due to Judge Thomas.

When I informed him that I was leaving in July, I recall that his response was that now I would no longer have an excuse for not going out with him. I told him that I still preferred not to do so. At some time after that meeting, he asked if he could take me to dinner at the end of the term. When I declined, he assured me that the dinner was a professional courtesy only and not a social invitation. I reluctantly agreed to accept that invitation, but only if it was at the very end of a working day.

On, as I recall, the last day of my employment at the EEOC in the summer of 1983, I did have dinner with Clarence Thomas. We went directly from work to a restaurant near the office. We talked about the work I had done, both at education and at the EEOC. He told me that he was pleased with all of it except for an article and speech that I had done for him while we were at the Office for Civil Rights. Finally, he made a comment that I will vividly remember. He said that if I ever told anyone of his behavior that it would ruin his career. This was not an apology, nor was it an explanation. That was his last remark about the possibility of our going out or reference to his behavior....

It is only after a great deal of agonizing consideration that I am able to talk of these unpleasant matters to anyone except my closest friends. As I've said before these last few days have been very trying and very hard for me and it hasn't just been the last few days this week. It has actually been over a month now that I have been under the strain of this issue.

Telling the world is the most difficult experience of my life, but it is very close to having to live through the experience that occasion this meeting. I may have used poor judgment early on in my relationship with this issue. I was aware, however, that telling at any point in my career could adversely affect my future career. And I did not want early on to burn all the bridges to the EEOC.

As I said, I may have used poor judgment. Perhaps I should have taken angry or even militant steps, both when I was in the agency, or after I left it. But I must confess to the world that the course that I took seemed the better as well as the easier approach.

I declined any comment to newspapers, but later when Senate staff asked me about these matters I felt I had a duty to report. I have no personal vendetta against Clarence Thomas. I seek only to provide the committee with information which it may regard as relevant.

It would have been more comfortable to remain silent. I took no initiative to inform anyone. But when I was asked by a representative of this committee to report my experience, I felt that I had to tell the truth. I could not keep silent.

From Anita Hill's Opening Statement to the Senate Judiciary Committee on Clarence Thomas October 11, 1991, United States Senate Judiciary Committee, Washington, D.C. (Text Source: Electronic Text Center, University of Virginia Library).

RACE RELATIONS BY GROUP

AFRICAN AMERICANS

While high judges and many white Americans argued during the 1990s that racism was a thing of the past, corporate America continued to have embarrassing revelations of patterns of discrimination and racial insensitivity. In 1994, Denny's restaurant chain paid $45.7 million to settle a class action discrimination suit filed on behalf of its African American customers. The Walt Disney company shelled out $1.5 million to settle a lawsuit brought by Jesse Jackson's Operation Push against its radio affiliate, KLOS in Los Angeles. In 1998, the FM station's popular "Mark & Brian" Show held what it called the "win a black hoe" contest in which the DJs distributed dark-painted garden tools to lucky listeners. The 22-hotel Adams Mark chain settled several civil suits and a Justice Department complaint out of court after one of its hotels allegedly forced black guests to wear orange wrist bands to enter the hotel but allowed whites to come and go as they pleased. In 1998, Nationwide Mutual Insurance Company and Nationwide Mutual Fire Insurance Company agreed to pay $5.3 million to settle a class-action lawsuit brought by 10,000 homeowners in Toledo, Ohio, who claimed they were "redlined" out of insurance coverage from the firm because they lived in predominately black neighborhoods. Avis car rental agreed to pay $3.3 million to settle suits alleging that the corporation took no action to correct abuses by one of its franchisers who turned away black customers by requiring them to show proof of employment or credit cards with higher maximums that he did not ask of white customers. Most revealing of all was the November 1996 agreement whereby oil giant Texaco settled a longstanding class action suit from its minority employees that had alleged systematic racial bias in their pay and work assignments. The corporation agreed to pay $176 million but, as was true in almost every case of this type, they stipulated that they would not admit blame. Even the Coca-Cola

Company, headquartered in the same city as the Rev. Martin Luther King Jr. museum and memorial in Atlanta, Georgia, agreed to pay $192.5 million to its black employees to settle a racial discrimination suit in 2000.[43]

Racial discrimination remained an issue even at the highest levels of the corporate pyramid. According to some studies, salary disparities between some minority groups and white men actually widened as the riches of the go-go 1990s were not equally shared around the office. According to the Federal Bureau of Labor Statistics, Hispanic women earned almost 70 percent of what white men earned in 1993, but this margin widened by 1998 when Latinas made only 60 percent of their white male counterparts. Other studies indicated that programs adopted by leading corporations to better recruit and retain minority employees (such programs were embraced by at least 370 of the 500 largest corporations in America) were not seen as increasing opportunity by most minority employees.[44]

The contrast between the sanguine beliefs among white Americans, that racism was dead and everyone was now equal, and the disenfranchisement, poverty, and marginalization that many African Americans still experienced, bred a general mistrust of "official" organs of information. Such mistrust of mainstream media outlets flourished in the 1980s and 1990s as successive epidemics of AIDS, crack, increasing incarceration rates, and deteriorating urban services created a confusing mosaic of problems. In the face of such complexity, simple conspiratorial theories that explain one or more of these problems in a way that has clear villains and causes become more and more appealing. By the early 1990s, a news poll showed that one in ten New York blacks said they believed AIDS was intentionally created in a laboratory to infect black people. An additional one in five said they thought such a theory might be true, but they were not certain of it. One in four African Americans in the same poll said they believed the government deliberately spread drugs in black communities. One in three agreed with the statement that "the government deliberately singles out and investigates black elected officials in order to discredit them," a view probably shaped by the highly publicized arrest and prosecution of Washington, D.C. Mayor Marion Barry.[45]

Such growing suspicion and cynicism toward government within the black community raised tensions in many neighborhoods. In the spring of 1992 in Minneapolis, a city not known for its racial tensions, when a teenage boy was shot while riding his bike in a middle-class black neighborhood, rumor quickly spread that he had been shot by a white police officer. Hundreds of people poured into the streets and pelted police and television news crews with rocks. A full-fledged riot was averted when a number of ministers and community leaders intervened and diffused the situation, spreading the word that the boy had not been shot by police but instead had been wounded by a 66-year-old neighbor who fired a shotgun at the boy from his front porch because he rode over his front lawn.[46]

Although President Clinton enjoyed tremendous personal popularity among African Americans, he was often denounced for ignoring his most loyal constituency. During his first term in office, critics outside the administration began to complain that although President Clinton had campaigned strongly on the need for confronting racism, once in office he had rarely raised the issue. Early in Clinton's first year, Henry Cisneros, the Secretary of Housing and Urban Development, admitted that his was a lonely voice urging greater attention to racial issues in the cabinet. Cisneros set as one of his first goals the relocation of many public housing units from urban cores to suburbs, a move that he admitted would provoke much backlash among more affluent white suburbanites, and a stronger enforcement of fair housing laws to curtail discrimination in renting and selling homes.[47]

Such criticisms were blunted largely because President Clinton enjoyed leading the nation during a decade of relative prosperity and economic growth. Much of this buoyed communities of color that traditionally had been the last to benefit from economic gains in the overall economy. According to one estimate, the total earned income of black Americans increased by one-third, from $243 billion to $367 billion from 1980 to 1996 even after adjusting for inflation. The benefits of this boom for African American communities was evident—in just one year, from 1995 to 1996, expenditures for new household appliances doubled.[48] In every year of Clinton's term of office from 1993 to 1999, the percentage of Americans living below the poverty line decreased. The President's Council of Economic Advisors highlighted the administration's success at delivering real economic progress in minority neighborhoods in their 1997 report, *Changing America: Indicators of Social and Economic Well-Being by Race and Hispanic Origin.*[49]

AFRICAN AMERICAN AND JEWISH RELATIONS

Lingering tensions between the African American community and Jews continually bubbled to the surface in the 1990s. The 1990 annual convention of the National Association for the Advancement of Colored People was held in Los Angeles, and there in the movie capital of the world it was probably inevitable that issues surrounding the entertainment industry would predominate. During a discussion of the movie industry, Legrand Clegg, chief deputy city attorney of Los Angeles, was warmly applauded when he reportedly blamed "Jewish racism" for the small number of blacks in positions of authority in Hollywood studios. About the same time, director Spike Lee came under intense criticism for his portrayal of a pair of Jewish nightclub owners who seemed to fall into the stereotype of Shylock, in his 1990 film, *Mo' Better Blues.*[50] Lee denied any intention to demean and insisted "I am not an anti-Semite." More pointedly, Lee accused his critics of holding him to a higher standard regarding racial stereotyping than they did for other directors.[51]

Opinion surveys conducted in 1992 showed a troubling rise in anti-Semitic attitudes among African Americans who already were twice as likely to hold negative views of Jews as whites. Such polls indicated that anti-Semitism was concentrated among two segments of the black population: those who were most educated and black youth. This trend was combated by some influential figures in the black community such as comedian and activist Dick Gregory, black leader Jesse Jackson, and philosopher Cornel West, who all publicly condemned anti-Semitism and called for greater attention to the problem within the black community.[52]

Anti-Semitism seemed endemic in the ranks of Louis Farrakhan's Nation of Islam organization. On November 29, 1994, Farrakhan's top aid and spokesman, Khalid Abdul Muhammad, gave a speech at Kean College in New Jersey that startled even those who had grown accustomed to Farrakhan's own anti-Semitic outbursts. In a three-hour speech entitled, "The Secret Relationship Between Blacks and Jews," Muhammad drew on the theories of Professor Leonard Jeffries, chairman of Black Studies at City College, who claimed whites, which he called "Ice People," especially Jews, descended from a different branch of the human tree. Muhammad called Jews "impostors [who] crawled around on all fours in the caves and hills of Europe...eating each other" and condemned Jews as "the bloodsuckers of the black nation," who controlled the government from the shadows and brought the Holocaust on themselves. Peppered throughout were references to "Jew York City" and "Columbia Jewniversity."[53]

After the Anti-Defamation League took out a full-page ad in the *New York Times* that quoted many of Muhammad's more poisonous claims, a train of respected black leaders, including Jesse Jackson, Benjamin Chavis (President of the NAACP), William H. Gray 3rd (chair of the United Negro College Fund), Congressman Kweisi Mfume, and others all rushed to condemn Muhammad and called on Farrakhan to repudiate his remarks.[54]

The continuing attacks on the Jewish community emanating from Farrakhan and his lieutenants were just a public expression of tensions that ran high between Jews and blacks in America, especially in New York City where several neighborhoods contained diverse collections of both immigrant Haitians, African Americans, and Hassidic Jews. The separatist ways of the Hasidim, who wished to be left alone and felt embattled in their small numbers (about 20,000 in a neighborhood of more than 130,000), did not contribute to lessening these tensions. Nor did their outspoken criticisms of the neighboring black community that even one of their defenders referred to as "smack[ing] of bigotry."[55]

These tensions broke into the open in the summer of 1991 when one of the cars in a motorcade accompanying the Grand Rebbe of the Lubavitcher Hassidic community ran a red light and jumped a curb, crushing two 7-year-old African American children. Gavin Cato was killed and his cousin, Angela, was gravely wounded. Police were quick to the scene as they were part of the motorcade and gave their attention to separating the growing crowd of angry bystanders from the driver of the car, while Gavin and Angela were left to wait for other responders. A rumor quickly spread that an ambulance from the Hasidic Hatzolah community had callously taken away the driver but left the children (which was partly true—police did direct the first ambulance to transport the driver whose presence they judged was provoking the crowd). Demonstrators protesting what they alleged was the unequal and privileged treatment accorded Brooklyn's Jewish community gathered around the Crown Heights neighborhood and began to confront police, and these confrontations escalated into rock throwing, burning of police cars, and looting. As the violence escalated, someone yelled "Get the Jew" and stabbed and killed Yankel Rosenbaum, a young ultra-Orthodox scholar. When Mayor David Dinkins arrived on the scene to try to "increase the peace," he was jeered and forced to retreat as bottles and rocks were thrown toward him. Hasidim saw angry and violent crowds and remembered European pogroms. African Americans saw yet another example of a power structure that values whites above them.[56]

The resulting ugly rioting in Crown Heights, tinged with anti-Semitic slogans and signs, continued for three nights and required more than 1,000 members of the riot squad and the arrests of hundreds to quell. Dinkins, New York's first African American mayor and its last Democrat of the twentieth century, was accused by newspaper editorials, police officers, and members of the Jewish community with not having acted vigorously enough to end the rioting, charges that clearly harmed his chances in the next mayoral election, which he lost to Rudolph W. Giuliani. A subsequent blue ribbon investigating commission in its 600-page report on the riot determined that Mayor Dinkins did not restrain the police, although it faulted him for not acting decisively enough to stop the riot.[57]

Months later, when the jury returned with a not-guilty verdict for the 16-year-old African American defendant accused of Rosenbaum's murder, it was the

Police in riot gear walk past a squad car overturned by rioters on August 21, 1991 in the Crown Heights section of Brooklyn. AP photo/David Burns, FILE.

Hasidim's turn to pour into the streets in an impromptu march chanting "No justice, no peace," and police prepared for yet more violence in Crown Heights, although there were just scattered reports of scuffles that night.

In the wake of the Crown Heights Riot of 1991, both black and Jewish leaders took steps to forge understanding and respect between hostile neighbors. Ten years of slow progress later, Crown Heights had joint Hasidic and African American picnics in a local park, a joint Halloween parade, and even the employment of black youth as Lubavitcher security officers. Black and Jewish leaders put each other on their speed dials, and over time both groups began voting similarly as a block in local elections. But such efforts only smoothed over the necessary daily interactions that existed alongside a raw mutual suspicion.[58]

OTHER EUROPEAN AMERICANS

If telephone polling data are to be trusted, during the 1990s, whites increasingly came to believe that racial discrimination was a thing of the past and consequently viewed attempts to redress the lingering effects of discrimination or combat hidden bias through affirmative action as "reverse discrimination." In a poll conducted in 1990, fewer than half of respondents (43%) agreed with the statement that "we have gone too far in pushing equal rights in this country." When the same pollsters asked the same question four years later, the number who agreed that equal rights had been pushed too far increased to 48 percent. A majority of those surveyed in 1999 (58%) believed that "African-American citizens have the same opportunities as white Americans" and another 17 percent said they were not sure if they did or not. A majority of those polled by the Democratic Leadership Council (DLC), a policy arm of the Democratic Party, agreed that "too often equal rights is just used as an excuse for not being good enough to succeed." Of interest, the DLC discovered a large partisan division in views on this matter, as more than two-thirds of Bush supporters agreed with this statement compared with 51 percent of Clinton supporters who thought this way.[59] Such collective beliefs were publicly expressed in 1996 when voters in California passed Proposition 209, banning all forms of affirmative action remedies to past discrimination.

A significant trend in the decade of the 1990s was a strong movement within the ranks of the conservative Christian denominations to confront both the racism still existing in United States and their own historical role in fostering it. In 1994, at a convention of Pentecostal organizations in Memphis, Tennessee, the all-white Pentecostal Fellowship of North America, a national organization of 21 Pentecostal denominations, voted to disband and merge into a new organization encompassing 10 million members, which for the first time since the 1920s brought together white and black Pentecostal denominations. Many participants were moved to tears when during a leadership meeting one of the white ministers unexpectedly washed the feet of a black bishop, asking forgiveness for the sins of the white church.[60]

Likewise, on their 150th anniversary, the largest Protestant denomination in the United States, the Southern Baptist Convention, approved a resolution at their annual convention repenting for the "racism of which we have been guilty" and asking forgiveness of all African Americans for their defense of slavery and discrimination. Notably, the resolution tied together the religious group's history rooted in slavery (it was founded when the southern branch of the Baptist church split away from its northern congregations because the northern church leaders had refused to appoint a slaveholder to a church post) with the problems of current times. "We lament and repudiate historic acts of evil such as slavery from which we continue to reap a bitter harvest, and we recognize that the racism which yet plagues our culture today is inextricably tied to the past."[61]

The United Church of Christ, one of the largest protestant denominations and one far more liberal than the evangelical churches, issued a pastoral letter, a rare church mechanism that had been invoked only twice before in the church's history, to all its 6,000 congregations in January 1991, warning that the increase in racial violence was a reflection of the racism that "permeate[s] most of our institutions." It described America as being a nation where "virtually no progress toward social and economic equality for African Americans has been made since the early 1970s" and where "quiet riots in the form of unemployment, poverty, social disorganization, family disintegration, housing and school deterioration, and crime" are the norm.[62]

Perhaps the most visible interracial movement of the decade was the rise of an ecumenical Christian religious movement calling itself the "Promise Keepers" that brought together hundreds of thousands of white and African American men in a what the movement viewed as crusade of religious rededication to "traditional family values." Organized in 1990 by the former coach of the University of Colorado football team, Bill McCartney, and several dozen other men, the Promise Keepers' membership rocketed into the millions by 1997, when it filled to capacity 62 sports arenas for their events. By that year, the Promise Keepers reported revenues of more than $100 million supporting 136 scattered offices and a payroll of 368. In October of that year, the Promise Keepers organized a "Stand in the Gap" rally in Washington D.C. that attracted similar numbers to the Million Man March of two years before and, like the former march, was specifically limited to male participants only.

The meteoric rise of the Promise Keepers was underwritten and nurtured by a network of mostly white conservative Christian evangelical organizations but took a turn past their politics when McCartney stressed the unique role the organization could play in overcoming racial divisions in American society. Racial issues were present at the outset, just not emphasized among other Christian initiatives, ranking as promise number six on a list of seven promises each member had to commit to. Promise six was: "A Promise Keeper is committed to reaching beyond any racial and denominational barriers to demonstrate the power of biblical unity." But as the organization grew, so did its rhetorical commitment to overcoming racial barriers. In 1996, McCartney frankly acknowledged the

A Promise Keepers rally in Veterans Stadium on July 11, 1998, in Philadelphia. AP Photo/ Chris Gardner.

problem of racism in America: "There is a spirit of white racial superiority in this country." He said, "It's insidious. It's worked its way into the fabric of society, and it's damaging souls." By that time each of its mass rallies featured both white and black speakers, each usually featured a sermon on the importance of fighting racism as a step toward Christian unity, and eventually the organization claimed that half of its executive board and more than a third of its employees were racial minorities. In 1996, the organization announced its year's theme for its ministry would be "Break Down the Walls," meaning the racial separation between whites and blacks, and it pledged $1 million to help rebuild black churches that had been destroyed by arsonists in the South. As quickly as it appeared, however, the Promise Keepers phenomenon declined and by the end of the decade it was just a remnant of its former self. Some observers even blamed the organization's emphasis on racial reconciliation as one reason for contributing to its steady loss of white membership and national interest.[63]

NATIVE AMERICANS

The 1990s began with a serious confrontation between agents of the federal government and the Mohawk nation straddling the border between Canada and northern New York State that raised important questions of native sovereignty. For many observers, the events in the Ganienkeh Indian Territory were reminiscent of the standoffs between federal agents and Lakota people in the Dakotas in the 1970s that escalated to gunfights, the deaths of several tribal members and two Federal Bureau of Investigation agents, and life imprisonment for American Indian Movement activist Leonard Peltier.

The trouble began with the crash of a Vermont national guard helicopter that injured a physician on board and that authorities claimed was downed by gunfire from Miner Lake, part of Mohawk territory. Federal authorities attempted to enter the area to investigate the shooting but were turned back by roadblocks set up by armed Mohawk. The standoff was complicated by the disputed nature of Miner Lake. Legally designated New York State land before 1977, it was turned over to the Mohawk community in exchange for the agreement by the Mohawks to quit their armed seizure of an abandoned elite girl's summer camp deep in the Adirondack Mountains. Mohawks declared the Miner Lake land to be the first parcel reclaimed from all the millions of acres stolen from the Mohawk people since precolonial times. Tensions mounted when federal prosecutors obtained more than a dozen warrants of arrest for tribal members accused of obstruction of justice. After 11 days of standoff, the Miner Lake Mohawks allowed federal agents onto their land for two hours to conduct a brief investigation.[64]

Two weeks later, another Mohawk community, St. Regis Reservation, was shaken by intertribal violence that took two lives as roadblocks set up to keep visitors from the casinos by antigambling traditionalists who had been fired on by a pro-gambling faction. Thousands of Mohawk residents of St. Regis fled the escalating violence while New York state police sealed off the reservation, although they did not enter it for fear of provoking more shooting. After five weeks of closure, the threat of immediate violence subsided and the majority of displaced Mohawks returned home, but the gambling issue was not resolved for three years when a compact was signed with the State of New York allowing casinos, although with the stipulation that New York police and officials would have access to the reservation.[65]

Questions of how much sovereignty native people have over their native lands continually appeared in numerous places and in a variety of ways throughout the decade. New York State attempted to crack down on businessmen who sold alcohol and cigarettes on native lands. Claiming that the state was losing as much as $100 million in revenue annually, Governor George Pataki ordered state police to interdict shipments of tobacco and alcoholic beverages to native reservations throughout the state, sparking demonstrations in favor of native sovereignty. Six weeks later, under legal and political pressure, New York dropped its efforts to tax these goods.[66]

In the Southwest, federal attempts to limit the scope of casino gambling also provoked conflict. In May 1992, federal agents descended on the Yavapai-Apache reservation near Fort McDowell, Arizona and seized video poker machines from the tribal casino. Soon hundreds of tribal members blockaded the federal agents with their cars until Arizona's governor negotiated a compromise whereby the gambling machines would be locked in a trailer at the site rather than being confiscated while legal arguments were heard. A month later the tribe relented and allowed the machines to be carted away as they opened negotiations with the state to expand their casino operations. Likewise, tribal leaders of the Miccosukee reservation near Miami, Florida defied state officials and a federal judge by taking over their bingo hall from a consortium of outside investors claiming tribal sovereignty and setting up roadblocks to keep state agents out of their small territory on the edge of the Everglades.[67]

Outside of these disputes, the overall relationship between tribal governments and the federal government seemed to improve over the course of the 1990s. When 700 tribal leaders met with the Bush administration's Interior Secretary, Manuel Lujan Jr., at a conference in Albuquerque, New Mexico, to discuss a Bush plan to devolve some of the authority and responsibilities of Bureau of Indian Affairs to tribal governments, there was much anger and suspicion as native leaders accused Lujan of not truly consulting with them but merely presenting policy decisions that had already been made and then parceling out information about these decisions in drips and drabs. Bush's plan stalled but was revived by President Clinton who tried to overcome the accumulated mistrust by summoning the heads of all 547 recognized tribal governments to the White House in 1994, the first such presidential gathering of all tribal leaders in history. At the same time, Clinton issued an executive order requiring government officials to treat native governments with the same protocols accorded to state governments and another making an exception to the Endangered Species Act by establishing a system of distributing eagle feathers recovered from carcasses on federal lands to tribes for ceremonial purposes. In the end, as had been the case with many administrations in the past, little changed in the paternalistic relationship between the Bureau of Indian Affairs and the 1.3 million native people it regulated.[68]

The deal-breaker in all these reorganization attempts was the question of what to do with the billions of dollars supposedly collected from those exploiting natural resources on native lands and administered in trust by the federal government for the tribes. This arrangement began with the Dawes Act of the 1880s under the assumption that native peoples were "incompetent" to manage their own affairs but continued to the present because it well served the interests of many land, timber, and mineral lease-holders and federal bureaucrats who maintained a cozy relationship with them. In 1994, the first broad audit of these accounts revealed that $2.4 billion was missing. In 1999, a tribal class action lawsuit seeking a full accounting bore fruit when a federal judge ordered Interior Secretary Bruce Babbitt to produce detailed accounts of the amount of money owed to the tribes and then later cited the secretary for contempt for what the judge called a "shocking pattern of deception of the court" in avoiding doing so. The special trustee appointed by Clinton to oversee this process resigned in protest of what he charged was the interior secretary's efforts to obstruct a proper accounting of money owed. Problems continued even after Congress authorized $41 million to build a computerized trust auditing and collection system. It was later discovered that the system did not work, although the Interior Department regularly provided false and misleading reports to a federal judge with oversight in this area claiming its efficiency. As it turned out, recovery of such money owed to native peoples would not be accomplished in the twentieth century.[69]

Native American advocacy groups targeted demeaning sports mascots, such as Cleveland Indians' "Chief Wahoo" and a host of college team names and symbols. Protest against Chief Wahoo was first organized by Russell Means of the American Indian Movement in the 1970s, but it had seemingly died down in the 1980s. In 1991, the United Church of Christ passed a resolution calling on its members to petition sports teams to abandon their offensive mascots, and a delegation of ministers met with Indians officials over the issue. The next year, protesters again targeted Cleveland Stadium and although their numbers were not large, they managed to put the issue in the media spotlight. Soon Jesse Jackson, meeting with baseball commissioner Bud Selig over the issue of the lack of diversity in baseball's front offices, also announced he was raising the issue of the grinning Chief Wahoo. The pressure was enough to force the Indians club to seriously consider dropping the chief when they moved into their newly built stadium, but in the end the chief moved with the team.[70]

The 800 protesters who picketed the opening game of the 1991 World Series between the Minnesota Twins and the Atlanta Braves did not convince the owner of the Atlanta franchise to change its name, but they did manage to convince the owner's fiancée, actress Jane Fonda, to stop doing the team's "tomahawk" gesture. Fonda was quoted in the national press saying "I'm sorry it offends them and I'm not going to do it anymore."[71]

Such protests seemed to be most effective among colleges and universities where the educational mission at least theoretically outweighed commercial considerations. The 1990s saw significant movement to eliminate the use of native mascots and nicknames in schools and colleges for the first time. The pioneers of this change came in Midwestern states, partly because in those regions, native organizations had been very vocal and active in campaigning against their use. Responding to a stream of complaints, the Michigan Civil Rights Commission declared that "any use of Indian names, logos and mascots should be discontinued because racial stereotyping of Native Americans is prevalent and destructive." It then conducted a study of the use of native names in public schools and found that 99 junior and senior high schools in that state had Indian nicknames and mascots, although it did not have the authority to actually order any of these institutions to change their names. The Minnesota State Board of Education did, however, and it declared that same year, 1988, that "it is the desire if the State Board of Education that no school district in the state of Minnesota shall have a mascot, namesake, official symbol, team name, newspaper, yearbook, or any official group or publication bearing the name of any American Indian symbol or cultural reference," and it announced that it would require each school district to issue yearly progress reports on their implementation. A total of 54 Minnesota schools resisted their state administration's directive and were subsequently sued by the Minnesota Civil Liberties Union. The Illinois State Board of Education took a more cautious approach, responding to individual complaints on a case-by-case basis (it asked the Naperville Central High School to consider dropping its "Redskins" moniker). In 1997, the Los Angeles Board of Education ordered all schools in the county to eliminate Indian mascots, symbols, and names. Dallas, Texas, followed suit in 1998.[72]

In 1991, the board of trustees of Marquette University in Milwaukee, Wisconsin set a precedent for other institutions and announced it was switching the name of its sports teams from "Redskins" to "Golden Eagles." Others soon followed suit: Juniata College, in Pennsylvania, stopped calling their athletes the "Indians" and became the "Eagles." Eastern Michigan abandoned the "Hurons" for the "Eagles." Tiny Simpson College in Indianola, Iowa, dropped "Redmen" and became "The Storm." St. John's University in New York City dropped the "Redmen" and became "The Red Storm." In 1996, Miami University in Oxford, Ohio voted to retire their sports teams "Redskins" name and replace it with "Redhawks." Progress to be sure, but by the end of the decade there were still 33 NCAA teams with Native American mascots and nicknames including: Fighting Illini, Fighting Sioux, Braves, Indians, Warriors, Redmen, Utes, Chippewas, Seminoles, Choctaws, Aztecs, Chieftains, and others.[73]

Such struggles over the deeply embedded and generally unquestioned symbols of American culture expanded in the 1990s because they both effectively hit a nerve among whites and forced them to confront the reality of America's history of Indian genocide and effectively demonstrated that popular culture was shot through with deeply biased images and messages that worked to render native peoples invisible or meaningless in the public arena. Such protests were most successful when they were sprung on those innocently and naively using symbolism that they did not recognize as biased or discriminatory. In 1996, the state of Minnesota enacted a law ordering all of its counties to change the name of all places containing the word "squaw." County boards struck the name "squaw" from 16 geographic features, although the commissioners in Lake County held out and refused to change the name of Squaw Creek, offering instead to name it "Politically Correct Creek."[74]

In 1992, the organizers of the Pasadena Tournament of Roses Parade, one of the largest annual public spectacles in America, seized on the year being the quincentenary of the first voyage of Christopher Columbus by inviting one of his supposed direct descendents, Cristóbal Colón, as the grand marshal of their parade. Californian tribes and other native advocacy groups protested the idea as insensitively promoting the memory of a conqueror known to use slavery, torture, and summary execution to subdue the first native peoples he encountered. Parade officials quickly scrambled to contain the protest and announce their plan to name Colorado Congressman, Ben Nighthorse Campbell, a Cheyenne, as a co-marshal. In the end, Congressman Campbell, in headdress and traditional dress, rode a horse and alternated leading the parade with Cristóbal Colón who led three floats depicting the explorer's ships, the Nina, Pinta, and Santa Maria. As many as a hundred protesters were unsatisfied with this arrangement and showed up at the parade to protest any honor bestowed on the memory of Columbus.[75]

ASIAN AMERICANS

In 1992, the United States Commission on Civil Rights reported an alarming increase in violence and acts of hatred against Japanese Americans. Although racial violence against Asian Americans was hardly anything new in America—10 years earlier Vincent Chin, a Chinese American was mistaken for a Japanese and was beaten to death by unemployed auto workers in Detroit and three years earlier a gunman invaded an elementary school in Stockton, California, killing five Indochinese children—the Commission noted signs of an increasing prejudice toward Japanese Americans in particular. Such tensions were aggravated by political debates such as that in Los Angeles where an amendment was proposed to the city's charter barring the city from contracting with foreign firms and would have forced Los Angeles to cancel a large contract with the Sumitomo Company of Japan to construct a section of its light rail mass transit system.[76]

Tensions between African American and Korean communities were not only exposed by the targets preferred by rioters in Los Angeles in 1992, where a majority of the property losses were incurred by Korean merchants and businessmen, but also on the other coast of America where conflict between ethnic groups was narrowly averted. What began as a routine case of suspected shoplifting and a conflict between a Haitian-American shopper and the owner of the Red Apple Market, quickly escalated into a community boycott of a small Korean grocery store in New York City. Shopper Giselaine Fetissainte, an immigrant herself, claimed to have been beaten by the shopkeeper and his family members after they accused her of stealing. The merchant, Pong Jae Jang, who had recently immigrated to the United States from Korea in 1983, claimed he merely restrained Fetissainte after she pocketed some items. Jang's English was functional but poor, which seems to have contributed to his misunderstandings with his black customers. Within hours, hundreds of angry neighborhood residents thronged the entrance to the store shouting at Jang and calling for a boycott. Although it was uninvolved in the incident that led to protests in front of Jang's store, the Korean-owned grocery across the street, Church Fruits, was protested and boycotted as well.

With approximately 1,500 Korean-owned stores in the city, newly elected African American mayor David Dinkins acted quickly to try to defuse what threatened to be a violently escalating situation. As boycotts against the pair of Korean-owned stores in the Flatbush neighborhood of Brooklyn, New York spread, Korean businessmen from around the area chipped in to help the embattled storeowners stay open, providing each store with a subsidy of $8,000 per month and free rent. Korean churches in Brooklyn organized shopping trips to the two stores. On the other side, protesters defied a court injunction and maintained pickets in front of the store for nine months until an appeals court ordered the New York police department to begin arresting all protesters who strayed within a 50-foot exclusion zone in front of the stores. At the conclusion of a week in which 13 protesters were arrested, more than a dozen gasoline bombs were discovered by police on the roof of the store. After one of the Korean brothers who ran the Red Apple store was acquitted of assault on Fetissainte, the protests finally died down.[77]

The historical tendency of many in the Asian American community to abstain from electoral politics weakened over the course of President Bill Clinton's reelection campaign in 1996. All told, it was estimated that Asian Americans voted in record numbers. And although they gave a majority of their votes and contributed $10 million to his campaign, Clinton shied away from rewarding this growing constituency with key appointments.

Such increased Chinese American political participation was facilitated by the formation of voting mobilization groups such as Asian American Voters Project and Chinese American Voter Education Committee. Historically, when Chinese did participate in electoral politics, they tended to concentrate political action on the local level. Even then, relative to other ethnic groups they were not politically active. In San Francisco, where Chinese communities were perhaps more politically involved than in many other areas and where Asian Americans made up nearly one-third of its population, Asians accounted for only one-fifth of registered voters in 1990. In spite of having 10 percent of California's population, there was not a single Asian American member of the California legislature from 1980 to 1992.[78]

Nevertheless, political gains were registered in the 1990s. Mike Woo, a 41-year-old ex-president of the Republican-affiliated organization, Chinese American Citizen Alliance, ran for mayor of Los Angeles and polled second out of two dozen candidates, with 46 percent of the vote. Woo was a Republican, but his candidacy was buoyed by an unexpected endorsement from President Clinton. In 1998, David Wu was elected to the House of Representatives from Oregon, only the third Chinese American in history to be elected to Congress. The slowly increasing political clout of the Chinese American community was finally rewarded when Clinton appointed California representative Norman Mineta to be secretary of commerce. Mineta became the first Asian American to sit in a presidential cabinet.[79]

Conservatives, fearing a tightening alignment of Asian Americans and the Democratic Party, seized on revelations that Clinton's campaign committee may have received donations from Indonesian and Chinese nationals, a violation of federal election laws. In 1996, Chinese American lobbyist Johnny Chung was prosecuted for allegedly funneling foreign cash into the Clinton campaign, including a $300,000 donation from the chief of Chinese intelligence. The Democrats were forced to return more than $2.25 million allegedly acquired from foreign sources. The important difference between Chinese national influences and Chinese American political support for Clinton was ignored, sometimes purposely, by those eager to use this scandal as an excuse to denounce "Asian"

Norman Mineta. AP Photo/Charles Dharapak.

influences on the Clinton administration. The conservative monthly, *The National Review,* even featured a cover illustration depicting President Clinton, Vice President Albert Gore, and the First Lady, Hillary Clinton, all with stereotypically Asian features.[80]

LATINOS

Mexican immigrants and their children born in the United States became a majority of California's population in the 1990s. In 1990, California had 72 cities with Latino majorities. The 1990s were also the decade in which Hispanics passed African Americans as the nation's largest minority group.

No state was more affected by the surge of immigration in the 1980s than California, which took in 35 percent of all documented foreign immigrants. By the early 1990s, the issue of immigration took on a more heated political character, as Governor Pete Wilson implied that the state's growing fiscal crisis was caused by the burden of providing services for immigrants, especially those who arrived without proper documentation and were deemed "illegal." In 1994, California voters approved "Proposition 187" by a 2-to-1 margin. Proposition 187 prohibited the provision of any state-supported services, such as medical care, child support, or even schooling, to those who could not prove they were citizens or legal residents of the state. Wilson's concern over foreign immigration touched a nerve, as the media focused attention on immigrants from other countries while overlooking the fact that nearly half of California's population growth came naturally from within the state and half of the remainder came from an influx of migrants from other parts of America, not from beyond its borders.[81]

As a wave of Haitian refugees who had arrived on U.S. shores, fleeing the militias who had overthrown the elected government of Father Jean-Bertrand Aristide, joined the continuing exodus of Chinese asylum-seekers, calls grew for tighter regulation of the border. In response to the rising clamor against such "illegal" immigration, the Clinton administration responded and helped draft the "Expedited Exclusion and Asylum Reform Act of 1993," which would have made it more difficult for such asylum-seekers to be designated as protected refugees and made it easier to swiftly deport them. Although this legislation did not pass, it indicated the direction that political winds were blowing at the time.[82]

The sensitive issue of "illegal" immigration derailed one of President Clinton's first cabinet appointments as Zoe Baird, his nominee for attorney general and the first woman to be tapped for the post, was forced to step aside when it was revealed that she had employed a Peruvian couple for two years as her nanny and driver, neither of whom had visas or work or residency permits and for whom Baird did not pay employment taxes until after Clinton was elected. Clinton and his key supporters in the Senate were willing to overlook the immigration issue and push Baird through to confirmation, but the force of the public and media denunciation of her was far greater than expected. As Baird herself said in her letter withdrawing herself from consideration for the post, "I am surprised at the extent of the public reaction"[83]

The complexities of racial politics at the end of the twentieth century were likewise apparent in the controversy surrounding President Clinton's struggle to find a nominee for the post of assistant secretary of inter-American affairs, the top diplomatic office for Latin America, who was acceptable to multiple ethnic constituencies. Clinton's first choice, Mario Baeza, a lawyer who had made his mark in consulting on the privatization of state-owned companies in the region, was popular with the Congressional Black Caucus, as he was of Afro-Cuban ancestry. Even before Baeza's nomination was announced, key Cuban American leaders privately protested that he was soft on the Castro regime and pointed to Baeza's having attended a conference on Cuban economic development in Havana as proof. Caught between two politically important Democratic constituencies, Clinton instead nominated Alexander F. Watson, a white career diplomat with a long résumé of service in the state department as the safest choice, pleasing no one but perhaps offending no one either.[84]

LAW AND GOVERNMENT

THE PARADOX OF RACIAL CATEGORIES

In 1993, the Federal Office of Management and Budget began consideration of a proposal to add a "multiracial" category to the established racial categories to be used in the 2000 census. Although little noted in the media at the time, this seemingly small change carried potentially large ramifications and eventually led to a heated disagreement among civil rights activists. Mainline civil rights organizations like the NAACP worried that such a change could, over time, diminish their political clout, but leaders of groups representing the children of interracial marriages marched on the capital in July 1996, demanding they be officially recognized and affirming their "multiraciality."

It was true that the numbers of people who identified as falling between the racial cracks in American society were steadily growing. In 1992, it was reported that the number of multiracial births was increasing faster than the rate for monoracial births. From 1960 to 1990, the multiracial population had increased by 547 percent. These phenomenon reached national attention in 1993 when *Time* magazine ran on its cover a picture of what it called "the face of America's multiracial future." The woman depicted, called "Eve," was actually a computer composite of different common racial features mixed in proportion to their statistical frequency in the future.

Such a change in the way people were counted and recognized was partly prompted by a change in how the national census was undertaken. Before the 1980 census, racial categories were assigned by the census enumerator. Beginning in 1980, Americans could describe themselves however they wished, although they had to check one of the established boxes indicating race: black, white, American Indian and Alaskan native, Asian and Pacific Islander, or "other." In addition to these categories, they could also describe themselves as "Hispanic." Once the act of racial assignment was transferred from the representative of the state (the enumerator) to the individual citizen, the act of choosing became something of a right while the question of what boxes to put on the survey slid from being a technical question of demography to an issue of equality.

The drive for a new "multiracial" category was also given momentum by a steady increase in the number of interracial marriages, which had doubled during the decade of the 1960s and tripled again in the 1970s. The Census Bureau reported that from 1970 to 1990, the number of interracial marriages tripled in the United States, although their overall numbers remained but four-tenths of 1 percent of all marriages or a total of 210,000 in 1990, most of them concentrated in the larger cities of the eastern and western seaboards. The pace of interracial marriages declined slightly from 1980 to 1990, but by then it was estimated that 3 million persons were united in marriage across racial lines. By the 1990s, some of the children of these unions organized into advocacy groups and success-fully lobbied seven state legislatures to place a "multiracial" category on official state documents that included race.[85]

The question of what the effect of adding a "multiraciality" category to the U.S. census would be was as complicated as the heritage of those advocating it. Native American tribes, many of whom received federal aid or other services in proportion to their population, worried because American Indians were shown to be the group most willing to adopt the new designation. Civil rights groups were likewise concerned that the new category could provide a convenient ex-cuse to end civil rights oversight of elections and desegregation orders in many communities. Theoretically, the potential numbers of people who might choose such a designation was quite large, as approximately three-quarters of all African Americans had at least one Native American or white person in their family tree. A nationwide study conducted by the Census Bureau in 1997, however, indi-cated that fewer than 2.7 percent of African Americans would choose to describe themselves in any other way than African American, whereas nearly 12 percent of Asian Americans might.

In the end, the multiagency task force charged with considering the impact of adding a "multiracial" designation chose instead to recommend against adding the category and in favor of allowing individuals to choose more than one box on the census form if they wished. The Clinton administration accepted the rec-ommendations and issued rules requiring the option of multiple racial category descriptions on all federal forms that classify race.[86]

WELFARE REFORM

President Clinton pushed through Congress a comprehensive "welfare reform act" that enacted many of the proposals first put forward in the Reagan admin-istration but blocked by Democrats in Congress. This legislation significantly reduced federal regulation of state-administered public relief and child welfare systems, allowing for a diversity of approaches to meeting the problem of pov-erty. A majority of the recipients of all welfare programs are white, but the poli-tics of this law's passage seemed to revolve around stereotypes of the minority dependence.

In a crowded field of presidential aspirants in 1992, Bill Clinton distinguished himself by breaking with his party's orthodoxy and denounced welfare as "one of [government's] worst failures" and promised to "end welfare as we know it" in order "to break the cycle of welfare dependency."[87] With such rhetoric ("It's time to make welfare what it should be—a second chance, not a way of life"), Clinton appeared to have stolen a page from the Republican playbook, a move that may well have won him the presidency.

The issue of welfare had been a vital partisan issue going back to the Nixon administration. Reagan incorporated images of welfare queens driving Cadillacs in his first bid for the Republican nomination in 1976 and continued to refer to the same discredited anecdote throughout his presidency. The issue clearly had great traction, largely because although a majority of the recipients of all welfare programs are white, the politics of welfare revolve around stereotypes of minority dependence. Like the word "crime," the word "welfare" was used as a form of coded language that appealed to voters who harbored prejudices that African Americans and other minorities were averse to work and prone to dishonesty, either stealing or looking to get ahead by cheating the government.

Many suspected that Clinton's commitment to the issue was little more than rhetorical when, nearly two years into his presidency, Clinton still had not sent his proposals to Congress. In fact, Clinton waited so long to move on the issue that Republican leaders in the House were able to reclaim the issue as their own and pushed the president to veto two versions of welfare reform legislation that were highly punitive, giving the GOP grounds to make the issue a centerpiece of their 1994 "Contract With America" campaign that carried their party to control of Congress for the first time in more than 36 years.

Both parties stood under the same banner of welfare reform, but the principles underpinning their programs remained far apart.

CIVIL RIGHTS

For the most part, the civil rights policies of the Reagan administration remained consistent until the inauguration of Bill Clinton in 1993. President George H. W. Bush did little to change the conservative direction of those civil rights agencies of the federal government that had been reoriented away from affirmative action remedies by his predecessor and on occasion moved to defend them. In late 1990, Bush vetoed a civil rights bill (a compromised form of which was eventually passed as the Civil Rights Act of 1991) that attempted to reverse a series of Supreme Court decisions that had weakened the legal protections against job discrimination contained in the 1964 Civil Rights Act.

RACE AND THE WAR ON DRUGS

Early in January 1990, Marion Barry, the mayor of the District of Columbia, was arrested in a D.C. hotel room with his girlfriend after a substance reputed to be crack cocaine was found. Undercover police officers reported that they had clear evidence of the mayor's drug use, having planted a hidden camera in the room whose incriminating images were later broadcast on network news programs. Barry initially accused the police and his political enemies of having entrapped him, but he later held a tearful press conference and confessed his "human weaknesses."[88] Barry was charged with multiple counts of perjury and possession, although in the end he was convicted of a single charge of drug possession and served six months in jail. Barry resigned as mayor after his conviction but ran again for the office in 1994 and won a fourth term. Throughout this period, Barry was the subject of far more media and national attention than scores of other locally elected officials caught in compromising circumstances, no doubt because he was African American and because of the racially identified drug, crack cocaine.

Since President Reagan's so-called War on Drugs of the early 1980s, federal drug laws discriminated against minority communities by more harshly punishing crack users, who tended to be people of color, than users of powder cocaine, a majority of whom were white and middle class. Federal sentencing rules mandated that possession of five grams of crack be punished by five years in prison. Possession of the same quantity of cocaine resulted in only a one-year sentence; a five-year sentence required the possession of 500 grams of cocaine, 100 times as much to trigger the same sentence as crack. Moreover, whereas all other lengthy drug felonies require that prosecutors prove that the possessor intended to sell or distribute the drug, the sentencing law governing crack does not require proof of intent to distribute. In 1994, 90 percent of people convicted of possession of crack were jailed, whereas fewer than one-third of those convicted of possession of powder cocaine were jailed. The effect of these disparities dramatically increased the proportion of African Americans in federal prisons. According to criminal justice experts, African Americans composed only 13 percent of regular drug users in the nation, but represented nearly three-quarters of those given prison sentences (74%).[89]

Many critics of the criminal justice system pointed out these disparities, but their appeals seemed to have little impact until, in early April 1995, the U.S. Sentencing Commission issued a formal recommendation that prison terms for the use or sale of crack should be lowered to be in line with those mandated for the use or sale of powder cocaine. As the U.S. Sentencing Commission was established by Congress partly to insulate the process of sentencing from the whims and demagoguery of politicians, its recommendations became legal policy unless Congress acted within the next session to overturn them.

In the fall of 1995, however, the Republican-controlled Congress, led by Newt Gingrich, pushed through a law reversing the United States Sentencing Commission recommendation to reduce the sentencing disparity between crack and powder and instead returned the sentencing guidelines to the discriminatory status quo.

Within 24 hours of Congress's vote, inmates in more than two dozen federal prisons in four states organized protests that included breaking windows, throwing chairs, assaulting prison staff, setting fires, and even taking control of some parts of their prisons. Such a reaction was not unexpected, as at the time nearly two-thirds of all federal prison inmates were serving time for drug crimes. In what was probably the most widespread prison uprising in American history, 26 people were injured, millions of dollars of damage was done, 28 federal prisons were locked down and the Federal Bureau of Prisons warned that unless the sentencing disparity was addressed somehow, even more violent prison riots might erupt.[90] In spite of the dangerous conditions inside federal prisons, the energetic lobbying on the part of Jesse Jackson, and the Congressional Black Caucus against the sentencing bill, President Clinton, entering an election year and perhaps motivated by a fear of appearing weak on crime or drugs, reluctantly signed it into law.[91]

THE FATE OF AFFIRMATIVE ACTION

In early 1995, Senator Bob Dole, the front-runner for the next-year's Republican presidential nomination, seemed to be favoring the issue of affirmative action as a political lever with which to distinguish himself from President Clinton. Dole asked the Library of Congress to count the number of affirmative action programs that existed in the executive branch (the answer was 160), but before he could make much of an issue of their findings, Clinton stole his thunder by ordering a general review of all affirmative action "preference" programs, saying that he wanted to keep those programs that actually worked to remedy the effects of past discrimination.[92] Clinton said, "After nearly 30 years of Government-sanctioned quotas, timetables, set-asides, and other racial preferences...the race-counting game has gone too far," Dole then upped the ante, introducing legislation, "The Equal Opportunity Act of 1995," which would prohibit the federal government from giving favored treatment to any group defined by race or sex. Republican congressional leaders reportedly scheduled the bill to come to a vote nearly a year later when it could be a more prominent issue in the presidential campaign.[93]

Responding to the shrill claims made by white Republicans that affirmative action programs were creating a general employment climate of "reverse racism" that limited the opportunities of white men across the nation, President Clinton ordered a full executive department review of all affirmative action initiatives to find any that were abusive, corrupt, unnecessary, or patently unfair. In doing so, however, Clinton seemed to be ignoring other evidence that employment discrimination against minorities was a continuing problem. A Labor Department study revealed that employment discrimination against white men was an exceedingly small problem. Rather, the numbers continued to point to the ongoing privileges whites enjoyed. In 1995, the Federal Glass Ceiling Commission reported that all but 5 percent of the highest tier of corporate positions were filled by white men.[94]

In California, Governor Pete Wilson, sensing the political momentum of the issue and considering a run at the Republican presidential nomination himself, noisily endorsed a state ballot initiative that would end all racial preferences in public contracts and even admissions policies in California's state university system, saying, "Let us begin to undo the corrosive unfairness of reverse discrimination."[95] Wilson kept up the drumbeat on the issue later that year by issuing a public letter to Californians in which he pledged to root out affirmative action programs throughout the state and pointedly called on President Clinton to "summon the courage" to do the same.[96] In protest, civil rights groups contemplated calling boycotts on California grapes, wine, and produce, but in the end chose not to go that far. The National Urban League, however, canceled its planned annual convention of 20,000 delegates in Los Angeles, costing the city somewhere between $6 and $10 million in lost tourist revenue.[97]

As in earlier presidential campaigns, race served as the hidden backdrop to the 1996 campaign, conveyed through code language and symbolism. To Patrick Buchanan, the conservative maverick who unsuccessfully sought to elbow ahead of Bob Dole for the Republican nomination, race was an unstable tool. Buchanan deftly appealed to conservative southern whites with the language of "America's cultural heritage," states' rights, immigrant invasions, and the need for English-only laws, but he also tried to distance himself from more unsavory white supremacist groups that supported his candidacy. In February 1996, Buchanan spoke before a Louisiana audience that included David Duke, former Klansman and neo-Nazi leader who lost his own bid for Louisiana governor in 1991, but attracted a majority of white votes in the state, and narrowly escaped being photographed alongside Duke. Later, one of Buchanan's campaign co-chairmen was pressured to resign from the campaign when his connections to white supremacist organizations were publicized and a number of his advisors and campaign workers were found to have worked for, or been members of, racist organizations including David Duke's own "National Association for the Advancement of White People." Such friends may have caused Buchanan trouble in some parts of the nation, but in Louisiana they certainly did not hurt much, as Buchanan won the Republican caucuses in the state. A week later he surprised pundits by defeating Dole in the important New Hampshire primary.[98]

Dole had been a vocal opponent of affirmative action in Congress, but he chose Jack Kemp as his running mate in 1996. Kemp, a congressman from upstate New York, was a rare Republican who had opposed the conservative movement to amend state constitutions to ban affirmative action programs. Clinton cruised to an easier-than-expected victory over Dole and secured a second term.

Politicians found affirmative action a fertile field in which to grow their voters, and the justice system reassessed them as well, although at its more deliberate and measured pace. After a hiatus of nearly five years, the constitutionality of government affirmative action programs again came under attack before the Supreme Court. In the late 1980s, the Mountain Gravel and Construction Company of Colorado won a federal contract to build and maintain certain highways in that state. Part of the terms of the contract gave Mountain Gravel bonuses if it hired minority subcontractors, and it subcontracted the job of building guardrails to Gonzales Construction, a Hispanic firm. A rival company that had actually submitted a lower bid, Adarand Constructors, sued the federal government alleging that affirmative action incentives that had led Mountain Gravel to reject its bid were in violation of the Fifth Amendment to the U.S. Constitution, which required that everyone receive "equal protection of the law."

Lower federal courts followed recent Supreme Court precedents and rejected Adarand's complaint on the basis that the federal government's use of race was not held to the same highest "strict scrutiny" standard of review that individual states were under the Fourteenth Amendment (which applied only to states and not the federal government). Rather, it applied the lower "intermediate" standard of review called for by the Supreme Court in *Fullilove v. Klutznick* (1980), which allowed programs that were clearly within the government's legitimate purpose of overcoming the legacy of racial discrimination and did not place an "undue burden" on businesses that were not minority-owned. Indeed, it seemed for a time that a slim majority of the Supreme Court was willing to grant greater latitude to federal government programs that could show a legitimate purpose for racial preferences. In a case brought by a white-owned radio station challenging a Federal Communications Commission program that favored granting licenses to minority broadcasters, *Metro Broadcasting v. F.C.C.* (1990), five justices allowed the program to proceed without evidence showing that Metro had itself discriminated in any time in the past.

Adarand Constructors appealed and the Supreme Court surprised most observers by reversing its own recent precedents and ruling that the federal government, like the states, must be judged according to the "strict scrutiny" standard, which allowed such minority set-aside programs only if they addressed a "compelling" government interest and did so in the narrowest and most focused means possible. Justice Sandra Day O'Connor, writing for the majority, declared the higher standard necessary because, she argued, it was not possible for justices to discern whether racially based programs were in fact charitable or malicious. Because "there is simply no way" of determining which programs are nobly intentioned and which are not, the courts must use the strict scrutiny standard to "smoke-out" bad uses of race. Justice John Paul Stevens, who along with Justice Ruth Bader Ginsberg dissented, ridiculed the majorities' willingness to equate "invidious" racial distinctions with "benign" ones. Nothing could be more obvious, wrote Stevens, than "the difference between a "No Trespassing" sign and a welcome mat."[99]

Justice Clarence Thomas, in his separate concurring opinion, took this a step further and used the opportunity to state plainly that in his view all racial appeals, whatever their motivation, were equally objectionable: "I believe that there is a 'moral [and] constitutional equivalence,'...between laws designed to subjugate a race and those that distribute benefits on the basis of race in order to foster some current notion of equality.... In my mind, government-sponsored racial discrimination based on benign prejudice is just as noxious as discrimination inspired by malicious prejudice." That segregation laws and minority set-aside programs shared a moral equivalence was considered by many a surprising view to be expressed by the former head of the Civil Rights Division of the Justice Department.

The Adarand decision forced the Clinton administration to initiate a review of all federal government programs that had preferences or inducements for minority advancement. As a result of the Justice Department review, in November 1995, the Defense Department ended its practice of reserving contracts for bidding by minority firms, a program that had awarded more than $1 billion to minority contractors in the previous year.[100]

The ruling in the Adarand case was just another step in a continuing trend of limiting the government's ability to address the legacy of segregation and the effects of racial discrimination, whereas, by every social measurement, it was clear that the destructive consequences of inequality were not withering away on their own. One of the most active arms of government in attempting to increase opportunities for minorities was the nation's public colleges and universities, many of which continued to craft admissions programs that would favor the recruitment of minority students. These affirmative action admissions programs were challenged across the country, and five cases from five different circuit districts made their way to federal appeals courts between 1996 and 2001. In the wake of the Supreme Court's 1978 *Bakke* decision that held the University of California system's affirmative action programs to a strict scrutiny standard and all but outlawed quota systems that reserved seats for minority applicants, universities had experimented with many different approaches to enhancing the diversity of their student bodies. Many of these programs did little more than recognize disadvantaged minority backgrounds as a positive factor in a complicated admissions formula. New challenges to these programs carried the ruling of *Bakke* and *Adarand* forward by arguing that having a racially diverse student body was not a "compelling government interest" in education and therefore not a sufficient reason to allow the use of race in any form in the admissions process. By the time the Supreme Court weighed in on the issue, two federal courts had found that racial diversity on campus was a compelling reason to allow affirmative action admissions programs, and two had concluded that it was not and struck down all uses of race in admissions.

The Supreme Court resolved the conflicts in the lower courts with two landmark cases, both dealing with the admissions policies at the University of Michigan. In *Grutter v. Bolinger*, a majority of justices for the first time clearly stated that the goal of having a racially diverse campus was important enough to constitute a "compelling state interest" and to pursue a "race-conscious" admissions program. In a companion case, however, *Gratz v. Bolinger* examined the technical details of the undergraduate admissions policy at the university. The court reaffirmed that campus racial diversity was of high enough importance to allow an exception to the Constitution's guarantee of equal protection of the laws, but that programs such as Michigan's, which arbitrarily gave an advantage to any minority applicant, were not narrow enough to meet the "strict scrutiny" standard and were illegal. Rather, each applicant had to be considered individually on all their merits, including their heritage, for an admissions program to pass muster.[101]

FOREIGN POLICY

Just as President Reagan's foreign policy toward South Africa had become a racially divisive issue domestically in the 1980s, during the Bush and Clinton years foreign policy questions continued to be of great concern and symbolic importance to many Americans, especially African Americans. In 1992, in response to a famine and civil war that killed hundreds of thousands, President George H. W. Bush ordered American troops into Somalia as the leading element of "Operation Restore Hope," a military intervention restricted to protecting aid workers and convoys distributing food. A year later President Clinton shifted the mission from support for famine relief to "nation-building," a move encouraged by black leaders including the Congressional Black Caucus. Even their support weakened, however, when the U.S. military quickly became embroiled in factional fighting in the capital Mogadishu, leading to the deaths of 18 American marines. Black leaders privately critical of Clinton's handling of the military deployment felt forced to back him as some conservative white congressmen opposed Clinton's policy in racist terms. One Republican congressman was quoted as referring to Somalis as "primitive" and criticized the idea of nation-building because, as he put it, there was "nothing in Somalia to rebuild or reestablish in the first place.... Somalia has been a basket case ever since its independence was declared back in 1960."[102]

The administration's debacle in Somalia certainly increased its reticence to become involved in the tragedy unfolding in Rwanda in 1994. Rwanda was a tiny Central African nation whose culture and political life was split along ethnic lines between tribal Tutsis and Hutus. On April 6, 1994, Rwandan President Juvénal Habyarimana was assassinated when his plane was shot down as it approached the Kigali airport. The death of President Habyarimana, a Hutu, initiated reprisal killing against the Tutsi minority. Ten Belgian United Nations peacekeepers were sent to protect the Rwandan prime minister who was seen as an obstacle to the genocidal plans of the extremist Hutus in the government, and all 10 peacekeepers and the prime minister were murdered. Soon all opposition politicians were being rounded up and slaughtered. Day by day the extent of the killing widened, although President Clinton and his top officials scrupulously avoided using the word "genocide" to describe the unfolding events in Rwanda. It was not until the middle of May, after half a million Rwandans had been killed, that the United Nations formally acknowledged that "genocide" was occurring.

Accusations that the American government followed a racist immigration policy were highlighted by the refugee crisis coming from Haiti in the 1990s. Haitians by the boatload began arriving with increasing frequency with the overthrow of the democratically elected government of Jean-Bertrand Aristide by a military cabal in September 1991. Responding to the flood of Haitian asylum-seekers, President George H. W. Bush ordered the expedited repatriation of tens of thousands of Haitian refugees being held at the American Guantanamo Bay military base in Cuba, and the interdiction and summary deportation back to Haiti of all found at sea without bothering to sort out those dissidents destined for persecution at the hands of the Haitian junta. American civil rights leaders denounced the obvious racial double standard of American immigration policy that allowed automatic residency status to any Cuban able to set foot on American soil, but interdicted all Haitians without consideration of the consequences of returning them to Haiti. The NAACP and the Congressional Black Caucus both protested and called for Congress to pass a measure that would grant Haitian refugees temporary protected status while their personal circumstances and risk of return could be determined. Because of their lobbying and raising the issue as one of racial justice, civil rights organizations were able to move at least part of Congress. In February 1992, the House of Representatives passed legislation to end the summary repatriation of Haitian refugees, but the bill was not acted on by the Senate.[103]

In May 1994, as the stream of Haitian refugees continued, the Clinton administration tried to soften the Bush interdiction policy by announcing it would consider Haitian political asylum requests at special processing center ships operating at sea. It then narrowed the difference between the way Cubans had been swiftly welcomed and Haitians excluded by announcing that henceforth Cubans caught on the seas would be taken to Guantanamo for detention and processing.[104]

RACIAL PROFILING

During the 1990s, racial profiling on the part of police moved from being a well-known problem in minority communities to being an issue of public concern. Police forces across the nation endowed with expanded search and seizure powers, indiscriminately detained and searched people of color. New Jersey's police had so frequently violated the civil rights of black and Latino drivers that they were placed under the supervision of a federal judge.[105]

Although police officers throughout the United States have been no better able to set aside their own prejudices than any other citizens, what were once individual acts of police discrimination became institutionalized policies with the advent of racial profiling in the 1980s and 1990s. Racial profiling has its roots in criminal profiling that was first used to identify behaviors that might reveal a tendency to commit a certain crime rather than to identify potential criminals by their race. In the 1960s, the federal government attempted to fight a rash of airline hijackings by establishing a screening system at airports based on the documented characteristics of airplane hijackers. Profiling based on psychological patterns was honed into an art by the FBI in the 1970s in tracking down serial killers. But a dangerous step was taken in the 1980s as part of the Reagan administration's "War on Drugs" when profiling systems that had been used very selectively to identify specific criminals were widened to provide a legal basis for the detention, questioning, and search of anyone who might commit a crime. As one expert on the history of racial profiling observed, these profiles were a step beyond anything ever attempted before because "these profiles were designed to be *predictive* of crime, not *descriptive* of particular criminals."[106]

In the mid-1980s, as part of a vast drug interdiction effort in south Florida, "Operation Pipeline," characteristics of motorists found carrying large quantities of drugs noted by a local patrolman were compiled into a profile used by the Drug Enforcement Agency to train agents. Official training materials used in this program focused on racial minorities, especially Hispanics and Jamaicans. Soon police departments throughout America, but especially in major cities where "stop and frisk" tactics were common, increasingly stopped and searched minority motorists. In California and New Jersey, the stopping of black and Latino motorists became so frequent that a number of class action lawsuits were filed to challenge the practice.

In 1994, arguments were heard in a case alleging that the New Jersey Highway Patrol was systematically stopping and searching African American motorists. A thorough survey of driver patterns and patrol records performed by researchers from Temple University introduced as evidence in the case revealed that slightly more than one-third of all motorists stopped and questioned were African American, although fewer than one-in-eight of motorists who used those roads were African American. The evidence persuaded both a state judge and an appellate court that New Jersey's state police were indeed practicing racial profiling on a wide scale. Similar suits in Maryland, Illinois, and Colorado revealed the broad extent of racial profiling on the highways of their states, as well as the ineffectiveness of such techniques. A subsequent court-ordered survey of traffic stops, searches, and arrests in New Jersey revealed that although police believed minorities were the most likely to possess drugs and stopped them more often, whites were in fact almost twice as likely to be found in possession of drugs as blacks and five times more likely to have contraband as were Latinos.[107]

Although scholarly studies clearly showed the racial biases common in police officers' choice of whom to pull over, it was a series of high-profile actions in 1999 that brought the issue to the forefront of the national agenda. That year the superintendent of the New Jersey state police, who had long defended his department against charges of racial profiling, told a reporter that: "The drug problem is mostly cocaine and marijuana. It is most likely a minority group that's involved with that." Governor Christie Todd Whitman promptly fired him. That summer, the NAACP declared police racial profiling to be its number one concern. President Clinton responded to the increasing publicity over the issue by issuing an executive order requiring all federal police agencies to keep detailed statistics on their stops, searches, and other activities to determine the extent of racial profiling. Not all leading politicians, however, agreed that racial profiling existed or that it was a problem. In California, Governor Grey Davis, at the urging of the state's police unions and fraternal organizations, vetoed a law that would have required all police departments to compile statistics on their traffic stops in order to assess possible racial disparities.[108]

HATE CRIMES

Partly because of the passage of individual state laws enhancing punishments for crimes committed with malice toward someone's race, gender, religion, and, in some states, disability or sexual orientation, there was more reporting and attention paid to ugly acts of racial violence. In March 1997, a 13-year-old African American boy, Lenard Clark, was beaten nearly to death and left in a coma by white teenagers who objected to the boy's straying into their white working-class Chicago neighborhood of Bridgeport, a neighborhood made famous because it was the home district of Mayor Richard Daley and had been walled-off from surrounding black neighborhoods by the careful placement of freeways. News of the attack made national headlines and prompted President Clinton to ask the nation to pray for Clark during one of his regular Saturday radio addresses.[109]

In 1994, the Student Press Law Center, a Washington, D.C. institute that monitors and supports campus newspapers in American colleges, reported that the number of "skirmishes" both verbal and physical, provoked by slurs of one's race, sex, or religion was rising in proportion with the increasing numbers of minority students in higher education.[110] Boston College had one of its largest protest meetings of the decade, more than a 1,000 students overflowing its largest auditorium, after a dozen leaders of minority student groups simultaneously received racist hate e-mail. Later it was learned that similar hate e-mail incidents had recently occurred at several other American universities. In 1998, Congress passed a bill expanding the categories of hate crimes and threats that must be reported to the federal government, expanding the 1990 Hate Crime Statistics Act that required all law enforcement agencies to report all crimes based on racial, religious, ethnic, and sexual bigotry.[111]

Although evidence accumulated that hate crimes were becoming a growing national problem, the movement for federal and state legislation that would enhance the penalties for crimes motivated by hate of another's race, gender, religion, ethnicity, or sexual preferences did not succeed until after the perpetration of a hate crime of shocking proportions. The movement to adopt such laws was suddenly stalled in 1992 when, in *R.A.V. v. St. Paul*, the justices of the U.S. Supreme Court unanimously struck down a typical hate crimes law, the Minnesota "Bias-Motivated Crime Ordinance" on the grounds that it violated constitutional First Amendment rights to free speech. In 1990, the city of St. Paul passed the Bias-Motivated Crime Ordinance that criminalized the display of any "symbol, object, appellation, characterization or graffiti, including, but not limited to, a burning cross or Nazi swastika" that one could reasonably expect to cause "anger, alarm or resentment in others on the basis of race, color, creed, religion or gender." In the case before the court, a group of teenagers had lashed together some broken chair legs into a cross and burned them on the lawn of their next-door neighbor. When the local judge threw out the case on First Amendment grounds, prosecutors appealed and succeeded in convincing the Minnesota Supreme Court that the ordinance did not imperil free speech but was legally equivalent to prohibiting "fighting words"—words that had long been held not to merit any legal protections. The U.S. Supreme Court, however, noted that the Bias-Motivated Crime Ordinance did not equally criminalize all such "fighting words." As Justice Anton Scalia wrote for the court, "Displays containing abusive invective…are permissible unless they are addressed to one of the specified disfavored topics. Those who wish to use 'fighting words' in connection with other ideas—to express hostility, for example, on the basis of political

affiliation, union membership, or homosexuality—are not covered"; and therefore
the city of St. Paul, was, in effect, punishing some views while allowing others. As
Scalia concluded with a clever turn of phrase, "Let there be no mistake about our
belief that burning a cross in someone's front yard is reprehensible ... but St. Paul
has sufficient means at its disposal to prevent such behavior without adding the
First Amendment to the fire."[112]

The next year after striking down St. Paul's type of hate-crime legislation, the
Supreme Court upheld another, making clear to legislatures across the country
what sort of laws they could pass. On October 7, 1989, 10 African American
teenagers were socializing in Kenosha, Wisconsin, when their conversation
turned to a scene from *Mississippi Burning*, a 1988 film they had just watched together. The film told the story of the FBI investigation of the murder of three civil
rights workers in 1961, in which a Klansman beat a black child who was praying.
When a 14-year-old white boy, Gregory Reddick, rode past on his bike, one of
the youths, Todd Mitchell, who actually had not watched the movie, asked the
others, "'You all want to f—k somebody up? There goes a white boy; go get him,'"
and then took part in a beating that left the younger boy in a coma. Eventually
three assailants were charged and convicted for assaulting Reddick and received
prison sentence ranging from 2 to 10 years. Mitchell's sentence was the lightest,
but he was also charged under Wisconsin's new hate crimes law that added additional penalties to crimes in which the perpetrator "intentionally selects the
person against whom the crime ... is committed or selects the property which is
damaged or otherwise affected by the crime ... because of the race, religion, color,
disability, sexual orientation, national origin or ancestry of that person or the
owner or occupant of that property."[113] Under this law, Mitchell's prison sentence
was doubled from two to four years.

Although the Wisconsin Supreme Court had struck down the law under which
Mitchell's sentence was stretched by referring to the U.S. Supreme Court's precedent in *R.A.V. v. St. Paul*, the highest court did not follow suit and instead
unanimously found that such laws did not "chill" or impinge on free speech but
only framed the sentencing for common criminal actions, which was clearly con-
stitutionally permissible. Indeed, the law had long held that thoughts and moti-
vations were relevant to sentencing and that states could decide that some sorts
of crimes were more threatening to peace and order than others and therefore
should be more harshly repressed.

Perhaps the largest hate crime of the decade was the bombing of the Alfred P.
Murrah federal building in Oklahoma City in 1995 that killed 168 people, including children in a daycare center. Timothy McVeigh was the man who planned
and executed the bombing. Although he was never shown to have closely associated with far right hate groups such as the paramilitary *posse comitatus* or Christian white identity movements, nevertheless he was deeply influenced by their
worldview. While in the army, he was reprimanded for discriminating against
subordinate soldiers who were African American by assigning them the dirtiest
jobs even though they were not the lowest in rank. Like others on the far right,

he viewed the government's assault on the religious cult, the Branch Davidians, in Waco, Texas in 1993 to have been the modern equivalent of the first shots on Concord Green justifying armed resistance against a hopelessly corrupt, tyrannical government (although in this case controlled by a secret cabal of Jews rather than the Imperial officers of England).[114]

After the Oklahoma City bombing, Congress quickly passed and President Clinton happily signed the Hate Crimes Enhancement Act of 1994. Many individual states either added or strengthened their own hate crimes laws so that by 1998, only 10 states had no statutes on their books specifically punishing hate crimes. The largest of these, Texas, came close to passing a hate crime bill modeled on the one in Wisconsin that had passed constitutional muster, but after easily passing the lower chamber it was bottled up by a Republican-controlled Senate committee and died. Texas governor George W. Bush refused to endorse the bill, saying only, "I will look at the bill when it makes it my desk, if it makes it to my desk." Later, when campaigning for president in 2000, his opponent, Senator Albert Gore, would make much of Bush's lack of support for hate crimes legislation.[115]

VOTING RIGHTS

On the last day of their 1995 term, and one month from the 30th anniversary of the passage of the Voting Rights Act of 1965, five justices of the Supreme Court narrowly restricted states' ability to draw congressional boundaries in such a way as to maximize the number of minority representatives. In a case arising from Georgia's 11th congressional district, a seat then held by Democratic black firebrand Cynthia McKinney was challenged as being unconstitutional because it was drawn for the purpose of enhancing black voting power. The district had been carved out of Atlanta neighborhoods as part of a 1992 Justice Department redistricting plan to create three "majority-minority" districts in the state, out of eleven, which would bring minority representation more in line with the demographics of the state, which was nearly one-third African American. Such redistricting procedures, begun by the Voting Rights Act of 1965, had become quite common by the 1990s, but were now under attack by whites claiming their constitutional guarantee of equal protection under the laws was violated.

In this case, *Miller v. Johnson*, the slim majority of Reagan and Bush appointees, including the court's only African American, Clarence Thomas, agreed with the white plaintiffs and declared Representative McKinney's district to be in violation of the constitutional rights of whites. According to Justice Anthony Kennedy who wrote for the majority, it did not even matter that the eleventh district was not circuitous and snakelike as gerrymandered districts tend to be (as a previous case from 1993, *Shaw v. Reno*, seemed to suggest was the deciding question), only that in drawing it up the state legislature had "subordinated traditional race-neutral districting principles... to racial considerations." This was a tortured principle in the context of Georgia's history where the racial gerrymandering of districts to exclude African Americans had been widely and openly practiced since the Civil War. Noting that the creation of such "minority-majority" districts under the Voting Rights Act had doubled the number of minorities elected to Congress from 26 to 52, dissenting justice John Paul Stevens wrote, "I do not see how a districting plan that favors a politically weak group can violate equal protection."[116]

In the wake of this decision, many congresspersons suddenly found that their congressional districts were under legal attack. At the time, only three of Congress's 39 African American legislators had been elected in districts with a white majority, and all three of these were outside of the South. Congresswoman Nydia Velazquez, a Democrat representing Brooklyn, New York, and the first Puerto Rican woman elected to Congress, was the first to be threatened with a copycat lawsuit. She was given legal support by the Puerto Rican Legal Defense and Education Fund. Velazquez was not alone. Over the next year, eight other districts with predominately African American and Hispanic populations were overturned by federal courts.[117]

Ironically, when the five Republican-appointed justices of the Supreme Court dismantled majority-minority districts, they also overturned a successful electoral strategy of the Republican Party. It was initially the Bush administration, following an amendment to the Voting Rights Act passed in 1982, that pressured the Justice Department to concentrate minority voters, who mostly voted for Democrats, into single districts so as to enhance the electoral chances of Republicans in neighboring districts where races had historically been close. In some states, such as Texas, North Carolina, and Florida, such efforts had helped achieve the Republican landslide of 1994 that put Republicans in control of Congress for the first time in 40 years.[118]

Jesse Jackson reflected the pessimism of many civil rights activists at the time of *Miller v. Johnson* when he predicted that the Supreme Court's ruling would throw half of the minority members out of Congress within a couple of years. In fact, the numbers of minorities in Congress changed little, although some particular states witnessed significant swings.

DEATH PENALTY

Another area where the justice system appeared to fail to be colorblind was in the allocation of death penalties. By the end of the 1990s, 42 percent of the 3,600 people condemned to death were African American in a nation where they comprised just 13 percent of the population. Since the Supreme Court ended a four-year legal hiatus of death penalties in 1976, the racial disparities in both those executed and the racial combinations of perpetrator and victim were obvious and persistent. From 1977 to 2000, one-quarter of all those executed in America were blacks who had victimized whites. In the same period, just 1.7 percent of those put to death were whites who had murdered blacks.[119]

Many antideath penalty activists pointed out both of these huge disparities and the seeming arbitrariness of who was sentenced to death. In 1997, the American

Bar Association (ABA) approved a resolution calling for a national moratorium on all executions until the issues of accuracy of verdicts and possible racial bias could be fully investigated. The ABA's resolution urged all states to strive "to eliminate discrimination in capital sentencing on the basis of the race of either the victim or the defendant." The ABA's call was soon reinforced by the United Nations, whose special rapporteur on extrajudicial, summary or arbitrary executions concluded that "race, ethnic origin and economic status appear to be key determinants of who will, and who will not, receive a sentence of death" in the United States.[120]

In spite of all the evidence indicating clear racial disparities in capital punishment, most whites continued to support it. Polling from the 1980s through the 1990s showed a remarkable stability of white attitudes toward capital punishment along with clear disparities in perceptions between Americans along lines of race. Polls in the mid-1980s showed that 70 percent of whites favored the death penalty, a proportion unchanged a decade later. White America's enthusiasm for putting prisoners to death did not diminish even though only 32 percent thought the ultimate sentence was "carried out fairly." African Americans overwhelmingly (73 percent in one poll in 1991) indicated that they believed blacks were more likely to receive the death penalty for the same crimes as committed by whites. Sensitivity to such issues of racial justice were probably the prime reason why, in most polls, fewer than half of African Americans supported the death penalty.[121]

An increasing number of death row commutations and reversals highlighted the problems with the system, but greater public attention to the issue came from the newfound attention it was given in Hollywood. In 1995, *Dead Man Walking*, an Oscar-wining biopic of the antideath penalty crusader Sister Helen Prejean, humanized those on death row, even a man guilty of a vicious murder. *The Hurricane*, released in 1999, starring Denzel Washington as middleweight fighting world champion Rubin "Hurricane" Carter whose conviction for a murder in 1966 was overturned 20 years later, played at a timely moment as legislatures and governors across the nation were grappling with the issue.[122]

Nowhere was the apparent randomness and irreversibility of prosecutorial mistakes as obvious as in a succession of cases in Illinois where men scheduled to be executed were exonerated by new evidence. In 1998, Anthony Porter, a black man who had a long criminal history and was convicted of murdering two people on the south side of Chicago, was just 48 hours from death when his execution was stayed in order to review whether he was mentally retarded. While this motion was considered, new evidence was uncovered by Northwestern University Professor David Protess and his journalism students that exonerated Porter and his conviction was overturned. The key eyewitness in the case swore an affidavit saying that he did not, in fact, see Porter shoot anyone at the Washington Park pool, but he said he did only because Chicago police intimidated him into accusing Porter. Other witnesses, including one new eyewitness, were found who provided convincing evidence pointing to a local drug dealer who later confessed to the crime.[123]

In the wake of the Porter exoneration, the 12th man since 1976 condemned to die in the state but later determined to be innocent, the Illinois state senate considered a bill to impose a moratorium on all executions, but it was killed in committee. As pressure for reform mounted and another wrongful murder prosecution unraveled, this time of a police officer implicated by a jailhouse informant, Illinois Governor George Ryan gave an emotional speech in which he said, "How do you prevent another Anthony Porter—another innocent man or woman from paying the ultimate penalty for a crime he or she did not commit? Today I cannot answer that question." Ryan ordered that all death row inmates scheduled for execution be issued reprieves while a special investigative committee reviewed all of their cases, paying special attention to advances in the use of DNA analysis of material evidence.[124]

In May 1999, the Nebraska state legislature became the first in the nation to pass a bill ordering a moratorium of all executions while an investigative committee reviewed the death penalty procedures in the case, looking especially for evidence of racial bias. Nebraska had a similar situation to many other states: 3 of its 10 condemned prisoners were African American or Indian, a ratio that did not seem to alarm Nebraska's first-term Republican governor, Mike Johanns, who vetoed the measure. Other states were moving in the same direction; legislators in 16 of the 38 states with death penalties debated similar bills.[125]

Perhaps the most protested pending execution of the era was that of the black radical and former journalist Mumia Abu-Jamal who was on Pennsylvania's death row after being convicted of killing Philadelphia police officer Daniel Faulkner in 1981. Hundreds of protesters were arrested simultaneously in front of the U.S. Supreme Court and the San Francisco court house in early 2000. The popular rock/rap group Rage Against the Machine adopted Abu-Jamal as their own crusade, holding sold-out fundraising concerts for his legal defense. Antioch College in Ohio invited Abu-Jamal to be its commencement speaker, an event later protested by several hundred visiting police who attended and turned their backs when a tape of Abu-Jamal was played. A week later, thousands of protesters rallied for a commutation of Abu-Jamal's sentence in New York's Madison Square Garden, and large protest rallies were centered on the Republican National Convention held in Philadelphia in the summer of 2000. In 2001, a federal judge overturned Abu-Jamal's death sentence in favor of a life sentence.[126]

MEDIA AND MASS COMMUNICATIONS

On June 1, 1993, Asian American journalist Connie Chung joined Dan Rather as co-anchor of the prestigious CBS Evening News. Whereas Chung represented a visible break with the entrenched Walter Cronkite archetype for television anchors, her appearance did not signify a new era in opportunities for minority journalists. Many social critics speculated that Chung's breakthrough was made possible because she fit a new, widespread "model minority" stereotype of Asian Americans in American culture.

In 1968, the Kerner Commission on Civil Unrest charged with uncovering the deeper roots of the urban rioting then plaguing American cities pointed one of its fingers at American newspapers, noting journalism's lack of minority representation as one cause of slanted and inflammatory reporting. During the 1970s, the American Society of Newspaper Editors (ASNE) encouraged its members to act to diversify their staffs and set as a goal having America's newsrooms contain the same proportion of ethnicities as the nation as a whole by the year 2000 (when 28 percent of Americans were members of an ethnic minority). By 1998, it was evident that this goal was beyond reach as fewer than 12 percent of journalists were people of color. Looking into the numbers, the problem appeared not to be one of recruitment as it was one of retention; one study found that for every 550 minority journalists hired each year in the mid-1990s, 400 quit, most because they perceived that their chances of promotion were poor. Indeed, 50 percent more African Americans, Asians, and Hispanics claimed this as a reason for their departure than white journalists did. Most minority journalists also complained of being unable to cover the stories they thought were important. Consequently, the ASNE revised its goal of making newspaper offices look like the nation they served, setting the date for this to occur to the distant year of 2025.[127]

In contrast to the nation's newspapers, television broadcasters had made much progress in diversifying their studios and offices. Minority employment in television broadcasting effectively doubled between the publication of the Kerner Report and 1998. But much of this improvement was not initiated by broadcasters themselves. Rather, the Federal Communications Commission (FCC) had required demonstrated employment diversity as a condition of licensing, leading to active affirmative action efforts at recruitment and retention on the part of America's television broadcast companies. But this requirement was overturned by one federal appeals court in 1998 and again by another in 2001, effectively taking the pressure off broadcast corporations to address the issue.

In the early 1990s, the future of Spanish-language broadcasting in America seemed dim in spite of the increasing Hispanic population and their above-average television viewership. After suffering years of losses, Hallmark Cards sold its controlling share in Univisión in 1992, disappointed at stagnant ad revenues, the high cost of developing domestic programming, and the low percentage (less than one-third) of Hispanic households who actually tuned in to Spanish-language television. Its main rival, Telemundo, declared bankruptcy in 1993. Both networks recovered and expanded after these lean years by slashing the number of shows produced in America expanding the amount of its programming originating from lower cost sources in Latin America.[128]

The 1990s saw the increased representation of Asian Americans on television, with Connie Chung anchoring the nightly news on CBS and in 1998 Lucy Liu having a major role on the hit television drama *Ally McBeal*. Other cultural developments, however, indicated that there was still much progress yet to achieve. Some critical observers of television noted that Japanese American figure skater Kristi Yamaguchi, champion of the 1992 Olympics, enjoyed far fewer commercial endorsement contracts than her white rival Nancy Kerrigan. Indeed, her most lucrative sponsorship was for pitching colored contact lenses that made her look less typically Asian.[129]

CULTURAL SCENE

SPORTS

Ever since Jackie Robinson broke the color line in baseball in 1947, the integration of professional sports had seemed to be a process smoothly propelled by the increasing size of payrolls and the rising benefits of fielding a winning team regardless of its color. Because most sports seemed to be steadily progressing toward racial equity, it was all the more shocking when a founder of the Shoal Creek Country Club in Birmingham, Alabama, site of the 1990 Professional Golfer's Association Championship, boasted that year that his club did not "discriminate...except [against] the blacks." This was an unwelcome reminder that golf was one of the last professional sports to eliminate a "Caucasian only" bar to participation, which it finally dropped from its by-laws in 1961. An extensive investigation by the *Charlotte Observer* (North Carolina) discovered that 17 golf clubs on the current PGA tour had all-white memberships. After Birmingham civil rights groups organized a boycott of the PGA tournament at Shoal Creek, at least four advertisers pulled their sponsorship, costing the sponsoring television network $2 million in lost revenue.[130]

Racism in golf reared up again with the meteoric rise of superstar player Tiger Woods. The difficulty professional golf had with its best player being a rich mixture of African, Thai, Native American, Chinese, and European heritage surfaced in 1997 when pro-golfer Fuzzy Zoeller referred to Woods as "a little boy" (boy being a common southern term of derision for black men) and said that he hoped that Woods would not serve fried chicken and collard greens at his victory dinner after winning the Masters' Tournament.[131]

The public was reminded of the long struggle to overcome the color line in professional sports in February 1993 when Arthur Robert Ashe Jr. died of AIDS at the age of 49. Ashe piled on a long list of firsts: the first black tennis player to be selected for the prestigious Davis Cup national tennis team in 1963, and the first to win a tennis grand slam event including the inaugural U.S. Open in 1968, the Australian Open in 1970, and Wimbledon in 1975. More than for his impressive list of on-court victories in an overwhelmingly white country-club sport, Ashe was remembered for his dignified protests against racism and injustice around the world, such as risking his professional career by campaigning for the expulsion of South Africa from the circuit of professional tournaments while it maintained its policy of racial apartheid (a policy that prevented Ashe himself from competing in the South African Open in 1968), or founding the first players union in the sport. Ashe continued his activism after his retirement from tennis against apartheid and discriminatory immigration policies that endangered the lives of thousands of Haitian political refuges who fled their country in flimsy rafts.

Racial controversy continued to haunt baseball whose fans had hoped that progress had been made since the Al Campanis controversy of 1987, when the Dodgers' general manager stated publicly that he did not think that African Americans had the "necessities" to become baseball managers and executives. But the question of what to do about racism again reappeared when Marge Schott, owner of the Cincinnati Reds, a team with but one black in its office staff of 45, went on the record defending her use of hurtful racist words including the comment that "I would never hire another nigger. I'd rather have a trained monkey working for me than a nigger" as being just "jokes" and "kidding." She also defended keeping a Nazi armband in her desk, saying that "Hitler was good in the beginning, but he went too far." Civil rights leader Al Sharpton seized on the issue and called for baseball players to refuse to play in Cincinnati's Riverfront Stadium unless Schott was removed as the Red's owner. Former baseball commissioner Fay Vincent told NBC journalist Bob Costas that he was not surprised by Schott's statements and that "baseball has a long way to go" and that baseball team owners lacked "a passionate commitment" to hiring African Americans and other minorities. Major league baseball's executive committee eventually suspended Schott from any participation in her team for one year, required her to attend a multicultural training class, and fined her $25,000 for her racist remarks.[132]

Race continued to roil the pot of baseball at the end of the decade, as Braves pitcher John Rocker was quoted in *Sports Illustrated* explaining why he would not pitch for a New York team: "It's depressing... The biggest thing I don't like about New York are the foreigners. I'm not a very big fan of foreigners. You can walk an entire block in Times Square and not hear anybody speaking English. Asians and Koreans and Vietnamese and Indians and Russians and Spanish people and everything up there. How the hell did they get in this country?"[133]

While many major league sports remained troubled by racial tensions, professional basketball in the 1990s featured perhaps the most universally admired sports star of the late twentieth century. Michael Jordan led his Chicago Bulls to three consecutive championships from 1991 to 1993, briefly retired to try his hand at baseball, then rejoined the Bulls and led them to three more titles from 1996–1998. Besides being one of the most dominating players in any sport, Jordan refashioned the meaning of sports superstar by appealing just as easily to white audiences as to black. In 1999, ESPN selected Jordan as the athlete of the century, edging out even Babe Ruth.[134]

Dallas Cowboys linebacker Dat Nguyen. AP Photo/LM Otero.

Likewise, Dat Nguyen, the star linebacker for the Texas A&M football team, became the first Vietnamese American to be picked in the NFL draft in 1999. Nguyen's parents and his five siblings fled Vietnam after the fall of Saigon and, after a perilous journey by boat to Thailand, were resettled in a refugee camp in Arkansas before moving permanently to fish the Gulf coast waters off Fulton, Texas, and adding Dat to their family. Considered small for his position by many scouts, Nguyen more than made up for his stature with his quickness, alert play, and fierce energy. He went on to a solid seven-year NFL career as a middle linebacker for the Dallas Cowboys, leading the team in tackles in three seasons. Nguyen's achievements were all the more remarkable as players of Asian descent are among the least represented in the National Football League. Before Nguyen, there had been a handful of players from Pacific islands, Chinese American Walter Achiu who played for Dayton in 1927, and Korean Americans Eugene Chung and John Lee who played in the late 1980s and early 1990s.[135]

MUSIC, FILM, AND LITERATURE

In the 1990s, Hip-Hop continued to shed its earlier political emphasis and embrace the ethos of the urban gangs and ghettos from which it increasingly found inspiration. "Gangsta Rap" became the mainstream of Hip-Hop and the source of its increasing profitability, although it soon provoked a backlash from white critics and moral guardians who denounced its seeming celebration of violence, misogyny, drugs, and lawbreaking.

In late 1990, a record store owner in Florida was convicted of obscenity for selling a copy of 2 Live Crew's album, *As Nasty as They Wanna Be,* becoming the fourth record-store clerk to be prosecuted in connection with the album. 2 Live Crew was arrested on obscenity charges after a performance in Hollywood, Florida, even though the show was restricted to those over the age of 21. Police in at least 13 states had warned record store owners not to sell the album or face arrest. It took more than two years of litigation before a federal appeals court voided obscenity charges against the Florida record store owner and the Supreme Court refused to hear the case, allowing the decision to stand, thus ending the matter in favor of free artistic expression.[136]

While 2 Live Crew drew fire for its pornographic lyrics, they were soon followed by a new trend in Hip-Hop that intensified a gritty appreciation of gangster life. In 1991, Ice-T released his album *OG: Original Gangster,* which in many ways set the standard for the genre. The following year he debuted *Body Count,* which provoked controversy with its hit single, "Cop Killer" in which a young tough describes his desire to murder a police officer. The song was protested by police associations who called for a national boycott and by President Bush who called the song "irresponsible." Sales were stopped by its distributor, Time Warner, who later re-released the album without the controversial song. Nevertheless, the MTV network invited Ice-T to be one of its presenters on its annual music award show that year and Ice-T defended his art from attack, saying, "Like metal, rap has always been maligned, misunderstood, underestimated.... It's here to stay, you know what I'm saying?"[137] Later that same year, Vice President Dan Quayle called on Time Warner to stop marketing Tupac Shakur's *Apacalypse Now,* alleging that it was the cause of the traffic-stop murder of a Texas state trooper by an assailant who was playing the tape in his truck at the time he was pulled over.[138]

Ironically, as rap moved further away from political themes of black power to celebrating the fast gangster lifestyle, it rapidly became popular with a crossover audience of white youths who soon came to be the largest segment of the market for rap albums. The album that most signaled this crossover trend was probably Snoop Doggy Dogg's 1993 *Doggystyle,* which became the first rap album to debut on the Billboard charts at Number 1.

Crossover moved in the other direction as well. White artists had been part of the Hip-Hop scene from the early 1980s. Acts such as the Beastie Boys had successfully bridged the rock and rap worlds, but remained most popular with white audiences. It was not until 1996 that Marshall Mathers (known by his stage name of "Eminem") became the first white rapper to burst to the top of the rap charts.

Other musical styles also found new crossover audiences in the 1990s. Long established Hispanic artists such as Tito Puente who served as the ambassador of Afro-Caribbean beats to America for decades and the famed lounge lizard sound of Juan Garcia Esquivel, were rediscovered by a new younger generation of listeners. Younger Latin music recording artists such as Gloria Estefan, Ricky Martin, and Jennifer López were discovered and became immensely popular with Americans of all ethnic backgrounds. Perhaps the most startling crossover phenomenon was the skyrocketing popularity of a song "Macarena" by Los del Río that became a cultural phenomenon as a dance craze that swept the nation, as sporting events and gatherings everywhere featured collective Macarena dances. The Macarena even served as the soundtrack for the culminating celebration of the Democratic National Convention in 1996.

In the 1990s, Hollywood embraced movies that explored issues of race and were the product of a new generation of minority filmmakers and actors. Spike Lee was perhaps the most outstanding example of this trend. Lee had written, produced, and directed two modestly successful films in the 1980s (*She's Gotta Have It*, 1986, and *School Daze*, 1988) but won both popular and critical acclaim with *Do The Right Thing* in 1990, a movie that dramatized the complicated racial and ethnic conflicts in Lee's native Brooklyn. Critics began comparing Lee with Woody Allen for his unmistakably original style, his rejection of easy answers to the problems his pictures posed, and the centrality of his own personality within his film.

Early in the 1990s, a concentration of movie releases by African American directors, all with an edgy, Hip-Hop sensibility, became identified as the "New Black Cinema." In addition to Spike Lee, at the forefront of this movement were a number of young first-time directors led by John Singleton, whose hit *Boyz n the Hood* (1991) was based on his own experiences in South Central Los Angeles, for which he was nominated for an Academy Award for Best Director at the age of 23. Allen and Albert Hughes, twenty-something brothers from Detroit, co-directed *Menace II Society* (1993), another film acclaimed by critics. Both Singleton and the Hughes Brothers developed their directorial skills by making music videos, a new segment of the film industry that had been invented only the decade before with the arrival of MTV.

Other ethnic groups also increased their role in the production of Hollywood films. Ang Lee who was born in Taiwan and later immigrated to the United States to attend college, emerged as one of the more important producer/directors of the 1990s with such films as *The Wedding Banquet* (1993), *Eat Drink Man Woman* (1994), and features such as *Sense and Sensibility* (1995), as well as the 2000 smash hit, *Crouching Tiger, Hidden Dragon*. Chris Eyre, a director of Cheyenne and Arapaho heritage, adapted Native American novelist Sherman Alexie's screenplay into *Smoke Signals* (1998), a refreshingly honest depiction of native identity.

Many cultural observers noted that these directors were producing the most innovative and interesting work to come out of Hollywood in years, but it was evident that the Hollywood establishment was hesitant to embrace them. There were howls of protest from many critics when Spike Lee was passed over for an Academy Award nomination in either the best picture and best director awards, especially after a poll of 80 film critics rated *Do the Right Thing* the year's best picture. Such grumbling intruded on the otherwise carefully orchestrated event itself when presenter Kim Basinger went off script and said after reading the nominees for best picture: "But there is one film missing from this list that deserves to be on it because ironically it might tell the biggest truth of all. And that's *Do the Right Thing*."[139]

Denzel Washington, an African American actor, had a decade of movie and television credits before his nomination for best actor in 1993 for his portrayal of *Malcolm X*, the first big-budget Hollywood movie directed by Spike Lee. When Washington's tour de force performance was passed over in favor of Al Pacino's role in *Scent of a Woman* in 1992, a few eyebrows were raised. Questions turned to protest in 2000 when Washington's portrayal of Rubin "Hurricane" Carter in the 1999 *The Hurricane* lost out to Kevin Spacey in an unprecedented "re-vote" of ballots after the Academy claimed to have lost 4,000 ballots.[140]

The trend toward increasing acceptance of multicultural literature by both popular audiences, literary scholars, and critics, first noticeable in the 1970s, continued to flourish in the 1990s. In 1990, Oscar Hijuelos became the first Hispanic American to win the Pulitzer Prize for Literature, being honored for his best-selling *The Mambo Kings Play Songs of Love* (1989). Ha Jin, a Chinese American novelist, won the National Book Award in 1999 for *Waiting*, a story set in China during the upheavals of the Cultural Revolution. Korean American Chang-rae Lee's novel, *Native Speaker*, was recognized as one of the decade's best first novels by the Hemingway Foundation through its PEN award. In academia, the long awaited publication of the landmark *Heath Anthology of American Literature* (1990) included a wide representation of ethnic literature and clearly marked the end of the day when the exclusion of multicultural voices from the American literary canon was defensible.

Many well-established African American writers continued to impress readers and critics in the 1990s. Toni Morrison completed her trilogy of novels *Beloved* (1987), *Jazz* (1992), and *Paradise* (1998), pleasing her many fans (*Paradise* was one of the best-selling books of 1998). Ernest Gaines, the descendent of Louisiana sharecroppers, who began publishing his stories around the bayous and plantations of the Delta region in the early 1970s, gained critical recognition for his *A Lesson before Dying* (1993), which won numerous book awards including a nomination for the Pulitzer Prize. Octavia Butler, one of the few African American women writing in the genre of science fiction, won long-deserved but late-coming recognition in 1999 for the second in her series of dystopian novels, *Parable of the Talents*, winning the Nebula Award for best science fiction novel.

Black poets were especially prominent in the 1990s, beginning with Maya Angelou's reading of her composition, "On the Pulse of Morning," at Bill Clinton's inauguration in 1993. Rita Dove, who had won the Pulitzer Prize for Poetry in 1987 for her collection, *Thomas and Beulah* (1986), was appointed the Poet Laureate of the United States in 1993. Ai, a black poet who adopted the Japanese word for "love" as her name in recognition of her complicated heritage, was awarded the National Book Award for Poetry in 1999 for her *Vice: New & Selected Poems*.

The decade also saw many young African American authors debut to wide acclaim. Terry McMillan, an African American author from Michigan, burst onto the bestseller lists in 1992 with her novel of professional black women and their complicated relationships in *Waiting to Exhale,* a novel that was made into a successful Hollywood movie three years later. Walter Mosely proved one of the more prolific authors of the decade with his series of mysteries set in his native Los Angeles featuring the tough but tender-hearted World War II veteran Easy Rawlins. Mosely's *Devil in a Blue Dress* (1991) was made into a hit movie starring Denzel Washington in 1995 and prompted Bill Clinton to cite Mosely as one of his favorite authors. Bebe Moore Campbell's *Brothers and Sisters* (1994), an exploration of the limits of friendship and loyalties across racial and sexual boundaries set in Los Angeles in the wake of the Rodney King riots, reached the *New York Times* bestseller list.

For all the progress made in bringing the experiences, voices, and perspectives of ethnic minorities to the American reading public, older stereotypes continued to retain some power and resiliency. In 1992, Michael Crichton's novel, *Rising Sun,* hit the bestseller lists and alarmed many critics who saw in it a dramatization of America's nativist fears of the Asian "other." A detective story that begins with the murder of a high-priced prostitute in the Los Angeles offices of a powerful Japanese corporation and veers into a Japanese plot to take over an American high technology firm, the book bristles with characters' commentaries about the Japanese economic menace. Apparently unsatisfied with allowing his characters to spout warnings of Japanese financial aggression, Crichton blurred the lines between fiction and nonfiction in an afterword in which he raises the alarm about Japan's "adversarial trade, trade like war, trade intended to wipe out the competition" and provides a bibliography for further reading into Japans plans to take over the world economy.[141]

Crichton's thriller was just the most popular of what was a large genre of Japan-bashing and fear-mongering that had produced at least 35 titles from commercial presses since the start of the 1980s. Many warned not of economic competition from foreign corporations, but of direct competition of foreign workers who flooded over America's borders illegally, "stole" American jobs, burdened public services without paying their share of taxes, and added to a dangerous criminal element. Most popular among these was Peter Brimelow's 1995 bestseller *Alien Nation: Common Sense about America's Immigration Disaster,* a book that explicitly points to the racial and ethnic character of inassimilable new immigrants as the source of many of America's national problems. Brimelow bemoaned what he saw as the loss of an "American nation [that] has always had a specific, white, ethnic core" and a "public policy [that] is now making the United States a multiracial society."[142]

Whereas one side of the Asian stereotype was that of competitive threat, the other was of overachievers. Joel Kotkin, in his best-selling book, *Tribes,* breathed new life into the tired "model minority" myth by extending its reach across the globe. His subtitle well illustrates this method: "How Race, Religion, and Identity Determine Success in the New Global Economy." Confucian principles, Kotkin argued, along with other clan-supporting ideologies, ironically made for more effective business networks in the modern economy and led to greater competitive success.

INFLUENTIAL THEORIES AND VIEWS OF RACE RELATIONS

In what was a throwback to a line of scientific thinking thought to have been thoroughly discredited in the 1950s and 1960s, Charles Murray and Richard Herrnstein coauthored *The Bell Curve* (1994), a study that revived biological explanations of apparent racial differences. Murray and Herrnstein's basic contention, through more than 800 pages of discussion of intelligence testing, was that a significant degree of the measurable differences in IQ between whites and blacks was a consequence of racial heredity; therefore federal programs like Headstart and other efforts to boost black achievement were doomed to failure. Perhaps because few authors were so bold as to make such claims in the 1990s, *The Bell Curve* provoked vast media attention and controversy in both academia and popular culture in 1994, and was featured on the cover of *Time, Newsweek, The National Review,* and other national magazines and splashed across the television talk shows.

Although most representatives of respectable opinion condemned *The Bell Curve,* its central arguments did bubble to the surface of public discussion in surprising ways. In November 1994, the president of Rutgers University, Francis Lawrence, addressed a group of faculty on the issue of standardized test scores and admissions policies and said, "The average S.A.T.'s for African Americans is 750. Do we set standards in the future so that we don't admit anybody with the national test? Or do we deal with a disadvantaged population that doesn't have that genetic hereditary background to have a higher average?" Students protested over the next months and called for Lawrence's resignation, culminating when 150 protesters sat on the floor of the Rutger's basketball court and refused to move, provoking racist cat calls from the sold-out crowd and the cancellation of the game with the University of Massachusetts.[143]

Ironically, as Murray and Herrenstein attempted to revive a discredited racial sociobiology, sociologists Stephen and Mary Thernstrom and social critic Dinesh D'Souza published much-discussed books arguing that racism was mostly eradicated from contemporary America. Thernstrom's optimistic, even pollyannish, conclusions were challenged by many other scholarly and popular books of the decade that instead found that America was continuing, in the words of the famed 1968 Kerner Commission Report, to move "toward two societies, one black, one white—separate and unequal." *Two Nations* (1992), by Andrew Hacker, and *Faces at the Bottom of the Well* (1992), by Derrick Bell, were the most notable contributions.

Randall Robinson, the director of Trans-Africa Forum, which had been one of the key lobbying organizations pushing the United States to divest from South Africa during the antiapartheid struggles of the 1980s, published *The Debt: What America Owes to Blacks* (2000). Robinson's book became a bestseller and reignited the reparations debate.

RESOURCE GUIDE

SUGGESTED READING

Ancheta, Angelo N. *Race, Rights, and the Asian American Experience*. New Brunswick: Rutgers University Press, 1998.

Baldassare, Mark, ed. *The Los Angeles Riots: Lessons for the Urban Future*. Boulder, CO: Westview Press, 1994.

Bell, Derrick. *Faces at the Bottom of the Well: The Permanence of Racism*. New York: Basic Books, 1992.

Cohen, Carl and James P. Sterba. *Affirmative Action and Racial Preference: A Debate*. New York: Oxford University Press, 2003.

D'Souza, Dinesh. *The End of Racism: Principles for a Multiracial Society*. New York: Free Press, 1995.

Gibbs, Jewelle Taylor. Gibbs, *Race and Justice: Rodney King and O. J. Simpson in a House Divided*. San Francisco: Jossey-Bass, 1996.

Hacker, Andrew. *Two Nations: Black and White, Separate, Hostile, Unequal*. New York: Maxwell Macmillan International, 1992.

Harris, Othello and R. Robin Miller, eds. *Impacts of Incarceration on the African American Family*. New Brunswick, NJ: Transaction Publishers, 2003.

Hill, Anita Faye and Emma Coleman Jordan, eds. *Race, Gender, and Power in America: The Legacy of the Hill-Thomas Hearing*. New York: Oxford University Press, 1995.

Johnson, Ollie A. III and Karin L. Stanford, eds. *Black Political Organizations in the Post-Civil Rights Era*. New Brunswick, NJ: Rutgers University Press, 2002.

Joyce, Patrick D. *No Fire Next Time: Black-Korean Conflicts and the Future of America's Cities*. Ithaca: Cornell University Press, 2003.

Kellough, Edward. *Understanding Affirmative Action: Politics, Discrimination, and the Search for Justice*. Washington, D.C.: Georgetown University Press, 2006.

Kwong, Peter and Dusanka Miscevic, *Chinese America: The Untold Story of America's Oldest New Community*. New York: New Press, 2005.

Marable, Manning. *Race, Reform, and Rebellion: The Second Reconstruction and Beyond in Black America, 1945–2006*. Jackson: University Press of Mississippi, 2007.

Martin, Waldo E. Jr. *No Coward Soldiers: Black Cultural Politics and Postwar America*. Cambridge, MA: Harvard University Press, 2005.

McClain, Paula D. and Joseph Stewart Jr. *"Can We All Get Along?": Racial and Ethnic Minorities in American Politics*. Boulder, CO: Westview Press, 2002.

Miyares, Ines M. and Christopher A. Airriess, eds. *Contemporary Ethnic Geographies in America*. Lanham: Rowman & Littlefield, 2007.

Morrison, Toni. *Playing in the Dark*. Cambridge, MA: Harvard University Press, 1992.

Ogletree, Charles J. Jr. *All Deliberate Speed: Reflections on the First Half Century of* Brown v. Board of Education. New York: W. W. Norton & Co., 2004.

Reed, Adolph Jr. *Stirrings in the Jug: Black Politics in the Post-Segregation Era*. Minneapolis: University of Minnesota Press, 1999.

Robinson, Randall. *The Debt: What America Owes to Blacks*. New York: Dutton, 2000.

Roediger, David R. *The Wages of Whiteness: Race and the Making of the American Working Class*. London: Verso, 1991.

Roediger, David R. *Towards the Abolition of Whiteness*. London: Verso, 1994.

Steele, Shelby Steele. *White Guilt: How Blacks and Whites Together Destroyed the Promise of the Civil Rights Era*. New York: HarperCollins, 2006.

Thernstrom, Stephan and Abigail Thernstrom, *America in Black and White: One Nation, Indivisible*. New York: Simon & Schuster, 1997.

Thomas, Gail E., ed. *U.S. Race Relations in the 1980s and 1990s: Challenges and Alternatives*. New York: Hemisphere Publishing Corporation, 1990.

Tuch, Steven A. and Jack K. Martin, eds. *Racial Attitudes in the 1990s: Continuity and Change*. Westport, CT: Praeger, 1997.

Reynaldo Anaya Valencia, ed., *Mexican Americans & the Law: El Pueblo Unido Jamas Sera Vencido!* Tucson: University of Arizona Press, 2004.

Wickham, DeWayne. *Bill Clinton and Black America*. New York: Ballantine Books, 2002.

FILMS AND VIDEOS

American History X (1998). Tony Kaye, director. New Line Cinema presents a Turman-Morrissey Company Production, New Line Home Video.

Amistad (1998). Steven Spielberg, director. DreamWorks Pictures in association with HBO Pictures.

Bamboozled (2000). Spike Lee, director. 40 Acres and a Mule Filmworks production; New Line Home Entertainment.

Boyz n the Hood (1991). John Singleton, director. Columbia Pictures Industries, Columbia TriStar Home Video.

Do the Right Thing (1989). Spike Lee, director. 40 Acres and a Mule, Filmworks production; New Line Home Entertainment.

L. A. Is Burning: Five Reports from a Divided City (1992). WGBH Educational Foundation, PBS Video.

Malcolm X (1992). Spike Lee, director. Warner Brothers Warner Home Video.

Smoke Signals (1998). Chris Eyre, director. Miramax Films, Shadowcatcher Entertainment production. Burbank, Cal.: Miramax Home Entertainment.

White Man's Burden (1995). Desmond Nakano, director. Chromatic Pictures Inc., HBO Home Video.

WEB SITES

ACLU Racial Profiling Project, http://www.aclu.org/racialjustice/racialprofiling/index.html.

American Indian Heritage Association, http://www.indians.org/.

Anti-Defamation League, http://www.adl.org/.

Chinese American United for Self-Improvement (CAUSE), http://www.causeusa.org/.

Civil Rights Leadership Conference, http://www.civilrights.org/.

Matters of Race, http://www.pbs.org/mattersofrace/.

National Association for the Advancement of Colored People, http://www.naacp.org/home/index.htm.

National Congress of American Indians, http://www.ncai.org/.

National Council of La Raza (a national Latino civil rights organization), http://www.nclr.org/.

Native Web, http://www.nativeweb.org/.

O. J. Simpson Murder Case, Court TV News, http://www.courttv.com/casefiles/simpson/index.html.

Southern Poverty Law Center, http://www.splcenter.org.

The Two Nations of Black America, A PBS Report, http://www.pbs.org/wgbh/pages/frontline/shows/race/.

Understanding Race, http://www.understandingrace.com/home.html.

William Jefferson Clinton Library, http://www.clintonlibrary.gov/.

NOTES

1. *Miami Times,* July 16, 1992, 8A.

2. *Washington Post,* March 7, 1998, A2; *New York Times,* February 28, 1999, WK19.

3. *Chicago Tribune,* February 18, 1999, 9.

4. *Pittsburgh Post-Gazette,* January 19, 1999, A6.

5. *Chicago Tribune,* January 21, 1999, A2.

6. *Chicago Tribune,* December 28, 1999, 1.

7. *San Francisco Chronicle,* May 22, 2002, A5.

8. *Chicago Tribune,* March 1, 1999, 6.

9. *New York Times,* April 30, 2000, 14.

10. *Washington Post,* May 13, 1992.

11. *Washington Post,* June 14, 1992.

12. *Washington Post,* January 5, 1978.

13. Although the Confederate battle flag is often referred to as the "stars and bars," historically the "stars and bars" referred to the official national flag of the Confederacy, not the flag designed by General P.G.T. Beauregard. *Philadelphia Inquirer,* April 20, 1983, A08; *Washington Post,* April 21, 1983, A2.

14. *Washington Post,* January 15, 1988, A3; *Chicago Tribune,* February 3, 1988, 7; *Chicago Tribune,* January 20, 1990, 4; *Lexington Herald-Leader,* October 4, 1990, A12.

15. *Chicago Tribune,* May 30, 1991, 12; *Miami Herald,* January 18, 1980, Broward Edition, 1; *Philadelphia Inquirer,* August 23, 1991, A13; *San Francisco Chronicle,* March 15, 1992, 3; March 28, 1992, A6; *Washington Post,* July 25, 1992, C1; *San Francisco Chronicle,* January 5, 1993, A6; *Lexington Herald-Leader,* April 30, 1993, A4.

16. *Detroit Free Press,* April 25, 1992, 6A; *Lexington Herald-Leader,* January 13, 1993, A3.

17. *New York Times,* July 23, 1993, B6.

18. Pomper, Miles A. "NOMINATION: Helms-Inspired Controversy over Moseley-Braun Nomination Is a Rare Break with Tradition." CQ Weekly Online (October 23,

1999): 2538–2538; Chuck McCutcheon and Miles A. Pomper. "NOMINATIONS: Moseley-Braun's Path To Confirmation Is Clear As Helms Lifts Roadblock." CQ Weekly Online (November 6, 1999): 2665–2665.

19. *Washington Post,* July 2, 1991, A1, A7; August 1, 1991, A1.

20. William Boot, "The Clarence Thomas Hearings: Why Everyone-Left, Right and Center-Found the Press Guilty as Charged," *Columbia Journalism Review,* 30:5 (January–February 1992), 25.

21. *New York Times,* October 21, 1991, 10.

22. *New York Times,* October 17, 1991, A26.

23. *Buffalo News,* October 18, 1991, C3.

24. *New York Times,* November 30, 1991, 1.

25. *Washington Post,* October 11, 1991, A1; October 12, 1991, A1.

26. Joe R. Feagin, Hernán Vera, and Pinar Batur, *White Racism: The Basics* (New York: Routledge, 2001), 123.

27. *The Los Angeles Riots: Lessons for the Urban Future,* Mark Baldassare, ed. (Boulder, CO: Westview Press, 1994), 74; Jewelle Taylor Gibbs, *Race and Justice: Rodney King an O. J. Simpson in a House Divided* (San Francisco: Jossey-Bass, 1996).

28. House Resolution 122, "Condemning the High Incidence of Police Brutality in the United States," 102d Congress, 1st Session, introduced April 11, 1991.

29. *San Francisco Chronicle,* December 26, 1992; May 25, 1992; *Newsweek,* February 16, 1998.

30. *The Los Angeles Riots: Lessons for the Urban Future,* 23, 161.

31. *San Francisco Chronicle,* June 1, 1992; July 14, 1992.

32. *New York Times,* May 5, 1992, A 1, 26.

33. *New York Times,* May 10, 1992, 1.

34. *New York Times,* June 14, 1993, A1.

35. *New York Times,* November 26, 1996, WC1.

36. "Overview of the Administration's Implementation of the Trafficking Victims Protection Act of 2000," Office to Monitor and Combat Trafficking in Persons (May 2002), http://www.state.gov/g/tip/rls/rpt/10531.htm.

37. *Philadelphia Tribune,* April 11, 1995, 1A.

38. *San Francisco Chronicle,* March 28, 1996, D1.

39. *New York Times,* June 25, 1994, 8.

40. *USA Today,* July 3, 1994; CBS News/New York Times Poll, February 1, 1997; Fox Broadcasting Company, September 27, 2007.

41. *Washington Post,* October 20, 1995, A1.

42. Haki R. Madhubuti, "Took Back Our Tears… " in *Million Man March/Day of Absence: A Commemorative Anthology* (Chicago: Third World Press), 3.

43. Dennys: *Chicago Tribune,* January 13, 1999, 10; Disney: *Los Angeles Sentinel,* October 18, 2000. Vol. 66:29. A19; Nationwide: *Call & Post* (Cleveland, Ohio), June 18, 1998, A5; Avis: *Los Angeles Sentinel,* January 7, 1998. Vol. 63:40, A3; Coke: *Washington Post,* November 17, 2000, A1.

44. *New York Times,* July 14, 1999, C4.

45. *New York Times,* October 29, 1990, A1.

46. *New York Times*, May 10, 1992, 23.

47. *New York Times*, July 8, 1993, A1.

48. *New York Times*, October 25, 1997, D1.

49. *Poverty in the United States, 1999*, U.S. Census Bureau (Washington, 2000).

50. *New York Times*, September 2, 1990, H7; August 16, 1990.

51. *New York Times*, August 22, 1990, A25.

52. *Chicago Defender*, December 28, 1991, 34.

53. Jeffries's work drew on that of Michael Bradley who based his research on the work of Carleton Coon, one of the last anthropologist defenders of the racist theory of polygenesis—that whites and blacks evolved at separately. Michael Anderson Bradley, *The Iceman Inheritance: Prehistoric Sources Of Western Man's Racism, Sexism And Aggression* (New York: Kayode Publications, 1991, 1978); *Forward* (New York), January 14, 1994, 1.

54. *New York Times*, January 23, 1994, 21; January 25, 1994, A12.

55. Philip Gourevitch, "The Crown Heights Riot & Its Aftermath," *Commentary*, 95:1 (January 1993), 33.

56. *New York Times*, August 21, 1991, B1.

57. *New York Times*, November 26, 1992, A1; July 21, 1993, B1–7.

58. *New York Times*, August 19, 2001, 1.

59. Times Mirror Center for the People & the Press (Washington, D.C.) May 1990, October 1994; General Social Surveys, Roper Center for Public Opinion and Research, (Storrs, CT) 1990; Democratic Leadership Council (Washington, D.C.) 1993. All cited surveys collected in the *Polling the Nations* database.

60. *The Philadelphia Inquirer*, October 20, 1994, A21; *New York Times*, August 4, 1996, E5.

61. *New York Times*, June 21, 1995, A1.

62. *New York Times*, January 15, 1991, B6.

63. *Pittsburgh Post-Gazette*, July 14, 1996, A12; "Seven Promises of Promise Keeper," http://www.promisekeepers.org/about/7promises, accessed December 5, 2007; *New York Times*, September 29, 1997, A12. See also Mike Hill, *After Whiteness: Unmaking an American Majority* (New York: New York University Press, 2004).

64. *New York Times*, April 14, 1990, 25.

65. *New York Times*, May 4, 1990, B2; May 21, 1993, 33.

66. *New York Times*, May 23, 1997, B1.

67. *New York Times*, May 17, 1992, 18; June 7, 1992, 27; June 11, 1993, A26.

68. *New York Times*, September 30, 1990, 22; April 30, 1994, 10.

69. *Washington Post*, March 2, 1999, A15; April 22, 2003, A8.

70. *The (Cleveland) Plain Dealer*, July 18, 1991, 3D; September 20, 1992, 2B; December 8, 1992, 1A; *Akron Beacon Journal*, March 6, 1993, B1.

71. *Washington Post*, October 20, 1991, d5.

72. *Detroit Free Press*, October 25, 1988, 1A; *Chicago Tribune*, January 26, 1989, 3; April 9, 1992, 1; *Washington Post*, February 17, 1999, A3.

73. *Washington Post*, May 3, 1994, E2; "NCAA Minority Opportunities and Interests Committee Report on the Use of American Indian Mascots in Intercollegiate Athletics to the NCAA Executive Committee Subcommittee on Gender and Diversity Issues," NCAA (October 2002); *Akron Beacon Journal*, October 18, 1996, B1.

74. *New York Times*, September 4, 1996, A16; *Washington Post*, August 3, 1996, A2.

75. *San Francisco Chronicle*, January 2, 1992, A2.

76. United States Commission on Civil Rights, "Voices across America: Roundtable Discussions of Asian Civil Rights Issues," Washington, D.C., February, 1992.

77. *New York Times*, May 14, 1990, B5; May 7, 1990, B1; September 23, 1990, 34; September 24, 1990, B1; February 1, 1991, A1.

78. Timothy P. Fong, *The Contemporary Asian American Experience: Beyond the Model Minority* (Upper Saddle River, NJ: Pearson-Prentice Hall, 2008), 306.

79. Birgit Zinzius, *Chinese America: Stereotype and Reality: History, Present, and Future of the Chinese Americans* (New York: Peter Lang, 2005), 238.

80. *New York Times*, March 23, 1997, A22; *The National Review*, March 24, 1997.

81. *New York Times*, December 3, 1991, A20.

82. *New York Times*, July 24, 1993, A26.

83. *New York Times*, January 14, 1993, A1; January 22, 1993, A14.

84. *New York Times*, March 2, 1993, A13.

85. *New York Times*, December 2, 1991, A1.

86. *New York Times*, July 8, 1994, A18, July 6, 1996, A1; May 16, 1997, A20; July 9, 1997, A12; October 30, 1997, A1.

87. *New York Times*, September 10, 1992, A20.

88. *New York Times*, January 22, 1990, A1.

89. *Washington Post*, October 5, 1995, A1; *New York Times*, October 28, 1995, A1.

90. *New York Times*, October 22, 1995, A1, October 23, 1995, B9; *Washington Post*, October 27, 1995, A1.

91. *Washington Post*, November 4, 1995, B1.

92. *New York Times*, February 24, 1995, A17.

93. *New York Times*, March 16, 1995, A1; July 19, 1995, A1; July 28, 1995, A17.

94. *New York Times*, April 5, 1995, A25.

95. *New York Times*, February 27, 1995, A13.

96. *New York Times*, June 1, 1995, A1.

97. *New York Times*, June 1, 1995, A1; *Washington Post*, July 3, 1995, A1.

98. *New York Times*, February 23, 1996, A1.

99. Adarand Constructors, Inc., Petitioner V. Federico Pena, Secretary of Transportation, et al., Certiorari to the United States Court of Appeals for the Tenth Circuit, No. 93–1841, Decided June 12, 1995.

100. *New York Times*, December 8, 1995, A24.

101. *Grutter v. Bolinger*, 539 U.S. 343 (2003); *Gratz v. Bollinger*, 539 U.S. 244 (2003)

102. *Washington Post*, October 3, 1993, A15.

103. Christopher Mitchell, "U.S. Policy toward Haitian Boat People, 1972–93," *The Annals of the American Academy of Political and Social Science*, Vol. 534, No. 1, 69–80 (1994); *Philadelphia Tribune*. December 20, 1991, 1A; *Los Angeles Sentinel*, February 26, 1992, A8; *Sacramento Observer*, March 18, 1992, A9.

104. "Influx of Cubans Forces Clinton To Halt Automatic Asylum." CQ Weekly Online (August 20, 1994): 2464–2465. http://0-library.cqpress.com.maurice.bgsu.edu:80/cqweekly/WR103405431 (accessed December 4, 2007).

105. *New York Times*, December 3, 2000, A1.

106. David A. Harris, *Profiles in Injustice: Why Racial Profiling Cannot Work* (New York: The New Press, 2002), 19–20.

107. *State v. Pedro Soto*, see Harris, *Profiles in Injustice*, 53–60, 80–81.

108. *New York Times*, June 20, 1999, SM 50; July 11, 1999, 23; June 10, 1999, A22; September 30, 1999, A20.

109. *Chicago Tribune*, September 20, 1998, 1; September 15, 1998, 12.

110. *New York Times*, May 1, 1994, A1.

111. *New York Times*, October 7, 1998, B8.

112. *R.A.V. v. St. Paul*, 505 U.S. 377 (1992).

113. *Wisconsin v. Mitchell*, 508 U.S. 476 (1993); *Chicago Tribune*, April 19, 1993, 6.

114. *New York Times*, May 5, 1995, A1.

115. *New York Times*, October 13, 1998, A17; May 16, 1999, 24.

116. *Miller v. Johnson*, 515 U.S. 900 (1995); *Washington Post*, June 30, 1995, A1, A18.

117. *Washington Post*, July 3, 1995, A1; *Pittsburgh Post-Gazette*, June 30, 1995, A1; *Washington Post*, June 14, 1996, A33.

118. *Washington Post*, June 14, 1996, A33. Gregory L. Giroux, "New Twists in the Old Debate on Race and Representation," *CQ Weekly*, August 11, 2001, 1966.

119. The Supreme Court temporarily halted all death penalties in its 1972 ruling in *Furman v. Georgia*, 408 U.S. 153; *Death Row U.S.A.: A Quarterly Report by the Criminal Justice Project of the N.A.A.C.P. Legal Defense and Educational Fund, Inc.* (Summer 2000), 6; Extrajudicial, Summary or Arbitrary Executions: Report of the Special Rapporteur…, 23 December 1997, UN document E/CN.4/1998/68.

120. *Building Momentum: The American Bar Association Call for a Moratorium on Executions Takes Hold* Appendix A, American Bar Association Resolution As Approved by the ABA House of Delegates February 3, 1997, American Bar Association Death Penalty Moratorium Implementation Project, 4th Report (August 2003).

121. Gallup Poll, March 2, 1986; Gallup Poll, June 26, 1991; CBS News/New York Times Poll, June 12, 1997.

122. *Chicago Tribune*, March 14, 1999, 21; March 3, 1999, 6; *Philadelphia Inquirer*, February 23, 2000, E1.

123. *Chicago Tribune*, September 15, 1998, 1; September 17, 1998, 5; February 2, 1999, 1; February 4, 1999, 1.

124. *Chicago Tribune*, January 30, 2000, 1; January 31, 2000, 1.

125. *Chicago Tribune*, May 27, 1999, 24; *New York Times*, May 21, 1999, A14.

126. *Philadelphia Inquirer*, February 29, 2000, A5; April 27, 2000, B1; April 30, 2000, A1; May 8, 2000, B1; *Philadelphia Daily News*, December 19, 2001, 1.

127. Pamela Newkirk, "Guess Who's Leaving the Newsrooms," *Columbia Journalism Review*, September–October 2000, 36. (Thanks to Lisa Halverstadt for suggesting this article.)

128. *Hispanic* (Washington, D.C.), January–February 1997, 39.

129. *New York Times*, January 16, 1994, S9.

130. *New York Times*, July 29, 1990, S1.

131. *Chicago Tribune,* April 24, 1997.

132. *San Francisco Chronicle,* November 30, 1992, C9; *Detroit Free Press,* November 30, 1992, 1D; December 4, 1992, 1F; February 4, 1993, 1A.

133. *Sports Illustrated,* Combined issue: December 27, 1999–January 3, 2000.

134. *Lexington Herald-Leader,* December 27, 1999, C2.

135. *New York Times,* April 5, 1999, D7.

136. *New York Times,* October 4, 1990, A18; *Miami Herald,* April 1, 1993, 1BR.

137. *San Francisco Chronicle,* July 29, 1992, A1; August 7, 1992, C2; September 10, 1992, E1.

138. *San Francisco Chronicle,* September 23, 1992, A6.

139. *Chicago Tribune,* March 28, 1990, 19.

140. *Los Angeles Sentinel,* April 12, 2000, A7; *New York Amsterdam News,* March 30, 2000, 21.

141. *New York Times,* February 9, 1992, A1.

142. *New York Times,* June 27, 1995, A16.

143. *New York Times,* February 8, 1995, B1.

Selected Bibliography

Abrahamson, Mark. *Urban Enclaves: Identity and Place in America*. New York: St. Martin's Press, 1996.

Abu-Jamal, Mumia. *Live from Death Row*. Reading, MA: Addison-Wesley, 1995.

Alexander, Amy. *The Farrakhan Factor: African American Writers on Leadership, Nationhood, and Minister Louis Farrakhan*. New York: Grove Press, 1997.

Baldassare, Mark, ed. *The Los Angeles Riots: Lessons for the Urban Future*. Boulder, CO: Westview Press, 1994.

Brown, Michael K. *Race, Money, and the American Welfare State*. Ithaca, NY: Cornell Univ. Press, 1999.

Bullard, Robert D. *Confronting Environmental Racism: Voices from the Grassroots*. Boston: South End Press, 1993.

Chavez, Lydia. *The Color Bind: California's Battle to End Affirmative Action*. Berkeley: University of California Press, 1998.

Dyson, Michael Eric. *Between God and Gangsta Rap: Bearing Witness to Black Culture*. New York: Oxford University Press, 1994.

Edley Jr., Christopher. *Not All Black and White: Affirmative Action and American Values*. New York: Hill and Wang, 1996.

Feagin, Joe R. *Racist America: Roots, Current Realities, and Future Reparations*. New York: Routledge, 2000.

Fix, Michael and Raymond Struyk. *Clear and Convincing Evidence: Measurement of Discrimination in America*. Washington, D.C.: Urban Institute, 1993.

Gooding-Williams, Robert. *Reading Rodney King, Reading Urban Uprising*. New York: Routledge, 1993.

Gutierrez, David G. *Mexican Americans, Mexican Immigrants, and the Politics of Ethnicity*. Berkeley: University of California Press, 1995.

Hacker, Andrew. *Two Nations: Black and White, Separate, Hostile, Unequal*. New York: Ballantine, 1995.

Hondagneu-Sotelo, Pierrette. *Doméstica: Immigrant Workers Cleaning and Caring in the Shadows of Affluence*. Berkeley: University of California Press, 2001.

Jennings, James, ed. *Race and Politics*. New York: Verso Press, 1997.

Katznelson, Ira. *When Affirmative Action Was White: An Untold History of Racial Inequality in Twentieth Century America*. New York: W. W. Norton, 2005.

Kelley, Robin D. G. *Yo' Mama's Disfunktional!: Fighting the Culture Wars in Urban America.* Boston: Beacon Press, 1997.

Klinker, Philip A. and Rogers M. Smith. *The Unsteady March: The Rise and Decline of Racial Equality in America.* Chicago: University of Chicago Press, 1999.

Lieberman, Robert C. *Shifting the Color Line: Race and the American Welfare State.* Cambridge, MA: Harvard University Press, 1998.

Lusane, Clarence. *African Americans at the Crossroads: The Restructuring of Black Leadership and the 1992 Elections.* Boston: South End Press, 1994.

McCall, Nathan. *Makes Me Wanna Holler: A Young Black Man in America.* New York: Random House, 1994.

McClain, Paula and Joseph Stewart, Jr. *Can We All Get Along? Racial and Ethnic Minorities in American Politics.* Boulder, CO: Westview Press, 1995.

Massey, Douglas S. and Nancy A. Denton. *American Apartheid: Segregation and the Making of the Underclass.* Cambridge, MA: Harvard University Press, 1993.

Menchaca, Martha. *The Mexican Outsiders: A Community History of Marginalization and Discrimination in California.* Austin: University of Texas Press, 1995.

Morris, Lorenzo, ed. *The Social and Political Implications of the 1984 Jesse Jackson Campaign.* Westport, CT: Praeger, 1990.

Morrison, Toni, ed. *Race-ing Justice, En-gendering Power: Essays on Anita Hill, Clarence Thomas, and the Construction of Social Reality.* New York: Pantheon, 1992.

Nagel, Joane. *American Indian Ethnic Renewal: Red Power and the Resurgence of Identity and Culture.* New York: Oxford University Press, 1997.

Neubeck, Kenneth J. and Noel A. Cazenave. *Welfare Racism: Playing the Race Card against America's Poor.* New York: Routledge, 2001.

Oliver, Melvin L. and Thomas M. Shapiro, *Black Wealth, White Wealth: A New Perspective on Racial Inequality.* New York: Routledge, 1995.

Omi, Michael and Howard Winant, *Racial Formation in the United States: From the 1960s to the 1990s.* London: Routledge, 1994.

O'Reilly, Kenneth. *Nixon's Piano: Presidents and Racial Politics from Washington to Clinton.* New York: Free Press, 1995.

Phillips, Kevin. *The Politics of Rich and Poor: Wealth and the American Electorate in the Reagan Aftermath.* New York: Random House, 1990.

Quadagno, Jill. *The Color of Welfare: How Racism Undermined the War on Poverty.* New York: Oxford University Press, 1994.

Reed, Adolph Jr. *Stirrings in the Jug: Black Politics in the Post-Segregation Era.* Minneapolis: University of Minnesota Press, 1999.

Shipler, David K. *A Country of Strangers: Blacks and Whites in America.* New York: Knopf, 1997.

Smith, Robert C. *We Have No Leaders: African Americans in the Post-Civil Rights Era.* Albany: State University of New York Press, 1996.

Smitherman, Geneva. *African American Women Speak Out on Anita Hill-Clarence Thomas.* Detroit: Wayne State University Press, 1995.

Sonenshein, Raphael J. *Politics in Black and White: Race and Power in Los Angeles.* Princeton, NJ: Princeton University Press, 1993.

Steinberg, Stephen. *Turning Back: The Retreat from Racial Justice in American Thought and Policy.* Boston: Beacon Press, 1996.

Terkel, Studs. *Race: How Blacks and Whites Think and Feel about the American Obsession.* New York: New Press, 1992.

Thernstrom, Stephen and Abigail Thernstrom. *America in Black and White: One Nation, Indivisible*. New York: Simon and Schuster, 1997.

Waters, Mary. *Ethnic Options: Choosing Identities in America*. Berkeley: University of California Press, 1990.

West, Cornell. *Race Matters*. Boston: Beacon Press, 1993.

Williams, Linda. *The Constraint of Race: Legacies of White Skin Privilege in America*. University Park, PA: The Pennsylvania State University Press, 2003.

Wilson, William Julius. *The Truly Disadvantaged: The Inner City, the Underclass, and Public Policy*. Chicago: University of Chicago Press, 1987.

Wilson, William Julius. *When Work Disappears: The World of the New Urban Poor*. New York: Vintage Books, 1997.

Wu, Frank H. *Yellow: Race in America beyond Black and White*. New York: Basic Books, 2002.

Yinger, John. *Closed Doors, Opportunities Lost: The Continuing Costs of Housing Discrimination*. New York: Russell Sage Foundation, 1995.

Index

About the Author

TIMOTHY MESSER-KRUSE is Professor of History at Bowling Green State University.